THE DEVIL

&

DAVE CHAPPELLE

& Other Essays

William Jelani Cobb

Thunder's Mouth Press
New York

THE DEVIL AND DAVE CHAPPELLE
& *Other Essays*

Published by
Thunder's Mouth Press
An Imprint of Avalon Publishing Group, Inc.
245 West 17th Street, 11th Floor
New York, NY 10011

AVALON

ISBN-13: 978-1-56025-977-0
ISBN-10: 1-56025-977-9

9 8 7 6 5 4 3 2 1

Book design by Ivelisse Robles
Printed in the United States of America
Distributed by Publishers Group West

For Mary C. and Sissy

Contents

Part III. Black-Owned

Part IV. Past Imperfect

Introduction

There are no simple answers, only oversimplified ones. This, my first collection of essays, begins with this premise and with the understanding that truth is the best antiseptic going. This collection is my attempt to get to the bottom of things, or at the very least, a few layers deeper than we would've been otherwise. To paraphrase Steven Biko, I write about what I like, but also what I *dislike*. I cover the terrain of that which makes me laugh, sigh, hold my head in my hands, or bellow. I take my cues from every angle: film, history, music, books, politics, the obituary columns. Then do my best to separate the wheat from the chaff, the corn from the husk, and the boll from the cotton.

The *Art of War* holds that one is to *respond* to a situation rather than merely reacting to one. This collection marks my response to some of the goings-on in this era. Our times are filled with plastic prophets and genius visionaries, heroes and clay-footed idols. My task is to tell the difference between the vinyl and the leather. This much I know: my old man was an electrician. Sixty-one years of pulling cable and wiring panels made his hands like leather; I once bought a pair of vinyl gloves, and six weeks later the elements had worn them to a tattered parody. Leather ages, grows weathered and wizened; vinyl, on the other hand, cracks the first chance it gets. Leather is toughened hide; vinyl is the synthetic, store-bought alternative. Vinyl always smells like the absence of sweat.

In the period covered by this collection, I've responded to dozens of stimuli in the form of essays, reviews, and profiles. The work selected for inclusion here is a sampler's plate, my take on some of the pivotal periods and personalities of the years covered by the collection. If there is a theme connecting these pieces, it is my consistent attempt to see through that oldest of American traditions: the con game, the studied attempt to pass off vinyl as leather. No matter what the style of the hustle, or the prints, textures, fabrics, or materials they come cloaked in, they inevitably have one thing in common: the simple answer to the complex riddle of life—the mark of intellectual sweatlessness. We know, or ought to know by now, that the pea is never under the first shell we choose and the sleight-of-hand card trick can come from any dealer—cinematic, literary, musical, political, or otherwise. Within any of these habitats, the swindle, like the Bengal tiger, only attacks when our backs are turned. These essays represent my ongoing efforts not to be taken in by the fine print and money-back guarantees.

Many of these pieces appeared originally in my column *Past Imperfect*, which appeared on Africana.com between October 2003 and January 2005. They often deal directly or indirectly with race, not because the race angle is my personal shtick, but because Americans have a demonstrated glass jaw when it comes to the racial sucker punch. That fact has made black writers—and a number of conscientious white ones—function like members of an intellectual bunco squad, policing the public from hoodwinkers and bamboozlers of all shades, sizes, and colors. Some of these essays were written when I was still a rookie and not yet hip to the inventory of social scams floating around us; still, I resist the urge to go backward and press further charges. The essays I've included reflect where my thinking was at a particular time, and there's no double jeopardy here.

The other theme tying these pieces together is the question of legacy and responsibility that confront us at each turn. The old preachers will tell you that you must know not only who you are, but also *whose* you are. I was born in 1969, and I write from a vantage point of that first generation that has—whether wisely or not—often taken freedom for granted. This is the meaning of the metaphor that James Baldwin crafted when he spoke of "the price of the ticket." The cost of arriving at our present location has been paid by four centuries of one's ancestors. So the question arises: what does one do with that inheritance? And what do we owe to one another and to those who come after us? In a phrase, *whose are we?*

I maintain a stubborn optimism about black people; I retain a deliberately idealistic belief that there is such a thing as a black community and that we are ultimately one another's responsibility. This collection is about the sweat equity in our present lives that is held by people who could never have imagined the scale of possibility that now lies before us.

I try to call to the carpet the myriad trickbags of the white world. But I'm not afraid to criticize black people, believing always that the truest Toms are those who keep their mouths shut in the face of impending tragedy. I speak with familiar authority of the brother who insists that we demand better of ourselves. And I demand that I stick to the fundamentals of the game, keep my eye on the ball, and remember that life is all about discerning which is vinyl and which is leather. I figure as long as I stay on the leather side of the issue, I'm doing all right. I don't pretend to be infallible in picking one from the other, but I keep this maxim in mind: leather is always the one that doesn't melt when you take a match to it.

Way Uptown & Way Down South, 2006

1

Troubling Waters

For half of the time period covered by this collection we have been at war. But the acknowledged war that the United States launched on the noun "9/11" is only one of the conflicts that we have witnessed. The essays in this section are explorations of the controversial moments in this time, the flashpoints and battlefronts within both black America and the world. The old Negro spiritual spoke of God "troubling the waters," as a reference to divine intervention. Perhaps more than anything else, Hurricane Katrina and its disastrous aftermath gave a new meaning to the phrase. The waters were indeed the trouble, and the people there were left waiting for interventions—divine, municipal, naval, or otherwise. Those waters have receded, but the metaphorical ones are still rising. And awaiting interventions of their own.

1

Nation-Time: Cotton Comes to Washington

In October 1995 Louis Farrakhan succeeded in drawing one million black men to Washington, D.C., to participate in his Million Man March. Beyond the spectacle of the event itself, the occasion brought to the surface tensions and contradictions and questions about the direction that had been developing in black America since the demise of the Black Power movement in the 1970s. The meaning of it all was nearly impossible to decipher at the time and has, if anything, grown more opaque in the decade since. This essay is excerpted from a longer manuscript on the march completed in January 1996.

Black men have failed to protect our women since the time of slavery. We either stay and are broken or we run away and leave them to look after the children and themselves. So each time a male child is born, they hope he will be the one to break this vicious cycle.

ERNEST GAINES, *A LESSON BEFORE DYING*

Only colored women know the extreme in suffering and humiliation. We know how many insults we have borne silently; we have hidden them from our men because we did not want them to die needlessly in our defense. And a woman loves a strong man, she delights to feel that her man can protect her, fight for her, If necessary, save her . . . thank God for Washington's colored men. They put new hope in their almost despairing women.

UNSIGNED LETTER TO *CRISIS* MAGAZINE, NOVEMBER 1919

July 20, 1995

Three black men, two young, one elder, are barreling through the barren big-city terrain of southeast Washington, D.C., in an ancient blue cab on a blast-furnace July morning. I had managed to push the impending eight-hour bid at work out of my mind and drift into semisleep—that is, until the elder driver asked above the background noise of metal-on-metal grinding, "So are you brothers going to be at Farrakhan's Million Man March?"

Beginning as a scheme on the same level as Farrakhan's still-born five-year economic plan or his proposal to curb black incarceration by repatriating the convicted to Africa, the Million Man March has spiraled out to become the unspoken thread running through discussions of the race and its problems in barber shops, supermarkets, street corners, classrooms, and cabs. The question jars me back into reality, and a response is formulated. "Yeah, I'll be there," I repeat to myself.

Ignoring my response to his question, he sizes me up for the sales pitch. "See, with all this stuff going on, the crime and drugs and such, we *have to* be there. This is our city. It's not like we have to go to Chicago or something. This government can't afford to have nobody stand up to it now. Black or white, really. That's why they are going after the militias now. Farrakhan is standing up for his people and them crackers don't like that."

As the folk wisdom goes, "Just because you're paranoid don't mean that nobody's out to get you." A tinge of slightly irrational fear might just keep you alive in this world. For those of us hip, wise, or paranoid enough to keep a watchful eye out for the Man and all his myriad trickbags, the Minister Farrakhan is a wellspring of knowledge. He is, in effect, a voice in the urban wilderness, and hence this cabbie's missionary zeal in pushing the Million Man cause.

The missionary/driver devotes his full attention now to converting me, but his words have become merely a background buzz to my thoughts on the impending gathering in the nation's capital. We rumble past the Berry Farms housing projects. The spray paint on a wall reads: *"Niggas Are Living in a Jungle."*

September 13, 1995

Among the stickier semitruths to circulate within the black community is the idea that black women *raise* their daughters and *love* their sons, creating boys who will grow up to be men-children trapped in a perpetual and never-ending state of adolescence. But this maxim is sticky precisely because of the baggage that it carries. The black man, as conventional wisdom teaches, has been thoroughly emasculated by the ordeal of slavery, leaving his woman to act as head of household. The black woman, by benevolent mothering or by barbed matriarchal tongue, has ultimately perpetuated the saga of these nonmen.

In any case, among black people in this country there is no image more powerful than that of the disempowered black male. Take note, for instance, of the deft manipulation of that fact, which provided the margin of salvation for trife black men from (Tom) Clarence Thomas's "high-tech lynching" through the trials of deracialized ciphers Michael Jackson and O. J. Simpson. Black people are almost physically and emotionally incapable of ignoring the "strange fruit" politic, because the specter of lynching has been so firmly ingrained in our collective memories.

The flipside of the sacrificial black male is the myth of the unscathed black woman. Part of the reason that so many people think it necessary for black men to go to Washington to get their acts together is the assumption that the women had already done so—or have never even needed to do so. The problem is that as long as we believe in such mythology, it will remain impossible for us to grapple with the fact that it is no easier for black women to get in touch with their humanity than it is for black men. And thus, black women will remain imprisoned within a compliment.

COTTON COMES TO WASHINGTON

Black nationalism in America lapses into romantic and escapist moods and will continue to do so for as long as it depends on emotional slogans, the messianic complex for the leader, or empty militant aggressiveness . . . the ability of the Negro movement to proceed beyond its present impasse depends upon finding the solutions to these problems.

HAROLD CRUSE, *REBELLION OR REVOLUTION?*

It should be clear to us now, some thirty-plus years after Malcolm X put the question to us, that some of us got ballots and a hell of a lot of us opted for bullets. Right now it looks like the ballots are being cast into the wind and all the bullets are headed in our direction *from our own guns.* The march is Farrakhan's chance to carve out his own personal "I Have a Dream"—"Ballot or the Bullet." For all his eloquent oratory, the man has yet to coin a phrase that will resonate with his name throughout the ages. And in this age of the two-minute synopsis, sometimes a catch phrase is all you get. This is the backdrop against which he will construct a sound bite to bequeath to the pop culture of generations yet unborn. For Jesse & Co., this may be his last chance to show that he can hang out with the in-crowd.

The historical symmetry of the march is almost eerie. For those who care to connect the historical dots, exactly one hundred years ago black people found themselves in the position of watching their hard-won gains from the Sixties (albeit the 1860s) be eroded. Booker T. Washington stepped onto the scene assuring black people that the key to uplift was industry and labor—a line that wealthy northern industrialists loved. But the catch was that we had to stop making political demands and work on economic "self-sufficiency." A year later, the U.S. Supreme Court handed us *Plessy v. Ferguson,* the precedent that breathed life into Jim Crow. Economics over politics, no direct political agitation, and a country bolting rightward. It came as no surprise, then, that historian Paula Giddings dismissed the agenda of the march as "nineteenth-century solutions for twenty-first-century problems."

But to call Farrakhan simply an Islamic knock-off of Booker T. Washington is ultimately an oversimplification. His niche in black leadership didn't fall to him by default, and unlike Booker, he no longer outright disses the idea of political work—part of the march platform is an attempt to register two million black voters. Farrakhan emerged from the shadow of Wallace Muhammad, Elijah's reformist son, in 1977. Since that time, Farrakhan has eclipsed his former superior and rebuilt the Nation of Islam (NOI) by the sheer force of his will. For at least the ten years that I've been following his upward trajectory, Farrakhan has been shrewdly playing his cards as the solo voice of the dispossessed. Thirty years ago there would have been a half dozen nationalist organizations vying for the attention of we ghetto dwellers. Today, and for at least the last decade, the Nation has been the only show going. So when Farrakhan dusted off and polished up the March on Washington idea for resale, it caught on like a California brushfire—if for no other reason than because it was the only game in town.

The show and the inevitable tides of cash that it will generate have led people to tag this as the Million Dollar March. Weeks ago, Farrakhan's bootstrap machine was replete with 1–900 numbers ($3.99/minute) and ten-dollar registration fees for attending. Okay, this march is black-financed. Beautiful. Still, this is the latest in a series of pay-per-view NOI events. Freedom has become very expensive. Gone are the days of Malcolm's 125th Street open-air rallies. Now it's strictly business: twenty-dollar tickets and indoor arenas. Bootstraps and bow ties. Bean-pie capitalism. The future documentary on the event will be titled *Eyes on the Price.*

The entire spectacle, the glittery pronouncements, the self-reverence and posturing, reminded me of a summertime tent revival, only in this case the good book is *The Wealth of Nations.*

THE SOJOURNERS

October 14, 1995

The sojourners began trickling into Washington a full week before October 16. Two days before ground zero, charged waves of social energy are rippling out from this urban epicenter. The electronic billboard above I-95 South glared warning of "MILLION MAN EVENT, OCTOBER 16, PREPARE FOR DELAYS" as early as October 11—a warning that was never issued for any of the major abortion or gay rights demonstrations.

Washington's streets are absurdly swollen. The chocolate city has, in all appearances, purged itself entirely of its vanilla extracts. Whether the march attracts a million or not is irrelevant at this point. Farrakhan has attracted enough people to launch himself into the forefront of the ad hoc committee known as black leadership.

Brothers from ghetto-bastard roughnecks to smooth-faced corporate refugees-for-the-day are working out elaborate grips on city streets and hotel lobbies. The streets are filled with the laughter and busy chatter of those who are filled by the strength of their collective selves. This whole is more than the sum of its disparate black parts.

There's a sort of pregnant vibe drifting over the city as the sun slips past the monuments and D.C.'s skyline. Even my stone-cold cynicism had begun to warm a little. Any black person who has lived in this country has heard a million times over the injunction for black people to unite. People routinely drop loaded verses like "Black people gotta unite" or "What we need is unity" that carry almost biblical significance. The saying goes, "We struggle to unite and unite to struggle." I wasn't sure which half of that dialectic marked where I came in on that day.

For us in the hip-hop generation, this is our first witnessing of the extended congregation of the First African United Church. It was last convened in 1963 on this same territory. Beyond the tangibles, the qualitative results of this gathering, everyday people—the holy-ghosted grandmothers in storefront churches, the brown faces staring out the window of the number 36 bus, and brothers lining endless boulevards—will see success in the simple fact that it occurred at all.

We spill out onto the streets, a massively charged black throng. The Muslim star and crescent are nearly ubiquitous as people scurry toward their hotels. The sheer mass of the body makes it possible to believe that nearly 10 percent of the black men in America are here. A stranger grabs my hand unexpectedly and gives me a Muslim greeting. "*Salaam alaikum,* brother." Jarred from my thoughts, I pump his hand and respond enthusiastically, "*Walaikum salaam.*"

GOING TO THE TERRITORY

October 16, 1995

Inhale deep. I'm pushing past the tree-lined aisle of Seventh Street, in northeast Washington, D.C., and breathing out frigid streams of October air. I can see my quick-moving shadow slip past the still-glowing streetlights. The setup is like something from a noir flick: a dark, rain-slick street, men huddled against the cold, moving in silent uniformity—like a mass of black G-men. In the distance we can see the dimly lit dome of the U.S. Capitol building. It looks almost gloomy and abandoned in the lingering darkness. We are being led by sound, not by sight. We can hear strains of Marvin Gaye asking, *What's Going On?*

We turn the corner onto the Washington Mall and see that the grounds in front of the capitol are completely full—and it's only 6:00 a.m. The resounding "Yes sirs!" of the Fruit of Islam are echoing through the mall. There are no speakers at the main podium yet, so the massive sound system runs through Isley Brothers and Earth, Wind, and Fire classics. By 6:30 the sun still has not risen and people are shadowy figures in the dark. A massive group of men from Chicago, led by a single man in a wheelchair, march in ranks into the gathering and use the title of the Public Enemy song "Brothers Gonna Work It Out" as a rally cry. Around 7:00 a.m., just as the sun has begun to creep up over the monuments, there is the Islamic call to prayer. The call of *"Allahu Akbar"* (Allah is great) soars over the mall in a beautiful, lilting voice. Almost spontaneously, the crowd breaks into a chant of "Long live the spirit of the Million Man March."

Early on, Marion Barry, Washington's politically resurrected mayor, steps up to the podium and announces the District of Columbia's support for the M^3. Barry was another textbook case for atonement. He managed to pull off a return from the dead that would have left Lazarus green with envy. Just one term removed from his crack-addicted demise in 1990, Barry launched a massive "Look at me now" campaign gaming on the fact that Washington is a city of glory for few and stifled aspiration for many. He played up the redemptive angle and emphasized the fact that more than anyone else in the city's fishbowl political structure, he could relate to "the least and the last." He registered ex-convicts. He registered the homeless. The least and last were responsible for him becoming, once again, the mayor of Washington, D.C.

Around noon, the women supporters of the march begin speaking. M^3 has pulled together a list of black women luminaries who are at least comparable to their male counterparts. Rosa Parks, Queen Mother Harriette Moore, and Maya Angelou put in appearances. By this time, the activities on the platform have taken a backseat to the bonding going on out in the crowd. People yell out their city, and when someone from the same city hears, they wade through the crowd and hug each other and then begin talking excitedly as if they were lifelong friends.

Angelou's regal bearing and eloquence draw attention back to the huge screens that are set up about three hundred feet apart. She manages to captivate us though the excitement of the event has dwindled our attention spans to milliseconds. "The night was long, the wounds were deep, the pit was dark, the walls were steep." She makes a teary segue into "Still We Rise," and nearly breaks everyone out there down.

It's midafternoon and a trilogy of preachers (including Joseph Lowery of the Southern Christian Leadership Conference (SCLC), which helped diss Farrakhan during the '93 march) has just reblessed the gathering with a blistering flurry of hallelujahs and et ceteras. Then, out of the blue, Al Sharpton departs from the previous eight-hour apology-thon and issues a challenge to all present to radically change Congress in 1996. "O. J. is home, but Mumia ain't," he points out, referring to death-row inmate Mumia Abu-Jamal. The tension is spiraling upward. The emcee is playing wait-and-see games, announcing for the past hour and a half that Farrakhan will be speaking "soon."

Jesse Jackson arrives to a mediocre smattering of applause. Seven years ago Jesse had seven times as many people in his camp as are arrayed at this gathering today. His seven million votes seem a lifetime ago amid the aura of marginality that has come to hang over him like a storm cloud. If people are generous, they think of J. J. in terms of where he's been and what he's done—not who and what he's become now. The words "opportunism" and "camera" have a way of filtering into conversations where our country preacher is concerned. Now salting the wounds of his eroded public presence is the fact that behind closed doors, the big-money black folks who underwrote Jesse's '88 bid are making eyes at

Colin Powell, an enigma that I wouldn't even attempt to drag into this discussion.

Jesse starts off by striking a spiritual note, but then steams off like a freight train in the opposite direction of his predecessors. When the day is over, Jesse's speech was probably the best one and definitely the only one that paid as much attention to personal responsibility as it did to the social and political structures that oppress black communities. He begins by invoking the names of the civil rights movement's deceased and segues into the discussion of racism. "Racists attack us for sport . . . but rabbit hunting ain't fun when the rabbits start fighting back." In rapid-fire succession, he points out the ills besieging the black community: redlined communities, media attacks, infant mortality, "second-class schools and first-class prisons," and unemployment. Black men, and the shortcoming for which we must atone, do not occur in a vacuum. Toward the end, he switches to the atonement theme, but anybody who is paying attention knows that Jesse has just attempted a coup onstage.

Still, for all of Jesse's substance, it is his form that gets him over. Facts be damned, the biggest responses come from Jesse's rhyming couplets. When all else fails, resort to poetry.

The impatient crowd greets Ben Chavis with near-hostility. He devotes his ten-minute presentation to laying to rest any idea of "separating the message from the messenger." God, he says, called this march through none other than the honorable minister Louis Farrakhan. No one, he informs us, will *ever* tell black people who they can or cannot meet with again.

At 4:17 p.m. Mustafa Farrakhan Muhammad, the son of the man who has summoned this event into existence, bears witness that there is no god but Allah and that Elijah is his divine messenger. To those in attendance as well as those on the platform, he issues a reminder that Farrakhan is the only one who will always come to the aid of black leaders. "My father is not a racist, not a bigot, not an anti-Semite. Farrakhan is in your midst today with a vision, and a people without vision will perish."

The enormous, bellowing sound that greets Farrakhan when he appears on the huge screen in front of me dwarfs the ovation that his name inspired the night before. There is something indescribably out of sync about seeing Farrakhan, completely surrounded by stern-faced Fruit of Islam forces, calmly walking down the steps of the capitol past a platform that features Betty Shabazz, Jesse Jackson, and members of the Congressional Black Caucus and up to a lectern to address one million people. Allah has prepared a podium for him in the presence of his former enemies. In my mind, I don't think I've ever conjured up two images that seemed to be more at odds than the glittering white steps and the bow-tied cadre of black men.

THE SHOW

Louis Farrakhan is black America's most prominent conservative spokesperson. He has chosen as his resonant sound bite for the ages the title "A More Perfect Union." It lacks the fiery ultimatum quality of "The Ballot or the Bullet" and the visionary faith of "I Have a Dream," but it might work anyway. By the time he reaches the stage, the sun is a heavy orb descending and streaking the sky orange. Farrakhan issues his meek thank-yous almost as if he's oblivious to the magnitude of his own creation. He thanks the women involved. He thanks Bob Johnson of BET (Black Entertainment Television). He thanks the media for making mischief. Then, out of nowhere, he slides into a treatise on numerology.

My cynicism returns in a flood. I *know* we didn't come all this way for something from the Psychic Friends Network. The Washington Monument is 555 feet tall. Put the number one in front of that and you get 1555, the year (according to the NOI) that black people first arrived in America. He draws Jefferson,

Washington, and Lincoln into a grand Masonic conspiracy theory that would have made the cab driver's heart swell with pride. Twenty minutes into his speech, he remains firmly fixed in tarot-card nationalism. Finally, ten minutes later, he drops the metaphysics and attacks those who would like to separate the messenger from the message. "You can't separate Newton from physics. You can't separate Moses from the Torah." All prophets are flawed, he announces. "And if my heart is so dark, how can my message be so clear and bright?"

Right then it hits me like a ton of bricks that of all the things I've decided Farrakhan was over the years, I've never really caught the integrationist streak in him. "A More Perfect Union." Farrakhan has dug up the preamble and comes full blast with a rationale for cutting black folks in on the action. Not that it is new. Nothing about the presentation is what you could call new, but "A More Perfect Union" might as well be ripped straight out of the SCLC handbook. He even implies that he should be seen as a great patriot because he's willing to point out the flaws in America. The basic argument of most integrationists is that America can only be redeemed by allowing black people full access to this country's abundant resources. The Million Man March has been tailor-made for Farrakhan to show off his bourgeois integrationism, because, after all, they aren't demanding anything, not even redress for legit grievances. Before the show is over, he is theorizing that God let black people be lynched, burned, and raped in order to transform us into a sort of racial Christ figure. "Undeserved suffering is redemptive, because only those who know the depth of hell can appreciate the heights of heaven."

• • •

There is a trickle of people moving backward. It's late and many of those in attendance will have to drive all night to reach their destinations. Farrakhan's speech stretches on for two and a half hours, though it begins to fade in and out of my attention after the first fifteen minutes. Before it's all over, it plays Wheel of Fortune with the letters in the word "atonement," deconstructing it into absurdity and juggling multiple metaphors. But I may well be the only one selectively listening. The frantic olive-branching of America while consistently berating black men has worn me down. Other men, though, are moved to tears by Farrakhan's melodic pronouncement. By the time he begins the now-famous pledge, I am one of the bodies streaming away from the capitol and looking to get out of town. I look over my shoulder for a final glance at the event, and slip past the barricades back out into the shadowy dusk.

EPILOGUE: OCTOBER 17

Looking back on the march days later, I realized that the reason this event was so spiritually resonant was that with treasured few exceptions, this was the only time in the history I have witnessed in my twenty-six years that black men have been able to breathe easily and treat one another as brothers. Even so, I still could not reconcile gathering one-twelfth of America's black men in one place and essentially letting America at large off the hook. Add to the long list of the black community's "ins" (sit-in, pray-in, etc.) our first ever "sorry-in." We came, we saw, we apologized.

None of us is perfect, but the brand of atonement that was marketed at the Million Man March was based upon trying to get black men to sign off on a collective guilt trip. Nobody in their right mind could argue against "personal responsibility," but listening to the bulk of the speeches given that day it would have been easy to draw the conclusion that black men are the ultimate reason that black communities are in disarray—especially when Farrakhan got to the part about white folks respecting us if we just cleaned up our neighborhoods and "did for self." It's never been that simple.

Rather than a "Day of Atonement," I have decided that this should have been called a day of us getting to know our better selves. There was a universe separating the public atoning that went on at the podium and what was going on out in that teeming mass of men. Walking down the streets you could almost point out the men who had been at the march. And those who wore "One in a Million" buttons would stop and kick it with other men and women who asked them about the march or wanted to tell them how proud they were of them.

I have noticed that we very rarely allow ourselves to indulge in our complexities, to avoid either/or categories, to remain both critical and supportive simultaneously. Contrary to what Ben Chavis might think, the message and the messenger are not necessarily joined at the hip. In the tradition of our better selves, on October 16 we took home with us that which was sustaining and left the bitter bullshit parts alone.

The march may have given the nod to Farrakhan for the time being, but to whom much is given, much is demanded. The major criticism of Marcus Garvey was that his flamboyant style and fiery oratory enabled him to sell a romantic vision of African redemption to black people that he could never have delivered. When Garvey's check bounced, he left a vast chasm of disillusionment in his place. The same may go for Farrakhan. The director's chair is also the hot seat.

Time and history demand that a community always makes sure that its symbols have substance to back them up. The immensity of feel-good politic generated by the march and the lack of political substance to accompany it reminded me of a health crisis that occurred a few years back. There was a starch that was taken off the market because poor people were eating it as a regular part of their diets. The starch had minimal nutritional value, but it did do one magical thing: it was cheap, and a small bit of it made people feel full for hours. Ultimately, though, what it did was allow people to feel very good while they simultaneously starved to death.

January 1996

• • •

In October 2005 Farrakhan and company recognized the tenth anniversary of the march by launching an event dubbed the Millions More Movement, which had as its aim bringing a million black people—men, women, and children—to the National Mall. It was clear even early on that this call lacked the timing, originality, and energy of the 1995 march. Dubbed the "Millionth March" by observers who were tired of number-based movements, its biggest headlines came with the announcement that Rev. Willie Wilson, the national chair of the march, would step down from that position after launching into a bizarre antigay sermon. The tirade, which featured a graphic description of lesbian sexual practices and the lubricants involved, was particularly inflammatory given the awkward invitation extended to black gays and lesbians to participate in the march.

Even with the broader invitation, the second march was dwarfed—both numerically and politically—by the first one. The intervening decade raised serious doubts about the politics of atonement. Jesse Jackson had been tarred by the public exposure of a child he fathered out of wedlock. The ensuing controversy diminished his ability to respond to the disenfranchisement scams run on black voters during the 2000 presidential election. By 2005 he had all but ceased to be a force in national politics. Marion Barry served a term as mayor, left politics, and returned to be elected to city council. He tested positive for cocaine and marijuana in 2005. Ben Chavis joined the Nation of Islam and was appointed minister of the famed Mosque Number 7 in Harlem—the institution once presided over by Malcolm X. Chavis departed shortly after his appointment under a cloud of sexual harassment allegations and became a director for Russell Simmons's Hip-Hop Summit Action Network.

Farrakhan traveled to Libya to arrange a finance deal with Muammar Qaddafi. In the late '90s he struck up a close relationship with the murderous Abacha regime of Nigeria. His close association with a figure who was such anathema in the arena of American—even African American politics—effectively squandered the political capital he derived from the march, and, tellingly, black elected officials once again felt it safe to distance themselves from him without fear of backlash from their constituents. Of the original cast, only Al Sharpton's fortunes have risen. Having organized the response to the police brutality crises in the wild late 1990s New York (the sodomizing of Haitian immigrant Abner Louima, the murder of West African–born Amadou Diallo), Sharpton became an indispensable part of the New York Democratic Party organization. In 2004 he addressed the national convention following his failed bid for the presidential nomination.

For those reasons—and lots more—the 2005 Millions More gathering resembled a reunion tour for an aging band more than any kind of dynamic call to action. It gave occasion to few memories or blueprints for the future. And even fewer footprints in history.

November 2005

2

41 Shots

In February 1999 four New York City policemen in the Bronx opened fire on an unarmed African immigrant named Amadou Diallo. Nineteen of the forty-one shots fired hit Diallo. His death brought to the surface the racial implications of the tough-on-crime politics of Giuliani-era New York. The then-mayor handled the case with a degree of bureaucratic callousness that was the hallmark of his administration and his public career—at least until the events of September 11, 2001, recast Rudy Giuliani as a great American hero. At least to those who had never encountered the New York City police in a tiny corridor in the Bronx.

One life canceled nineteen times over. In this, the post-Diallo New York, there is no such thing as hyperbole. Exaggeration has taken a tragic backseat to the everyday of our reality. There are no more innocents among us. It has been ninety-four days since four white officers of the NYPD's Street Crimes Unit fired forty-one shots at Amadou Diallo, an unarmed West African immigrant, and still his execution hangs over this city like a municipal death shroud. As well it should. You can hear it on the street, smell it, taste it nearly—the volcanic discontent brewing in New York's vaunted avenues. The protests, the rallies, the organizing efforts have stretched from the arctic cold of February into the spring thaw and show no signs of abating. The protesters number in the tens of thousands, the arrested are easily in the hundreds.

Diallo's death has become a historical watershed, a bookmark for this particular page in our history.

This is what I will remember: standing before city hall holding a placard that read something to the effect of "End Giuliani's Fascism," while a white man screamed to me that he wished the cops had shot the man *fifty*-one times. I will remember a young white woman who told me that, sure, Giuliani was a little heavy-handed, but we were blowing things out of proportion. There are no more proportions. Not after hundreds of police gathered before the Bronx courthouse to cheer and whistle for the four cops as they entered the building for a hearing. Not after the patrolman's benevolent association gave police commissioner Howard Safir a vote of no confidence for failing to put the officers back on active duty quick enough.

One would have suspected that the case would eradicate the doubts regarding the brutal ways in which black and brown New York are policed, but, alas, no. More than anything else, the legacy of the Diallo shooting will be that it revealed the fault lines in the city as rarely before. That it displayed the gaping cracks in what David Dinkins has called a "gorgeous mosaic." These lines are not merely racial or ethnic, but bureaucratic as well. There are many whites of conscience, many of whom protested and were willing to be arrested to make a point about the brutality that seems endemic to New York's alleged finest. But there are many more whose silence is tacit consent, an unspoken willingness to tolerate brutal police behavior in the city's darker wards in exchange for an overall decrease in crime. These are the quarters where, for so long, the claims of police brutality have been dismissed as exaggeration, as overstated accounts delivered by supersensitive minorities. There were forty-one verified shots fired at an unarmed black man. The brutality of this scene, by its nature, defies exaggeration.

Rudolph Giuliani is, above all else, a man completely lacking in compassion—a quality that should be prerequisite for those whom we allow access to such power as his. Giuliani blew into office in 1994, evoking images of Al Pacino in *City Hall* pledging to once again make the city into a palace. It seems almost surreal that a mayor of a major metropolis at the end of the twentieth century could respond to this shooting by demanding that police be given the infinitely destructive hollow-point bullets that, he deduced, would make firing so many shots unnecessary. The conclusion that Giuliani—on the level of his basic, spiritual circuitry—is incapable of understanding human suffering when that human being is draped in black skin seems inescapable. Moreover, the mayor, as a man who is notoriously willing to accept credit for every minute improvement in the city, appears equally unwilling to accept blame. But the nine-millimeter lynching of Diallo and the brutal rape of Abner Louima nineteen months earlier are intricately related to Giuliani's tenure in city hall.

It is no coincidence that such absurdly violent behavior followed the election of a man who had led a rally of white police officers in which then-Mayor David Dinkins was referred to as a nigger and a bathroom attendant. It is no coincidence that a gunslinger mentality would pervade the police force after Giuliani formed a committee to investigate brutality in the wake of Louima's assault only to disband it, throw out its recommendations, and call their ideas "weird" after he was reelected. This is the inevitable reaping of what has been sown.

But make no mistake, white elected leaders are not the only ones indicted by Diallo's death. The case shines the spotlight on the pathetic state of black leadership within the city. In the intervening months since that tragic night in the Bronx, the black leadership of the city has yet to produce a coherent agenda regarding this case. Calvin Butts, pastor of the Harlem gospelic powerhouse Abyssinian Baptist Church, opened his building for the organizing of protests and spoke at several rallies regarding the case—each time denouncing police brutality—only to Tom-mishly fall into Giuliani's arms in a scripted hug a few weeks later at an interfaith "healing" service. His Queens clerical counter-part and Giuliani partisan, Floyd Flake, pronounced a few uncon-troversial platitudes immediately after the killing and faded from sight. Both men prefaced their criticism of the police department by saying they believed the overwhelming majority of cops were good and decent professionals—a sentiment that is as unverifiable as it is simpleminded, ignoring the systemic roots of police vio-lence directed at blacks. One doesn't need an advanced degree in history to recall that every major race riot in New York this cen-tury has had police violence toward blacks at its root.

It is the irony of ironies that Al Sharpton has emerged in these months as the man most capable of bringing together a multiracial audience, united in their outrage. Sharpton comes off as a provocateur, a flamboyant bidder for the admiration of the crowd, but, nonetheless, as a man who is not without his uses. No group is without its own absolute, immutable partisans, and in New York Sharpton has invented himself as the epitome of black partisanship. Still, he is far more adept at the art of public provocation than the tedious sciences of social and political change. Ultimately, the case seems chain-linked to the mayoral ambitions of all involved.

Thus, it has come to this: a humble dead man's memory looming in the consciousness of a city and the mass of municipal players lacking the imagination or will required to achieve true justice. An innocent man has died, a city has been torn, powerful men have fallen short, and suddenly, all hyperbole has become understatement.

March 1999

3

White Negro Please: Eminem's Race Blues

In the pantheon of disposable American heroes, Marshall Mathers is the man of the moment. Having turned a media double play on the big screen and the airwaves with the high-grossing biopic *8 Mile* and its ubiquitous soundtrack, M. M. (or Eminem) is poised to parlay his anointed fifteen minutes into an epic run of at least an hour or two. Already canonized in the pages of the *New York Times* and virtually ordained by the glossies, digging Eminem has become the current hipness litmus. Frank Rich, in the midst of a pathos festival in the pages of the *Times,* praised Em's lyrical flow and originality. En route to proclaiming Eminem as fun for all ages, he offered this observation: "In a country in which broken homes, absentee parents and latchkey kids are endemic to every social class, he can touch some of the hottest emotional buttons. He can be puerile, too, but what else is new in pop music?"

No less an authority on hip-hop than Andrew Sullivan observed on Salon.com that "Eminem's music is some of the most challenging, inventive and lyrically brilliant in recent times. His movie . . . was an excellently written and directed product. There's no mystery why it did so well."

With the minor concerns of his antigay and violently misogynistic lyrics airbrushed into obscurity, courtesy of endorsements by critics (and Elton John—dude, what gives?), Em's slouchy way and disaffected scowl are set to become our modern equivalent of Elvis's hip tic.

With a 250-word lead-in out of the way, conventional journalism about Eminem holds that this paragraph is where I'm supposed to start talking about his disturbing significance to our particular cultural moment and detail the important questions that his ascent raises. Long pause. Truth told, beyond asking the obvious questions (i.e., Yo, they, like, got white people in Detroit) the response from the hip-hop cognoscenti and more than a few quarters of black America has been an audible yawn. True, the rapper's cultural cache has earned him placement on the covers of underground hip-hop publications, but their treatment of him has had way fewer hosannas than the mainstream magazines and papers that have branded him as the second coming of Elvis Marciano.

Compare Rich's and Sullivan's assessments to this unsolicited testimonial from a black writer on the Afrofuturism Listserv: "I know that we are on the list to talk about futurist themes in black cultural production. And right now with all this Eminem talk I think the eradication of white hegemony would be quite futuristic. Does anyone have any links to any articles where the writer has actually told the truth about this %$#@!())&???"

In the race to imbue Eminem with some enduring

significance—beyond the receipts he adds to the national cash register—the fact that he is not all that culturally significant to hip-hop has gone almost completely unnoticed. He is not a stylistic innovator a la Busta Rhymes or Snoop Dogg, or a master narrator like Slick Rick. His subject matter is daring, but benchmark acts like Public Enemy, Eric B and Rakim, Queen Latifah, and A Tribe Called Quest were responsible for dilating hip-hop's understanding of what could be rapped about. Mainstream American pop has been dipping into black culture for reinvigoration since the days of burnt cork; that a white rapper has made millions is nothing new.

Eminem's market dominance has occurred for the same reasons that Jayson "White Chocolate" Williams of the Sacramento Kings has the best-selling jersey in the NBA, and I'm awaiting the day that music critics start praising Eminem for having "sound fundamentals" when it comes to rapping. Both Em and Williams are the beneficiaries of a type of cultural affirmative action for white men, which is to say that neither of them is unqualified, but both are object lessons in the benefits of diversity. (Toddlers too small to grip a microphone or hold a basketball now will in future days remember the first time they heard Eminem flow or saw one of Williams's pyrotechnic, no-look passes and realized that they, too, could succeed in a black-dominated world.)

Eminem is neither the first commercially successful white rapper—the Beastie Boys lay claim to that distinction, nor the first to be charged with the Elvising of hip-hop (that would be Vanilla Ice). He fits into a pantheon of white artists that include moderate successes like Third Base (a riff on the famous "Who's on First?" routine) and the Irish American trio House of Pain, who played up their Gaelic ancestry as an ethnic counterpoint to the Afrocentrism that dominated hip-hop at the time. But the question remains: who IS on first? Eminem is in scoring position because he is, for what it matters, probably the most talented white rapper yet to emerge. But comparing Eminem to the lineage of white wordsmiths is approximately as patronizing as calling Miles Davis "a fine Negro musician" or referring to Denzel Washington as "that black guy with the Oscar."

Eminem is undoubtedly clever, but cleverness is as common to rappers as lying is to politicians. His cadence (or flow) is infectious, but not in the same league as vocal masters like Rakim or Notorious B.I.G. Em has a lyrical gift, but leave him in the same room with the West Coast's Ras Kass or the Brooklyn freestyle master Supernatural and you'd have a repeat of the Larry Holmes–Gerry Cooney fight back in '82. Nor does Eminem himself have any illusions about his standing in the pantheon of rap, having stated in interviews that he doesn't consider himself to be in the top tier of rappers in terms of skill.

What Em is selling—and what has resonated with his legions of fans, salivating critics, and assorted media apostles—is a narrative of a worthless childhood in the postindustrial wasteland of the former Motor City. With his brooding, swaggering persona, replete with prereq tattoos, oversized gear, and bleached-out follicles, Eminem has been appointed the voice of Anglo angst à la Kurt Cobain. Call it Columbine chic.

In a country where class distinctions are consistently glossed over and the white poor are virtually invisible, save for the sardonic exploitation of Jerry Springer, Eminem's trailer park blues have way more significance to white suburban America than hip-hop as a genre. For what it matters, Eminem's tales of alienation (i.e., his existential query, "How can I be white when I don't even exist?") descend from the visceral autobiographical narratives of rappers like Scarface, Notorious B.I.G., and Tupac Shakur. At its best, hip-hop has been a vehicle for expressing—and transcending—the frailties and the pain of life in the negative space of America. That reality may have been lost on many prior to the Eminem movement. To be accurate, Eminem may fit into that tradition of lyrical catharsis and boulevard jeremiads, but he certainly didn't create it. Plus, Em's matricidal ramblings are beyond the pale even for hip-hop; gangsta rappers, like their celluloid counterparts, will consistently take hiatus from issuing colorful death threats to pay homage to dear old Mom. (See Tupac's "Dear Mama" or Biggie's loving nod to his mother on "Juicy.")

Epidermal novelty explains why mainstream critics, baby boomers, and other people who are not in hip-hop's core demographic but who are purchasing Eminem records took a first listen and got hooked. To cut to the quick: white pain is now the flavor of the month, and if oppression (class, that is, not race, sexual orientation, or gender) leaves a guy with some rough misogynist and homophobic edges, what can you expect? He's *poor*, for God's sake. Sympathy for the black poor (and the stories they tell) may have gone out with big hair and leg warmers, but a *white* poor guy raises questions that are both unsettling and alluring to Market America (i.e., Didn't FDR take care of that problem?). One can imagine Rich and Sullivan sipping Merlot in their respective dens while grooving to the *8 Mile* soundtrack and asking, "Yo, they, like, still got white people in Detroit?"

The digital mytho-history of the film *8 Mile* plays up this class angle—with substantial echoes of Prince's cult classic *Purple Rain*. Trailer park denizen Jimmy Smith—a stand-in for our lyrical hero—inhabits a perpetually overcast world where opportunity missed a rent payment and lost its lease. Down but not completely out, B. Rabbit—Jimmy's performance alter ego— struggles nobly to be judged by the content of his lyrics, not the color of his skin. Jimmy has no racial reckoning of his own to do, because racism is black people's problem in *8 Mile*. Jimmy loves everybody. He even takes up for a gay guy at work. The climactic scene in which B. Rabbit outs his black male rival as a middle-class brat with a thug complex reminded me of that scene in

Rocky II where another of America's low-income icons beats the ten count to take the title from that rich, flamboyant black guy. When you get right down to it, how bad can black people with money have it?

With his gift for crossover appeal (though he's crossing class, not race lines), it's fitting that Eminem hails from Detroit—the city where Berry Gordy first came up with his formula for selling black music to white America. The cocktail of white poverty and hip-hop is a heady mix right about now, and both Eminem and his black producer, Dr. Dre, are laughing all the way to the bank—and isn't that what really matters? The boy made a name for himself by suggesting he was chocolate on the inside, but he made a fortune from an audience invested in seeing him as white to the bone. Marshall Mathers: Credit to his race.

January 2003

4

The World Is Yours

People be asking me all the time, Yo, Mos, what you think is getting ready to happen with hip-hop? I tell them, Whatever is happening with us. We are hip-hop—you, me, everybody. So hip-hop is going wherever we're going.

MOS DEF, "FEAR NOT OF MAN"

A true fact: DJ Kay-Slay has in his possession a classified mix tape featuring Colin Powell and Beanie Sigel freestyling over the track from Nas's "The World Is Yours." Heads from the State Department and Roc-a-Fella Records were talking some ill, market cross-fertilization-type shit, saying this was gonna help both of them blow up in those parts of the world that we routinely blow up. In coming weeks Alan Greenspan is expected to announce the new laissez-faire plan to deregulate the medical, weapons, and food industries known as the "Can't Knock the Hustle" initiative. The Federal Reserve has hired street promotion teams to blanket Wall Street with flyers stating that the new initiative drops on July 1. And we ain't even gonna speak on that Li'l Kim–Condi Rice collabo where they drop jewels over the "Bombs Over Baghdad" track.

We know, or ought to know by now, that, in the words of the late Notorious One, *things done changed*. Flip on your TV, turn on the radio, open a magazine, and there's a good chance that there's a rapper floating on your medium of choice. Time was when heads were being ironic, or at least hyperbolic in speaking of the so-called hip-hop nation, but with a consumer base of 45 million people dropping somewhere around $10 billion a year on CDs, clothing, DVDs, magazines, and concerts—and $300 billion in purchasing power—hip-hop dwarfs the financial power of entire nations in the so-called Third World.

And don't think there ain't big implications for this kind of cash flow. Like Madison-Avenued focus-grouped novelties, rappers are created in accord with the reigning flavor of the nanosecond. Right about now, most rappers exist as living product placements, their gear, their rides, their whole setup as deliberately schemed as that can of Coke downed by your favorite action hero before he splits to do battle with the special-effected forces of evil. Only the mad niche-marketers of American hypercapitalism could conceive of the modern rap video—basically a commercial in which products advertise other products.

Rappers have literally gone from being maligned boulevard poets à la Grand Master Flash and the Furious Five's *The Message* to acting as melinated sales reps for the American Dream. Hip-hop has highlighted the black impulse toward verbal and musical innovation and, at the same time, turned the most problematic, despair-riddled elements of American life into purchasable entertainment. The hip-hop industry is largely responsible for the global redispersal of stereotypical visions of black sexuality, criminality, material obsession, violence, and social detachment. That a brother can now fly halfway around the world and be greeted in the Czech Republic by young men who speak no English but regard you with a high five and say "What up, Nigga?" is a bitterly ironic testament to the power and appeal of African American culture in the age of high capitalism.

And the art ain't exempt, neither. Heads were once clear on the difference between a rapper and an emcee, when the verbal sales rep for the music industry was understood as distinct from the microphone controller.

The difference between an emcee and a rapper is the difference between smooth jazz and John Coltrane, the difference between studio and unplugged. Or to sample a line from Alice Walker, the difference between indigo and sky blue. Nelly is a rapper; KRS-One is an emcee twenty-five hours a day. Lauryn Hill is, straight up and down, an emcee's emcee; Li'l Kim is a rapper. The Fresh Prince was an emcee; Will Smith is a rapper. Nas has been an emcee since he breathed his first, but the P's (both Diddy and Master) are rappers down to their DNA.

The rapper is judged by his ability to move units; the measure of the emcee is the ability to move crowds. The emcee gets down to his task with only the barest elements of hip-hop instrumentalization: two turntables and a microphone. On that level, the Miami basspreneur Luke, who didn't even necessarily *rhyme,* was closer to being an emcee than Hammer, who did—or at least attempted to. The emcee writes his own material. The emcee would still be writing his own material even if he didn't have a record deal. A rapper without a record deal is a commercial without a time slot.

But to cop a line from Dead Prez, this really is bigger than hip-hop. Black people have been the smiling face of American capitalism for a long time. The difference, though, between Uncle Ben and Uncle L is that neither Ben—nor his girl, Jemima—ever endorsed GOP ballers like George Pataki (LL Cool J, that inveterate player of the stock markets, knows on which side his bread is buttered). The point is that the music is the canary in our collective mineshaft. It is "The Message" in an arena where we specialize in killing the messengers.

We know the arid facts: Rocawear's generating $300 million in sales annually, Reebok's S. Carter line accounting for 15 percent of the company's footwear sales, Rush Communications's status as the second largest black-owned entertainment company in the United States, and a white consumer base that accounts for 75 percent of hip-hop's sales numbers. And we could trip on the irony of this—a generation of black artists and label executives getting rich by selling black music to white America, learning from the generation of black rock musicians who died broke while their pale imitations copped platinum sales, if we didn't also know that the vitality of the art form is being drowned by the commercialized lyrics, the same-ol', same ol' gangsta-pimp formulas, and industry domination.

Not surprisingly, a Cuban emcee explained to me last year that hip-hop was created in the United States, but it no longer resides there. "American hip-hop," he all but epitaphed, "is dead." Its Third World siblings—at least in his telling—are alive and thriving. And the brother had a point. Hip-hop as we know it might not be deceased, but it's damn sure on life support. Think about how often you hear an emcee who makes you consistently stop the CD to replay his last line, and you'll see my point. But attempting to fix hip-hop in this here era of global grand larceny and economic terrorism might just be as bright as looking for a mop on the deck of the Titanic or facing west at sunrise. *To cut to the quick, your music is fucked up because everything else is, too.*

Hip-hop's so-deemed Golden Age, between 1988 and 1992, witnessed the ascent of Public Enemy, KRS-One, Queen Latifah, Big Daddy Kane, NWA, Salt-N-Pepa, A Tribe Called Quest, and Rakim. But it don't take a conspiracy theorist to see that hip-hop's artistic integrity started to decline at the same time that the United States declared victory in the Cold War and all opposition to the global reign of American capitalism collapsed. Dig, if it wasn't obvious before, we should've known which way the wind was blowing when characters like Eazy-E started showing up at Republican Party fund-raisers. Materialism has always been a theme in hip-hop, but in this millennium artists don't speak of the idle longing for gold chains and white-walled caddies, but give straight-up lyrical balance sheets of shit they actually own. So the question is, what becomes of an art that is born of poverty when its primary voices belong to the top 1 percent of the economic brackets?

And yeah, I know, before we start speaking on the virtues of the underground, let's bear in mind that Rawkus, the hip-hop industry's version of Miramax, was started by James Murdoch, son of Rupert Murdoch, the owner of the Fox News network—the same people whose yellow propaganda helped fan the flames of Desert Storm: The Sequel. The same people who forbade the mention of the name Osama Bin Laden on air lest the country be reminded that he—not Saddam Hussein—had bombed the World Trade Center.

In hip-hop the commercial niche-artist has drowned out an array of nonmarketed voices for the same reason that Barnes and Noble ran your local bookstore into the ground, Wal-Mart sent your neighborhood hardware store owner into early retirement, and that twenty-thousand-seat megachurch put the storefront preacher into financial purgatory. In a phrase: market economics. No wonder you got Jay-Z calling hisself the "rap version of T. D. Jakes." KRS-One broke this down for all posterity on "Step Into a World" when he kicked the line "I'm not the run of the mill, 'cause for the mill I don't run"—meaning that market logic demands that the industry go with what sells, not with what advances the art form.

Amiri Baraka points out in the classic *Blues People* that you can chart the precise political and social position of a people by the music they produce at a given moment. And by that standard the blues came into existence as the musical score to the Great Migration and the lives of the generation that lived through it. Listen to Martha and the Vandellas' "Dancing in the Street" or Aretha's "Think," and you recognize immediately that the soul music of the 1960s was the musical accompaniment to the civil rights movement. And Parliament classics like "Chocolate City" and "Up on the Downstroke" bear witness to funk's knee-deep connection to the black power movement.

Critics have lamented that hip-hop has no particular set of ideals attached to it, but you are dead wrong, or at least mad naïve to think the music exists outside a cultural movement—hip-hop is, among other things—the soundtrack of globalism. Not the kind of globalism marked by the people of color crossroading up in the Bronx in the 1970s, but the kind that allows you to buy McDonald's in Tibet. It's been pointed out that the United States has never been attacked by a country that has McDonald's—and it ain't no surprise that the first flag planted in post-Soviet soil was that of the red-yellow-white clown-faced burger dealers. And thanks to the struggles of the 1960s, black people—or at least some of us—have been admitted as junior shareholders in this corporation called America (you can almost hear the theme song from *The Jeffersons* playing in the background). In the bitter irony of history, Martin Luther King's assassination cleared the way for there eventually to be the first black CEO of Halliburton.

Free at last.

Free for all.

Hip-hop is not the first music to confront the implications of the market. Motown had lucre as a preeminent concern. The fabled "Motown Sound" was Berry Gordy's formula for getting into the pockets of white America. Gordy's Hitsville, USA, studio took Henry Ford's insights into mass assembly and applied it to black music in a way that made Gordy more a captain of industry than a pioneer in music. Gordy, in fact, hated Marvin Gaye's single "What's Going On," which was meant to be Gaye's artistic rebellion against the formulaic sound coming out of Hitsville, USA—but in true, ironic capitalist fashion, Gordy ordered ten more songs just like it once the song caught on. Still, hip-hop is the music produced by the first generation of black people to be (limited) shareholders in America, Inc., and necessarily brings a whole 'nother set of concerns to the foreground. The materialism of hip-hop is, on one level, a measure of the extent to which the American Dream has been purchased—as is—since the civil rights movement.

There's a reason that Tony Montana, from Brian DePalma's *Scarface,* is the patron saint of hip-hop. Recall the tagline for that flick was "He loved the American dream. With a vengeance." And this is the reason that Colin Powell and Condoleeza Rice have replaced the black dissidents Malcolm X, Muhammad Ali, and Martin Luther King (and Paul Robeson, too, if you want to be real about it) as the most recognizable African American political icons both domestically and abroad. Add into the equation Kenneth Chenault, the black CEO of Amex; Stanley O'Neal, the black CEO of Merrill Lynch; Richard Parsons, CEO of Time Warner, and you'll recognize that in the post–civil rights era, the dominant African Americans are all products of the American corporate machinery or American state authority. And they represent Product America in a way that Uncle Ben and Aunt Jemima never could, because they are not meant to be ironic.

So the question is not how hip-hop came to be where it is, but really, how it could be anything but this. Why have John Wayne as the face of swaggering American capital when you can have Jay-Z?

On this score, none is better than Jay. Think of Jigga as Horatio Alger with street cred, the world's first supply-side emcee. Sleep if you want to, but Jay's line "Mama ain't raise no fools / put me anywhere on God's green earth / I'll triple my worth" is the clearest statement of the capitalist credo since Calvin Coolidge declared that "the business of America is *business.*" Given his standing as the only multimedia don to rise up out of the infamous Marcy 'jects, you really *can't* knock the hustle. Or the hustler neither, as it turns out.

More than any rhyme spitter going, the life and career of Shawn Carter—the self-professed "Che Guevera with bling on"—indicates how far this game has been played. It might be facile to observe that the drug hustle is the pristine example of free market economics and that even Jay's cross-borough nemesis, Nas, was hip to the fact that "the rap game reminds me of the crack game" way back in the *Illmatic* era, but the observation bears repeating. Elizabeth Mendez Berry broke this down deftly in her review of *The Blueprint*:

> Jay-Z is convincing. When he raps, "I'm representin' for the seat where Rosa Parks sat / where Malcolm X was shot, where Martin Luther was popped" on *Blueprint*'s "The Ruler's Back," you almost believe him. When he rocks his Guevara shirt and do-rag, squint and you see a revolutionary. But open your eyes to the platinum chain around his neck: Jay-Z is a hustler. It may be that he recognizes the sex-appeal-by-association of guerilla garb. Or perhaps in the process of polishing his game till it gleams, it has begun to blind him.

From where I'm standing, *The Black Album* could've been one of the ten greatest in hip-hop history had the commercial diversions and mass market confections like "Change Clothes" and "Dirt Off Your Shoulder" not gotten in the way of his autobiography. Give the man credit, though. In an arena where artists routinely downplay the corporate interests that control their music, Jay came clean, telling his audience straight up that he'd dumbed down his lyrics to double his dollars (which presumes, ironically enough, that his audience is so enthralled that he can state he had to take it down a notch so they could understand him, or that they're so dumb as to not notice they've been insulted).

And all of this ultimately brings us back to that freestyle with Colin Powell. In the new millennium, hip-hop is foreign policy (why you think Cam'ron calls them cats "The Diplomats"?). One might double his or her dollars domestically, but in order to quadruple them you need to follow the flag of American capital abroad. In order to sell globally, you have to have MTV globally, or Amazon.com globally, or Virgin Megastores—again, globally. Plus the industrial bling glimmering from the chest of your rapper of choice is priceless public relations for America, Inc. Dig the slogan: *America the Beautiful: Where Even Niggas in the Projects Are Rich.*

We would do well to recall that jazz musicians were sent on CIA-sponsored world tours in the 1950s as part of the cultural effort to combat Communism. The U.S. Information Agency's support of Louis Armstrong's music was meant both as a cultural statement—introducing the world to America's sole classical music—and a political one: stating implicitly that even the most exploited of Americans were able to cultivate artistic genius in the grand, gold-paved streets of the U.S. of A. That young brother from Newark who came back from Operation Iraqi Freedom tripping off the fact that both the Iraqis and the Americans had Tupac CDs was speaking volumes about hip-hop's niche in the disordered New World. For all their in-family squabbling about violent, antisocial content, the voices of Official America desperately *need* hip-hop to be global—what else are you gonna sell when you open that HMV in downtown Baghdad?

Think about it for a second and you can't help but realize that we're asking hip-hop, of all things, to be exempt from the forces that have corrupted medicine, bought off the media, produced for-profit prisons, and stolen presidential elections. When you get down to the get-down, those aging white hippies smashing the windows of Starbucks during the G8 summit are doing more to re-create quality hip-hop than the last dozen anointed producers and industry-heralded emcees combined. The truth is that we already knew that no country with a McDonald's has ever attacked the U.S. The real scoop is that no country with Black Entertainment Television has either.

In the end, Colin and Jigga need to be on the same track, because they're already on the same page. Hip-hop is on life support for the same reasons that capitalism is doing victory laps around the globe. The victors have always gotten to write history—it's just that now they can produce its soundtrack, too. So when you find yourself nostalgicizing over the golden age of hip-hop, you might just want to cop that unsigned independent artist's latest self-produced CD or sample the latest offerings of the emcees from anywhere that the currency is worth one one-hundredth of the U.S. dollar. And pray like hell that you can't find them on Amazon.com.

June 2004

5

The Hoodrat Theory

In April 2004, students at Spelman College became embroiled in a national debate over misogyny in hip-hop when they criticized the rapper Nelly for a sexually explicit music video. Unaware of the controversy, the rapper had planned to organize a bone marrow drive at the college in hopes of finding a match for his sister, who was stricken with leukemia. In the ensuing conflict, Nelly opted to cancel the appearance and the drive, igniting a heated and long overdue controversy over the images of black women in hip-hop.

The flyers posted in Cosby Hall said it all: "We Care About Your Sister, But You Have to Care About Ours, Too." The slogan explained the position of the student activists at Spelman College, whose protests over Nelly's "Tip Drill" video led the artist to cancel his scheduled appearance for a bone marrow drive on the campus earlier this month. But in a real sense, their point went beyond any single rapper or any single video and went to the center of a long-standing conflict in the heart of the black community.

By now we have been drowned by the cliché defenses and half-explanations for "Tip Drill"—most of which fall into a formulaic defense of Nelly's "artistic freedom" while casting hellfire on the unpaid women who participated in the creation of the video. The slightly more complex responses point to the pressing need for bone marrow donors in the black community, saying that saving the lives of leukemia patients outweighs the issue of a single soft-porn music video. But rarely do we hear the point that these students were bringing home: that this single video is part of a centuries-long debasement of black women's bodies. And the sad truth is that hip-hop artists' verbal and visual renderings of black women are now virtually indistinguishable from those of nineteenth-century white slave owners.

History is full of tragic irony.

Full Disclosure: I am a history professor at Spelman College. I've also taught several of the students involved in the protests over the video. I don't pretend to be unbiased in my support for their actions. I openly supported the students who—and this is important—never uninvited Nelly or canceled the marrow drive. They did, however, request that he participate in a campuswide forum on the video's problematic images and stated that if he did not, the marrow drive could continue but his presence on campus would be protested. That Nelly's organization decided to cancel the drive rather than listen to the views of women who were literally being asked to give up bone and blood is tantamount to saying, "Shut up and give me your bone marrow."

This is the truth: hip-hop has all but devolved into a brand neominstrelsy, advertising a one-dimensional rendering of black life. But stereotypes serve to justify not only individual prejudices, but also oppressive power relationships. In the 1890s the prevailing depiction of black men as sex-crazed rapists who were obsessed with white women served as a social rationalization for the insanity of lynching. Nor should we forget that Jim Crow took root and evolved in tandem with the growing obsession with blackface caricatures of African Americans as senseless children too simpleminded to participate in an allegedly democratic society. It is no coincidence that the newborn NAACP made its first national headlines for protesting D. W. Griffith's white supremacist epic, *Birth of a Nation.*

In short, stereotypes are the public relations campaign for injustice.

In the case of black women, the body of myths surrounding their sexuality served to justify the sexual exploitation they experienced during and after slavery. And in so doing, the blame for adulterous relationships that produced biracial offspring shifted from married white slaveholders to insatiable black temptresses who led them astray. The historian Deborah White has written of the prevailing images of enslaved black women:

> One of the most prevalent images of black women in antebellum America was of a person governed almost entirely by libido, a Jezebel character. In every way, Jezebel was the counter-image of the nineteenth-century ideal of the Victorian lady. She did not lead men and children to God; piety was foreign to her. She saw no advantage in prudery, indeed domesticity paled in importance before matters of the flesh.

As long as black women could be understood to be sexually lascivious, it was impossible to view them as victims of sexual exploitation. Some went so far as to argue that black women did not experience pain during childbirth—evidence, in their minds, that they were not descendants of Eve, and therefore not human.

In 1895, when Ida B. Wells-Barnett began traveling abroad to publicize the horrors of American racism—and highlighting the recreational homicide of lynching—this same set of ideas was employed to discredit her. One editor charged that she was not to be believed, because it was a known fact that black women were inclined toward prostitution—among an array of other immoral pastimes. During the 1930s this image of the black Jezebel was dusted off to justify the forced sterilization of black women, who, it was believed, were sexually insatiable and prone to produce far too many offspring. Half a century later, Ronald Reagan's rhetoric about punishing "welfare queens"—basically Jezebels who traveled to the big city and moved into the projects—helped him solidify support among white voters who perceived welfare as a subsidy for reckless black sex and reproduction.

It would be easy to assume that sexist music videos are simple entertainment—not the equivalent of a body of myths that have been used to oppress black women—were it not for the fact that the lines between culture and politics are not always that easily distinguishable. Hip-hop is now the prevailing global youth culture and, in many instances, the only vision people have of African American life. In a twisted testament to the ubiquity of black culture, a student who spent a semester in China reported back that some of the town residents were fearful of the black male exchange students, having met very few black people but viewed a great many black-thug music videos.

Regardless of Nelly's intentions, videos like "Tip Drill" are viewed as yet another confirmation of the long-standing ideas about black women. On one level, the consistent stream of near-naked sisters gyrating their way through one video after the next and the glossary of hip-hop epithets directed at women—chickenheads, tip drills, hoodrats, etc.—highlight a serious breach between young black men and women. But on another level, it was affirming to see young men from Morehouse College and Clark-Atlanta University involved in the protests. All told, the students who organized the protests were not hating on a successful black man or ignoring the pressing need for bone marrow. They were highlighting a truth that is almost forgotten in hip-hop these days—a truth so basic that I wish I did not have to state it: anything that harms black women harms black people.

April 2004

6

The Quagmire Blues

History may not repeat itself, but it is prone to extended paraphrases. And that's why the ongoing war in Iraq increasingly seems like a contemporary remake of a tragedy epic called Vietnam. On one level, the United States' twenty-five-year involvement in Vietnam has become the standing metaphor for every military conflict since the fall of Saigon in 1975; Iraq is only the most recent military action to be called "another Vietnam." But on another level, this is anything but a pat comparison. There are too many parallels between the historical experience of Vietnam and our current, allegedly concluded, war in Iraq to be ignored.

The first American military presence in Vietnam began in 1950—on the heels of the Chinese Revolution—an attempt to assist the failing French effort at subduing the independence movement there. After France's crushing defeat at Dien Bien Phu in 1954, the United States took an increasing interest in Vietnam, concerned ultimately that a victory for Ho Chi Minh's forces would lead to the spread of Communism throughout Asia—the famous "domino theory." The cold war may be over, but domino politics are still in vogue. In 2003 the Bush administration attempted to create a reverse domino, selling the war as, among other things, a chance to create a stable democratic society in the Middle East that will then serve as a home base for spreading democracy throughout the region.

But systems of government tend not to spread in the same way as viruses—countries do not simply "catch" democracy from their neighbors. Building a democratic culture may take decades, and democracy, almost by definition, cannot be imposed from abroad. It has to be built from below. Now that Iraq has had freedom imposed upon it, the United States is in the catch-22 of having to spend billions supporting it through political infancy or cutting the apron strings prematurely and risking a repeat of anti-American groundswell seen in Afghanistan when the United States withdrew its support following the cold war. In either case, we will be living with Iraq for a very long time.

In this Vietnam remake, George W. Bush reprises the role of that other Texan populist, Lyndon B. Johnson. Like Johnson, Bush is attempting to fight an enormously expensive war while simultaneously financing expensive domestic programs. LBJ's War on Poverty programs were ultimately done in by the billions in Vietnam-related expenses, but the cost of maintaining well over one hundred thousand troops in Iraq—not to mention Afghanistan—hasn't dimmed the Bush administration's fervor for their most expensive domestic item: tax cuts disproportionately benefiting the upper reaches of the income bracket. And, for what it matters, the Bush administration's rationale for attacking

Iraq—the pursuit of "weapons of mass destruction" that posed an imminent danger to American lives—recalls LBJ's Gulf of Tonkin incident, the phantom attack upon American ships by North Vietnamese gunboats that Johnson used to gain a congressional resolution authorizing him to use "all necessary measures" to prevent further aggression.

In 1971 Daniel Ellsberg secretly leaked what came to be known as "The Pentagon Papers," the Rand Corporation's history of the Vietnam War, which confirmed the suspicions of critics that both the Kennedy and Johnson administrations had consistently misled the public about Vietnam. Ellsberg's whistle-blowing earned him the animosity of the Nixon administration (which sent the Watergate team to break into the office of Ellsberg's psychiatrist, seeking incriminating information). It's hard to avoid the echoes of Ellsberg when we see former terrorism czar Richard Clarke testifying that the administration had little interest in terrorism and essentially special-ordered intelligence linking Saddam Hussein to Osama Bin Laden to justify invading Iraq. At the very least, both men's revelations called into question the arguments in support of wars allegedly fought for our own protection. And it's no irony that Ellsberg himself took to the streets well before the war in Iraq began, telling the public that an invasion would be "a catastrophe."

In this scenario, Colin Powell gives a cameo performance as . . . Colin Powell. The secretary of state is the only cabinet-level Bush appointee who in fact knows what "another Vietnam" would look like, since he had a soldier's-eye view of the first one. Not surprisingly, Powell was wary about the prospect of an Iraq invasion. It's no secret that Powell's approach to diplomacy and war was shaped by his experience in Vietnam. Thus, his "Powell Doctrine" holds that the United States should commit its forces to war in numbers designed to overwhelm the enemy, in circumstances where soldiers can clearly distinguish enemies from allies, and only after domestic and international support for the action has been established. For what it matters, Powell has frowned upon using the military to achieve what are essentially political goals, and in situations where the yardstick measuring victory is unclear. In short, everything that defines the current—ongoing—war in Iraq.

In Vietnam, American soldiers found themselves enmeshed in a war where "victory" became an increasingly opaque concept. The North Vietnamese NLF (National Front for the Liberation of Vietnam) forces were clear that the war could be "won" simply by continuing to fight the American forces to a long-standing, demoralizing, and expensive stalemate. And this prospect was complicated by the difficulty in determining friend from foe, the unprecedented levels of domestic opposition to the war, and the fact that not even a military victory would ensure long-term political stability.

Last week's uprisings in Fallujah established that Iraqi bridges—along with Southern trees—bear strange fruit. Despite the grisly specter of charred Americans swinging from Fallujah bridges, polls indicate that the administration's Iraq plan is still clinging to a 3 percent margin of approval regarding the war. But this war is vastly unpopular abroad, and has squandered entirely the foreign goodwill that came in the wake of September 11. The unilateral bombing of Iraq has vastly undermined the United Nations' diplomatic authority and created a precedent for bypassing the UN for other countries. Iraqi cities, filled with civilians, mosques, and apartment complexes, may yet be the equivalent of Vietnam's dense underbrush—an intractable hiding place for insurgents plotting guerilla attacks. And there's no Agent Orange for removing glass and concrete.

Both Dick Cheney and Donald Rumsfeld have voiced their wish to eliminate the "Vietnam Syndrome"—to conduct the conflict in Iraq in such a way as to wipe away the American knee-jerk reflex to call any possible war "another Vietnam." And on this level, the vice president and the secretary of defense might well be successful. This conflict may banish the ghosts of Vietnam: future generations will look at the looming prospect of invading an underdeveloped country to achieve ambiguous aims at the cost of a great many lives and say, "This is going to be another Iraq."

January 2005

7

The Cosby Show

In May 2004 the comedian Bill Cosby, speaking at an event organized for the fiftieth anniversary of the Brown v. Board of Education decision, launched into an unscripted diatribe directed at the faults of poor African Americans. The screed earned him a new standing in the screaming match that passes for dialogue in this country, but his statements raised as many questions as they supplied answers. In 2005 Cosby reiterated his comments in a city-by-city speaking tour—a tour that was canceled when a young African American woman in Cosby's hometown of Philadelphia directed allegations of sexual assault at the comedian.

The old maxim warns us to beware of priests who lose their faith but keep their jobs. By that logic, a whole lot of alleged spokespersons for black people should've been unemployed a long time ago. In the wake of Bill Cosby's now-famous "Pound Cake Speech" at the NAACP Legal Defense Fund's dinner commemorating the *Brown v. Board of Education* case, the comedian has been praised by white conservatives and black folk at large for essentially keeping it real. For airing dirty laundry. For saying in public what your uncle Bobby has been saying behind closed doors for years.

But hold on. Before you fix your mouth to sing Cosby's praises, consider this: the fact that some black people make similar comments in private does not make them any more accurate when they are spoken in public. When it all gets down to the get-down, black people are no more immune to believing stereotypes about African Americans than anyone else—and Cosby was guilty of podium-pounding about the grossest stereotypes of poor black people.

Even if you agreed with his hyperbolic claims of five-hundred-dollar sneakers taking precedence over Hooked on Phonics in the hood, even if you signed on to his twenty-first-century bootstrap prescriptions, ("You can't blame white people for this"), it's impossible to ignore the classist, bigoted, and reactionary underpinnings of his disdain for giving black children names like Shaniqua or Ali and his justification of police shooting people in the back of the head for "stealing pound cake." (I have to wonder what Cosby would say to me, a black man with a PhD and no criminal record who has nonetheless had police pull guns on him three times in his life—once by an officer demanding that I walk on the sidewalk and not the street.) In the wake of Amadou Diallo and Abner Louima, in the wake of literally dozens of black people being arrested and imprisoned on false evidence in Tulia, Texas, two years ago, these comments are not only ignorant, but also extremely dangerous.

Amid all the national clatter that Cosby's comments have generated, it would be easy to miss the fact that there is nothing particularly new about his indictments—his prescriptions fit into a century-old program of bourgeois behavior modification directed at poor black people from their purportedly better-off kinfolk. The historian Evelyn Brooks Higginbotham has come up with a name for this phenomenon, referring to the idea that personal etiquette is a form of racial uplift as "the politics of respectability." Since at least as far back as the days when W. E. B. Du Bois announced his Talented Tenth program, the Afrostocracy has felt it necessary to clean up, dust off, and lead their less fortunate cousins into the promised land of social acceptance.

Call this "Negro noblesse oblige." This concern wasn't totally altruistic: black elites recognized that in the reductive racial reasoning of the United States, the embarrassing behavior of poor black people would always compromise their own bourgeois standing. (This class tension led Tennessee to experiment with first-class and second-class sections within it's segregated railroad cars.)

And though the two clashed bitterly on matters of personality and policy, both Booker T. Washington and Du Bois found common ground in advocating moral uplift among the Negro masses. Du Bois lamented in the pages of his masterful *Philadelphia Negro* that moral corruption and vice were the major afflictions among the newly arrived Southern migrants. Booker T. Washington famously urged his followers to become models of thriftiness, cleanliness, and religious adherence, believing this would clear the way to racial uplift. During the same era, Elijah Montgomery, the founder of the all-black town of Mound Bayou, Mississippi, banned the sale of liquor in the area and conducted house-to-house investigations of the domestic arrangements of residents, ordering all couples who were not legally married to leave the district.

In the early twentieth century, organizations like the National Association of Colored Women and the Women's Convention of the National Baptist Convention, keenly aware of the prevailing stereotypes of black female sexuality, advocated a program of abstinence and "virtue" as a means of defending their own collective honor. A nearly obsessive concern with personal behavior ties together movements as diverse as Garveyism, the Montgomery bus boycott (whose leadership quietly jettisoned the case of a young black teen who had been arrested for refusing to give up her seat months before Rosa Parks when it was discovered that she was pregnant and unmarried) the Nation of Islam, and the activities of the National Urban League. (Urban Leaguers would meet newly arrived northern migrants with care packages that included soap, toothbrushes, and lists of life "instructions"—which included warning their arriving kin not to come outside with rollers in their hair or keep livestock in their yards.)

Taken on its face, a "morality" agenda—however that is defined—may have been useful, as unplanned pregnancy and crime did negatively impact black people's lives. The problem, however, lies in the idea that this "morality" would vanquish racism, which has as its underlying premise the inability to recognize any black person as moral in the first place. And "morality" has frequently been conflated with a simple, assimilationist ideal of white behavior, which is why Cosby could so easily lump naming a child LaQuita or speaking nonstandard English into the same category as theft and disdain for education. When you get down to it, how decent can you be when you saddle your kids with names like that? What kind of person— besides a whole lot of those who were fighting off police dogs in Birmingham—doesn't bother to conjugate correctly? The question is not whether or not we've overcome, but whether some of us are too ghetto to even deserve to.

This respectability politic also ties together Cosby's entire career, from his days playing a Rhodes scholar on *I-Spy* to his role as the successful obstetrician Heathcliff Huxtable on *The Cosby Show* and his noted criticism of Eddie Murphy for his use of profanity and sexual subject matter. In a society built upon one-dimensional, pathological views of black life, Cosby's body of work—and his support for historically black colleges—is commendable. But positive imagery and philanthropic good deeds don't justify what is essentially hate speech.

Truth told, reactionary, elitist, stereotypical, and inappropriate as they were, there was really nothing black-specific in Cosby's commentary. (I have long believed that the NAACP should give Jerry Springer an image award for pulling back the sheets on white American dysfunctionality.) Every ethnic group in this country has experienced this dynamic of intragroup embarrassment (there exists a glossary of terms for members of an ethnic group whose absence of social decorum seems to justify the prejudices directed at the whole), and rich people have been declaring poor people immoral since the days of feudalism. The irony is that we've only recently generated black people who were rich enough to be taken seriously.

Ultimately, Cosby was right: we can't solely blame white people for this contempt for the black poor. There are plenty of black people who are responsible, too. But most of them are not named Shaniqua.

May 2004

8

Fear Factor

*Three years after the 9/11 attacks on New York and Washington, D.C.,
the Bush administration found itself trying to scare up enough votes to
win the office that the Supreme Court gave him four years earlier.*

The horror of it remains undiminished a thousand days later.
For any of us, for *every* one of us, the images of September
11, 2001, have been permanently soldered into our collective
memory. Mental echoes of the day come back on you like bad
food and recurrent nightmares. And in this, the first presidential
election held in the post–9/11 era, the terrorist attacks loom over
campaigns like the towers once did over Lower Manhattan.

George W. Bush has never been accused of being historically
minded, and his administration is more secretive than even
Richard Nixon's was. (Bush began his term by issuing an executive order delaying the release of his father's presidential papers
for years and has classified thousands of documents relating to
his own years as governor of Texas.) But despite Bush's hostility

toward history, his administration is deeply invested in short-term memory.

Three years, to be precise.

The alleged war on terror has become central to George W. Bush's campaign, because he has virtually no domestic accomplishments to speak of. It was no coincidence that Dick Cheney growled ominously earlier this week that a vote for John Kerry would result in more terrorist attacks on American soil. You don't need *Fahrenheit 9/11* to take the temperature out here. Bush's campaign strategy can be distilled to a simple equation: fear = reelection. Or, in his case, election in the first place.

It was obvious what page of the playbook the GOP was reading from as early as 2002 when presidential adviser Karl Rove advised Republican candidates during the midterm elections to "run on the war"—showing that the Bush inner circle recognizes a long-term pattern: paranoia is one of the great threads of American political history.

This administration knows that the voting public has never turned a president out of office in the midst of a war. (Lyndon B. Johnson, who presided over Vietnam, the most unpopular war in American history, chose not to run for reelection in 1968, but had already won the 1964 election in the midst of that war.) And this explains why Bush and company have tried so hard to convince the public that an unnecessary invasion and occupation of Iraq is part of a war on terror. Establishing this point has required political doublespeak that would have left George Orwell's head spinning. George W. Bush has asked the public to indulge in illogical quotes like "We are safer even though Saddam Hussein did not have weapons of mass destruction," without asking the obvious question of what exactly we are safer from.

Just over a half century ago, another Republican won a presidential election by claiming he could defend America from a foreign menace that had found its way to American soil. The candidate was Dwight Eisenhower, the evil to be vanquished was Communism, and the common thread between 1952 and 2004 is fear.

If you heard George Pataki indict the Clinton administration for being soft on terrorism at the GOP convention last month, it wasn't hard to hear strains of Eisenhower accusing the Truman-era Democrats of being soft on Communism. Ike didn't have the benefit of color-coded charts to help the public calibrate its heart palpitations, but there were regional "un-American activities" committees providing the public with flash bulletins of the Communist threat du jour.

And the fear factor has not been left solely in the hands of presidential contenders. Joseph McCarthy was a little-known junior figure in the U.S. Senate when in 1950 he gave a speech declaring that he had in his hand a list of 205 Communists who had infiltrated the State Department. McCarthy's "list" was as nonexistent as the Iraqi weapons of mass destruction, but it helped the senator craft his public image as a strong, resolute leader in the war on Communism—and it got him reelected that year.

Dig a little farther back and you find more common threads. The threat to civil liberties and zealous conflation of "terrorism" with dissent that has characterized John Ashcroft's tenure as attorney general is not unique. Just after World War I—in the midst of the country's first Red Scare—A. Mitchell Palmer, the anti–civil libertarian attorney general of the United States, used the fear of "Bolshevik" sympathizers to launch the infamous Palmer Raids. The result was the suppression of dissent (and the harassment of even mainstream black newspapers) and deportation of hundreds of immigrants on dubious charges of subversion.

In the nineteenth century, politicians who were aligned with the Know-Nothing Party used fear of a Catholic conspiracy to subvert the Constitution to scare up votes. And a generation earlier, the fear that Free Masons would attempt the same thing drove the sweaty-palmed citizenry out to the polls. In the early years of the republic, the country was united in its fear that Tories—British sympathizers—would undermine the newly established independence of the United States.

None of this is to argue that terrorism is a false threat, but rather that the public has been falsely threatened by terrorism. The same politicians who ignored briefings clearly stating that Osama Bin Laden was determined to attack within the United States now expect the public to ignore the fact that bin Laden and Al Qaeda are still at large and focus on the fact that the false threat of Saddam Hussein has been removed.

The truth is that we don't need Karl Rove or Dick Cheney to remind us of what happened on 9/11. The despair and the horrific amazement of that accursed moment of history is still hanging in the air like smoke over Manhattan. That day in September 2001 inaugurated a new era in American history. But it did not give us a reason to see George W. Bush inaugurated for a second time in January 2005.

September 2004

9

Terror in Black and White

September 11 was far from the first instance of terrorism on American soil. Terror—and specifically racial terrorism—has roots almost as old as this country itself.

E ven before the death-colored clouds had cleared from the skies over Lower Manhattan, the words "worst" and "first" were already becoming synonymous. Three years after the terrorist attacks on New York and Washington, D.C., September 11 has become a sort of touchstone in the common consciousness, a moment of catastrophic unreality that was force-fed into our real world. Looking back at the all-too-recent events of that day, it's easy to understand why 9/11 seems to have blotted out all prior memory and conviction. In its scale and spectacle, it was unprecedented. Its repercussions have only yet begun to echo. It is both the context and subtext for this moment in history. The horror of 9/11 is the ghost in our bloodstream.

The idea that terror is new to American soil has been politically beneficial to the Bush administration, which, in the absence of any domestic accomplishments, has staked its future on "keeping America safe." In the wake of the terrorist attacks on the World Trade Center and the Pentagon, a misstatement made amid the trauma of so much death and destruction gradually calcified into a fact of public perception: this has never happened before.

But history is long and, truth told, terrorism in America is nearly as old as America itself. Only a century earlier, terrorists had actually succeeded in assassinating a president of the United States. William McKinley died in 1901, the shot by Leon Czolgosz, an anarchist assassin. And if we think of terrorism as organized acts of violence directed at civilians in order to instill fear and affect politics, then it is impossible to ignore the fact that racism and terrorism are inseparable in American history. On one level, race is irrelevant on this bleak anniversary—black remains are indistinguishable among the lost thousands cremated in terrorist flames in New York and Washington, D.C. But the past *is* relevant here. Race is the link connecting acts of terrorism from the guerilla raids fought over slavery in Kansas in the 1850s through the Oklahoma City bombing of 1995.

To cut to the chase, American history is a harvest of strange fruit.

It would be easy, at this distant remove, to forget that Timothy McVeigh, the homegrown terrorist who orchestrated the bombing of the Alfred P. Murrah Building in Oklahoma City that claimed 168 lives, did so in order to ignite a race war. McVeigh's attack was literally taken from the pages of Andrew McDonald's racist potboiler, *The Turner Diaries*. McVeigh himself had spoken at length about the federal government's role in usurping the rights of white people and argued that the government had become an instrument solely for furthering the interests of people of color and Jews.

At the time it occurred, the bombing in Oklahoma City was

referred to as the worst instance of terrorism on American soil. But that assessment required a certain historical nearsightedness to be true. The 1995 bombing was not even the worst act of terrorism in the *state*. The 1921 Tulsa race riot, in which bands of armed and deputized whites attacked black residents of the city, resulted in twice as many deaths as the Oklahoma City bombing, even by the most conservative estimates. That same year, white rioters burned the town of Rosewood, Florida, completely off the map. And earlier, just after the Civil War, Southern whites killed forty-six blacks, injured more than a hundred, and burned ninety-odd homes to the ground in Memphis—while Northern troops stationed in the city watched.

Nor can it be said that McVeigh was a historical anomaly. Just over a century earlier, the organized terrorist campaigns of alleged Southern Redeemers began with the goal of eradicating black political participation during Reconstruction. Early in the twentieth century, their racist campaigns were mythologized by Thomas Dixon and D. W. Griffith. As the late writer Ralph Wiley pointed out, McVeigh bombed a building in order to live out the plotlines of a novel in the same way that nineteenth-century terrorists attempted to live out the plotlines of *Birth of a Nation*. Griffith's masterpiece of racial propaganda was based upon Dixon's novel *The Leopard's Spots*. The success of *Birth of a Nation* inspired a resurgence of the Ku Klux Klan—which had nearly died out—and became the basis for their ritual burning of the cross (an act that had been invented for its dramatic value to the story). The terror directed at black people who had the audacity to take the Emancipation Proclamation at face value resulted in more than three thousand lynchings between 1880 and 1920.

The names, dates, and casualties of these assorted inhumanities are innumerable: the pandemic of rape directed at black women after Reconstruction, the litany of assassinations, the fatal bombing of the home of NAACP activists Harry and Harriette Moore in 1951, the bombing of Fred Shuttlesworth's home in 1956, the bombing of Martin Luther King's home that same year, the bombing of the 16th Street Baptist Church in Birmingham, Alabama, in 1963—a city so defined by racial terrorism that it was known as "Bombingham."

And, ultimately, even the prerequisites for black freedom start to fit the technical definitions: Sherman's march through Atlanta. Nat Turner's rebellion. John Brown's raid at Harper's Ferry. Sherman was an early proponent of the concept of "total war," which recognized no battle lines and few civilian zones. His famed march to the sea was designed both to instill fear in the Southern civilian population and to break the will of the Confederate soldiers miles away from their jeopardized homes. Nor are the revolts of Nat Turner and John Brown exempt. The difficult truth is that sometimes the charge of terrorism lies in the eye of the beholder.

None of this is meant to lessen the tragedy of the lives stolen on 9/11 three years ago—it is bad moral mathematics to even weigh any one tragedy against another—but it does raise questions about the current administration's use of the term *terrorist*. In the midst of a public stricken with post-traumatic stress syndrome and a presidency that has used fear as its primary political tool, we would do well to recall that terror has deep roots in American soil.

September 2004

10

Six in One Hand

Now it thundered and it lightnin'd, Lord and the wind, wind began to blow
Now it thundered and it lightnin'd, Lord and the wind, wind began to blow
Lord there was thousands and thousands of poor people
at that time didn't have no place to go

BIG BILL BROONZY, "BACK WATER BLUES (VERSION 1)"

The waters came down with a biblical fury, and it was—as it is always—the poor who were left to confront the catastrophe on her own terms. There had been years of warnings before the flood-waters exploded past the levees. They poured into the low-lying areas, sweeping away housing that had been substandard even before the rains began. Nearly a million people fled. More than a thousand perished. The refugees, overwhelmingly black, overwhelmingly poor, were placed in sites that were their own brand of disaster and, unable to leave once they entered, they began comparing the structures to prisons. And the terrible truth beneath this all was that this occurred precisely as it was supposed to: water follows the path of least resistance.

These events went down not in Louisiana in the past week, but in Mississippi in 1927. Swollen by heavy rains, the river began bursting through levees—built despite protests that they would only amplify the water's destructive capacity—between Illinois and the Gulf. The Republican official in charge—Herbert Hoover in this case—took a virtually hands-off approach, and the Red Cross refugee sites became models of Southern race relations, with blacks being forced to do laundry for the National Guardsmen and literally leased out to help rebuild the flooded plantations of the delta. The levees were repaired, though—as soon as the waters receded enough for black men to be gathered at gunpoint and forced onto labor gangs. (One black man refused to join the gang and was killed by a policeman.)

You don't need to read Genesis 6:5 to know that there have been echoes of bad history this week; to know that the past has come back upon us like bad food in the gut. Prior to Monday, anyone who argued that the country would essentially carry on business as usual while a major American city sank into the Gulf of Mexico would have been dismissed as part of the lunatic fringe. But this is one of those cases where it takes a broken clock to check the time.

You already got a clue as to which way the storm winds were blowing when the press images of blacks who "looted" stores were placed alongside those of whites who "found" bread and soda. In 2005 we have been taught to hedge our bets, to speak of racism as one possibility among other feasible explanations for the problems we witness. There will be attempts to disguise this as a problem of logistics or, at the most, the result of faceless bureaucratic neglect that has been corroding American cities for decades. Worst-case scenario: this political nonchalance will all be attributed to the indefensible armed gangs within the city.

But these are lies.

None of those explanations can explain why there were not press conferences from forty-six other governors pledging support for New Orleans. They will not explain why New York City did not send five hundred of its forty thousand cops to assist the submerged city. They cannot explain why George W. Bush—in a cameo of his performance on 9/11—did not respond to the disaster as it occurred and instead arrived on the fifth day of the flood.

In coming days you will be offered spin and staged photo ops designed to make your heart go sepia with regard for our "strong leadership." This is an illusion. Only the river-bloated bodies are real. Filter through the spin and you will meet a brutal truth: there are people who have died and people who are dying in Louisiana because they are black and they are poor. The truth is that neglect is the racial default setting—which is why those people were left behind in the city, both literally and metaphorically. The truth is that there was a silent amen exhaled across the country when Dennis Hastert floated the idea of not bothering to rebuild. Sixty-seven percent black; 30 percent of the population below the poverty line: cities like New Orleans are the reason we have red states in the first place.

Or maybe they will rebuild. And in future years we can look to a charming, romantic 2.0 version of the Big Easy, one where the problem population left in 2005 and never quite made it back inside the city.

• • •

Herbert Hoover graduated to the Oval Office from his post as secretary of commerce after the 1927 flood. As president he displayed that same cavalier approach to catastrophe as the Great Depression strangled ordinary citizens, and he continued to govern on behalf of the upper percentiles of the economy. The echoes of bad history are, at this point, deafening. This is not Mississippi in 1927. It is America seventy-eight years later. But I swear to God, its getting harder and harder to tell the difference.

September 2005

11

On the Stroll: Pimping Three 6 Mafia

The opening scene of the film *Hustle and Flow* features Djay, the low-wattage pimp masterfully brought to life by Terrence Howard, spitting his best game at a young, impressionable white hooker. At the conclusion of his motivational sermon, he pitches her services to a would-be john, who declines the offer. Two minutes later, without his assistance, the girl closes a deal with that same john. The implication of the scene is clear: a pimp without game is in precisely the same place as a lawyer without a lie or a hooker without heels. Nowhere.

But in a real sense the failure of a player to master his own game was what saved director Craig Brewer's film about a pimp having a midlife crisis from being a piece of unintentional satire or a series of purple satin clichés. It's important to note that the film was set in Memphis. The protagonist is a local small-time mack without even the sheen of a big-city backdrop to help him amplify his hustle.

Delusionally grand and ghetto-rich, the pimp in his most recent incarnation is a crossover artist. The past decade of American popular culture has witnessed such paeans to pandering as the movies *Pimps Up, Ho's Down* and *American Pimp* and the coffee table photo book *Pimpnosis*. A sampler platter of hip-hop artists working the pimp angle in their music would include 50 Cent ("P.I.M.P."), David Banner ("Like a Pimp"), Jay-Z ("Big Pimping"), Trick Daddy ("Pimp"), Nelly ("Pimp Juice"), Ludacris ("Pimping All Over the World"), and dozens of other lesser-acknowledged chroniclers of the player's life and trials.

And given that level of pimpology, it was only a matter of time before themes of hip-hop and ho' houses would find their way onto the big screen. That *Hustle and Flow* was delivered in the midst of a pimp renaissance of sorts but managed to steer clear of the most threadbare elements of what participants refer to as "The Life" goes to the credit of Brewer; John Singleton, who executive-produced the film; and particularly Terrence Howard. Beyond hip-hop, though, Hustle dates its pimp genealogy (or is it pedigree?) back to the era of *The Mack* and *Superfly*, and Melvin Van Peebles's *Sweet Sweetback's Baadaass Song*, cinematic ballads immortalizing the hustler as the man caught in the snare of a crooked system and excelling at the only angle he has left. But *Hustle and Flow* bears the same relationship to its predecessors that *Goodfellas* had to *The Godfather* and the cascade of highly stylized gangster flicks that followed it. Just as *Goodfellas* gave us gangster verite—the mafia minus the customized wardrobe and philosophical speeches, *Hustle and Flow* succeeded in stripping away the veneer of street-glam associated with pimping and replaced it with a type of Dirty South realism. This at a point when audiences had grown accustomed to seeing the pimp draped in riotous swaths of lush fabric, his clothes a civil war of clashing colors and textures. But Djay's world is one that is perpetually two weeks behind on the rent and even the brightest days are somewhat overcast. The prevailing fabric scheme here is the dingy white cotton of the protagonist's wife-beater tees.

With *Hustle and Flow*, Craig Brewer told what was essentially a hip-hop story. On one level or another, hip-hop has always existed as a hope of last resort for the dead broke. To hear them tell it, *Hustle and Flow* could be a cinematic retelling of the lives of any number of rappers—T.I., Jay-Z, 50 Cent, Notorious B.I.G., DMX, Ice-T, and Too Short—artists who turned to music as a hustler's plan B. But it's precisely because Brewer succeeded in making his lead character improbably sympathetic and three-dimensional that Three 6 Mafia's now-infamous Oscar performance goes down in the annals of artists who have played themselves in public.

There is a street credo that holds that game is sold, never told—meaning that one usually learns the meaning of a particular hustle by having first been a victim of it. The difference between the con man and his mark is, quite simply, the degree of life experience. Three 6 Mafia doesn't have a great deal of experience in the ways of Tinsel Town, and that probably explains why this particular con went down as it did. In short, Three 6 took home an Oscar and a left-handed compliment; one of those gifts went unnoticed and it wasn't the gold statuette.

The Oscars show has been lamented for its declining audience for years—which is the most prominent reason behind the selection of Chris Rock as the host of last year's awards. Three 6's performance was calibrated to give the academy the appearance of hip edginess. Awarding the Oscar for best song would, in the best of all worlds, grant a show known more for its rigid formality a degree of street cred. But, truth told, it had the opposite effect—making the academy appear all the more geriatric. For those in the know, Three 6 Mafia's status as the first hip-hop group to win an Oscar was a reminder that some two decades into the genre's becoming a commercial force, and seventeen years after Public Enemy's brilliant incendiary "Fight the Power" played Greek chorus to Spike Lee's *Do the Right Thing*, the motion picture industry has finally figured out that hip-hop exists. Their selection highlighted yet another reality about the double-edged sword that is hip-hop's commercial success: the increasing opportunity to detail the realities of black lives in this country has made it vastly less likely that anyone within the music will actually do so with any integrity.

By and large, commercially viable hip-hop presents a vision of African American life that is one-dimensional, a verbal cartoon made all the more dangerous by its professions of "realness." We know, but refuse to say that for every player on the boulevard, there is a sixty-year-old grandmother somewhere trying to instill values in her grandchildren. For every parable of brutality, there is someone who fell in love and someone who has made it through another day against great odds; there is someone who has just invested hope of a better life in a civil service exam and an old man who has just dispensed some hard-learned wisdom to a kid on his way up. But the sad truth is that Brewer—a white director—invested black Memphis with more depth, complexity, and humanity than anything in Three 6's entire body of work.

The most glaring example of this was the Oscar performance—complete with choreographed pimp fights and miniskirted hookers out on the Hollywood stroll—which was a checklist of the very clichés that Brewer's film had studiously avoided.

There was a second level of irony in that neither the Hollywood establishment nor mainstream hip-hop has a track record of dealing substantively with black humanity. So perhaps the question is not how that spectacle of hooker minstrelsy took place at the Oscars, but why it took so long for it to happen.

Rappers have been taking their cues from Hollywood for eons (which explains why there are so many artists named after movie characters and why virtually all of the film *Scarface* has been sampled onto hip-hop records). Still, it's tragic to consider that a generation of black artists and the overwhelmingly white film industry have found their common ground in racial clichés.

The post-Oscar parties saw a reporter asking the trio how much their grills cost (as if they would ask Tom Cruise how much he spent on his watch) and then sardonically marveling that their thirty-thousand-dollar dental jewelry cost more than her car. The reporter said nothing about ghetto grandeur, wasted investment, and conspicuous consumption, but then again, she didn't have to. It is possible to ridicule by inference. Think about the Oscar night in that light, and it starts to remind you of that GI in *A Soldier's Story* who was coaxed into dancing onstage with a tail attached to him for the entertainment of the white officers.

The echoed line of defense for the trio held up that aged cliché that "it's just entertainment." But when music becomes a means to grab the attention of the entire world and make a statement, when it holds the possibility to beam one's image to the farthest corners of the globe, it becomes much more than that. It is communication. That distinction may have been lost on the three rappers onstage that night, but it is precisely the difference between the mark and the con, the comedian and the minstrel. Ultimately, Three 6 Mafia unintentionally proved their own argument: that it literally *is* hard out here for a pimp. But not nearly as hard as it is for those of us who—whether we realize it or not—consent to work for one.

March 2006

12

Out of Time (Brian Barber's *Idlewild*)

I f you could grab hip-hop by its ends and wring it out you would find, along with the bullshit, bullets, bravado, and bling, that there would still be a modicum of brilliance. And a disproportionate share of that brilliance would belong to Andre Benjamin and Antwan Patton, known collectively as OutKast. In the fourteen years since their debut album, *Southernplayalisticadillac-muzik,* the duo has consistently expanded the parameters of the genre. Emerging at a point when the East Coast artists held sway over the art form and fermenting through the period of West Coast dominance that followed, OutKast laid the groundwork for the Dirty South revolution that now reigns in hip-hop.

The duo's willingness to poke fun at themselves and simultaneously broadcast the facts about the otherwise invisible drama going down in the black mecca of Atlanta gave OutKast a unique niche inside hip-hop. The Parliament-esque riffs, their tendency toward elaborate costumes (a throwback to the days when rappers actually considered themselves entertainers), and the playfully original approach to the rhyme ensured that it would take a good decade or so before hip-hop could think about catching up to the self-described ATLiens. It also figured that they would be the ones to liberate hip-hop cinema from its self-imposed ghetto exile. The wonder is that *Idlewild*, their first film together did not reach audiences earlier.

Idlewild is the product of writer-director Brian Barber's creative vision. Not coincidentally, it was Barber who crafted the idiosyncratic visual style of OutKast's music videos. His brilliant work on videos for the singles "Hey Ya" and "Roses," from Out-Kast's *Speakerboxx/The Love Below* release, made it clear that Barber's talents were spilling over the four-minute video format and he struck upon the novel idea that one could basically combine a cinematic narrative with a series of music videos and produce a credible musical. (As a nod to both *Idlewild* and Barber's music video roots, the artists appear onstage in full Depression era attire with feather-clad showgirls, but perform as rappers, not singers.)

That said, the originality of the concept was no guarantee that Barber could successfully execute a feature film. Note the case of Hype Williams, the South Queens graffiti legend turned video director who essentially revolutionized music videos in the mid-1990s, adding a new palette of color and deliberate distortion that biters and knock-offs have been trying to re-create for a decade. Williams's visual poetry helped transform what had been essentially a type of choreographed commercial into a legitimate artistic genre. But if anything, his neoblaxploitation flick *Belly* highlighted the falsehood that image is everything. While visually indelible—in one heist scene, Williams shoots his protagonists in a deep indigo tint to highlight the evil in their hearts—the tale falls apart in the telling. And that kind of narrative disaster served as a cautionary tale for Barber's *Idlewild*.

Set in a fictitious Georgia town during Prohibition, *Idlewild* is the story of Percival and Rooster, lifelong friends and performers at a juke joint called Church. There is a gleefully anachronistic perspective at work in Church, a place where the two-toned shoed players reference Cadillacs and revelers do the Lindy Hop. It is a place where people conduct what your grandmother would have called grown-folk business. If the Great Depression exists, it is segregated outside the borders of Idlewild. Barber's offering is steeped in a kind of Jim Crow vogue. Every aspect—from the clothes to the cars to the lingo he puts into his characters' mouths—is insistently elegant and rebelliously at odds with our vision of black life in Georgi. Percival and his father, Percy Sr. (Ben Vereen), are talented tenthers who operate a successful funeral home and appear in such grand style that refinement itself operates as a refutation of inferiority. If Barber's idealism is at odds with lived history of the Cotton Belt, so be it. The real point of this swirling color-coordinated world where, coincidentally, there is not a single white person to be found, is one that Ralph Ellison spent the better part of his career trying to drive home: that black culture could never sustain itself simply as a response to the racism of white people.

Barber passes a subtle nod to these games he plays with chronology by filling Percival's room with dozens of cuckoo clocks and jamming his bookshelves with tomes on the measure and meaning of time. And if the director was not already at his artistic credit limit, he throws in the additional element of surrealism—Rooster's liquor flask *literally* talks to him; Percival's music actually comes to life. His back-roads chase scenes are equally indebted to the gangster flicks of old and the computer-generated imagery of *The Matrix*. The result is a film that is more closely related to Morrison and Marquez than Mobb Deep and Method Man.

There is drama to be found in the town of Idlewild, but it has nothing to do with lynch mobs and sharecropping. When the philandering Rooster inherits Church from an uncle, he also inherits the club's debt to an upstart hustler named Trumpy, played by Terrence Howard. Rooster is also the only witness to Trumpy's murder of the previous proprietor. Percival must choose between remaining with his father, who is embittered by the death of his wife years earlier, and going on the road to pursue his music with love interest Angel Davenport, played by Paula Patton, while Rooster's hopes of digging the club out of debt hinge upon Angel's ability to draw in crowds. The script reveals moments of cleverness (Faizon Love, who plays Sunshine Ace, exclaims that a new brand of moonshine is "Selling like canned pussy,") but it also lapses into the occasional cliché, as when Rooster's wife shows up at Church with a shotgun to ward off rivals for her husband's attentions and the Holy Book given to Rooster by Cicely Tyson stops a bullet.

Ultimately, Barber's effort hangs together as cleanly as the suits he dresses his characters in. The film climaxes in a final confrontation between Trumpy and Rooster that leaves Angel dead on the floor of Church and Percival sequestered in the kind of grief that has turned his father inside out. But unlike his old man, he walks out of that world and onto the Chicago stage as the film dissolves into a concluding musical number a la *Purple Rain*, the film that, in all reality, *Idlewild* is most likely to be compared to. The tragedy of *Idlewild* is that hip-hop's under-standing of itself has become so constricted that—like OutKast's musical output—it may take years to appreciate the significance of what Brian Barber has put down. It is destined to become one of those cult flicks adored by later audiences despite the tepid response to it by critics and audiences thus far. If you could grab

Idlewild by its ends and wring it out, you would be left with a menagerie of eccentric images and wild visions of black life once upon a time in the deep South of our imagination. And a nagging nostalgia for the days when hip-hop was not afraid to dream.

August 2006

13

The Trouble with Harry

It was apparent when Maya Angelou stated, "I speak for Harry Belafonte," that something was wrong. Even before the poet spoke those five words, the absence of civil rights activist and entertainer Harry Belafonte from Coretta Scott King's funeral was noticeable to the closest observers. In the sanctuary of New Birth Missionary Baptist Church and beyond, people worried that some health crisis had prevented Belafonte from attending the funeral of his friend of forty-plus years. But the reality proved to be much more complicated.

Weeks after the funeral, Belafonte confirmed rumors that he had been invited to eulogize Coretta Scott King and then saw his invitation rescinded after George W. Bush confirmed that *he* would attend the funeral. The irony was as clear as it was bitter:

Belafonte had been disinvited from the funeral of a fellow civil rights activist precisely because he has stubbornly insisted on upholding the principles of the civil rights movement. It is difficult to make those kinds of charges—even from a distance.

There is no way to calculate the disastrous weight of April 4, 1968. Black America has yet to recover from Martin Luther King's assassination, and on some level it would be wrong to assume that it would be any different for his own kin. Add to that bitter equation the drowning death of A. D. King, King's younger brother, just a year after the assassination and then the brutal 1974 slaying of Alberta King, Martin's mother, by a gunman who opened fire in the Ebenezer Baptist Church sanctuary. And now, with Coretta Scott King's passing, it becomes clear that the King family has endured an inconceivable degree of tragedy and loss.

And yet sympathy cannot mute the disturbing questions that Belafonte's absence raised. This was bigger than an issue of who did or did not make it onto the invite list. His absence goes to the heart of a generational divide. It goes to the heart of a question about what one does with a legacy of freedom that has been earned for us by generations past. It is as much about a gap of spirit as it is of relative birth dates.

The radical psychiatrist Frantz Fanon once commented about the ambivalence that parents in his native Martinique felt when their children went off to be educated in France. The joy of brighter prospects was tempered by the fear that their children would return with disdain for the very traditions that had produced them. In black America that ambivalence is generational; it describes the mix of pride and concern that the now aged generation of the civil rights era feels toward those of us who were born in the wake of that movement. It is an ambivalence that even Martin Luther King Jr. recognized as the struggle was unfolding. Toward the end of his life, Martin Luther King worried about the wisdom of integrating black America "into a burning house." The logic was that segregation was a two-way street, keeping black people exiled from opportunities in mainstream American life—and at the same time filtering away some of the ugliest traits of this consumer paradise.

For what it matters—and it does, a great deal—this is the first generation of black people who are (limited) shareholders in America, Inc.'s black equivalent of a "me" generation. Randall Robinson lamented to me a few years ago that he always assumed that his radical social justice inclinations would be eclipsed as he grew older, that future generations would chide him for being a moderate. That hasn't happened. Instead he sees himself even further to the left than his younger counterparts.

In the case of Belafonte, this was literal, not metaphoric. His disinvitation came from the children of the movement. King's daughter Yolanda was born only a few weeks before the King home in Montgomery was bombed because of Martin's civil rights work.

Belafonte was played as a stand-in for a struggle that had gone out of style. Weeks before the funeral he had traveled to Venezuela and, in the company of President Hugo Chavez, denounced George W. Bush as "the greatest terrorist in the world." In 2002 Belafonte lamented publicly that Colin Powell had opted to play the role of literal "house Negro" to George W. Bush. He told CNN's Larry King that Powell's willingness to go along with a disastrous and unnecessary war in Iraq was a betrayal of the moral mandate that had made it possible for him to hold the position of secretary of state.

Martin Luther King III later stated that there was a "mix-up" that left Belafonte off the dais, but coming months after the fact, his explanation was viewed skeptically. It was far too convenient that, in the confusion, the only person removed from the ceremony was the most stringent critic of the Bush administration. There are some mix-ups that are just not supposed to happen. You don't forget to invite the man who paid for your father's funeral.

You don't forget to invite the man who helped your mother pick out the suit your father was to be buried in.

And therein lies the angle.

Belafonte is still an idealist in an age of pragmatism. The dictates of politics, not the moral fiber of struggle, informed the decision to disinvite him from the funeral. He later commented that "I saw all of the power of the oppressor represented on the stage, and all those who fought for the victories that this nation was experiencing and enjoying sat in the outhouse, sat out in the field, sat removed." And perhaps that was the point.

But the seams showed in other places, too. The funeral was held in the house of Eddie Long, a megachurch pastor whose New Birth Missionary Baptist Church boasts twenty thousand members. Long is part of a new generation of preachers of the "prosperity gospel," which emphasizes financial and material blessings over the traditional social justice concerns of the black church. He is a supporter of George W. Bush and the so-deemed war on terror and an advocate of a constitutional ban on gay marriage. Bernice King, the youngest child of Martin and Coretta, is an assistant pastor there, and Long recently began billing himself as the heir to the legacy of Martin Luther King Jr.

The sheer size of the event weighed in the decision to hold the ceremony at Long's massive church, but it remained an uneasy fit. The woman being memorialized was a committed pacifist who supported gay rights and challenged economic inequality at every turn. (Weeks after the funeral Long's invitation to give the commencement address at Atlanta's Interdenominational Theological Center created a storm of controversy, as students charged that he had abandoned the tradition of moral struggle in pursuit of financial reward.)

And even prior to Coretta Scott King's death, a feud had erupted among King's children over the future of the King Center in Atlanta. While she was recovering from a stroke that had left her unable to communicate, the family split over a plan to sell the center to the National Park Service. Two of the children, Martin III and Yolanda, favored the sale, while Dexter and Bernice vehemently opposed it. The center had fallen into disrepair and required some $11 million in renovations. It became the focus of a federal investigation into its financial dealings—while both sons drew six-figure salaries from their employment there. Martin and Dexter then filed lawsuits against each other, with the former changing the locks on the center to bar his brother from the facilities.

The family has, in recent years, launched a litigious battle for control over Martin's words and image. But they have not displayed the same zeal for Martin's activist legacy. The center is scarcely mentioned when it comes to addressing HIV, incarceration, family dissolution, or any of the issues confronting black America in 2006. The Kings famously sued the newspaper *USA Today* for reprinting the "I Have a Dream" speech in recognition of Martin Luther King Day, but then turned around and licensed Martin's image for a software commercial that had nothing to do with their father's ideals.

Those realities made it all but impossible to see Belafonte's absence as an isolated oversight in the hour of grief. He came to be a part of a larger pattern that has repercussions far beyond the children of the most famous American of the twentieth century. Massive public regard for Martin and Coretta has blunted a great deal of criticism for these decisions, but that won't be the case forever. History is a witness and seldom judges lightly those individuals or generations who are lulled by inherited victories into taking freedom for granted.

May 2006

14

Pimp-Slapping Oprah (Or We Still Wear the Mask)

Wе could have known that it would come to this way back in 1896. That was the year that Paul Lawrence Dunbar dropped a jewel for the ages, telling the world "we wear the mask that grins and lies." The poet's point was that beneath the camouflage of subservient smiles, black folks of the Jim Crow era were hiding a powder keg of other emotions, waiting patiently for the chance to detonate. The thing is, Dunbar never got the chance to spit bars with 50 Cent or throw in a guest collabo on a Mobb Deep album. If he had, then he would've known that grins and lies were only half the story.

These days, camouflage is the new black. Hip-hop now operates on a single hope: that if the world mistakes kindness for weakness, it can also be led to confuse meanness with strength. That principle explains why there is a permanent reverence for the thug within the music; it is why there is a murderer's grit and a jailhouse tat peering back at you from the cover of damn near any CD you picked up in the last five years. But what hip-hop can't tell you, the secret that it would just as soon take to its deathbed, is that this urban bravado is a guise, a mask, a head fake to shake the reality of fear and powerlessness in America. Hip-hop will never admit that our assorted thugs and gangstas are not the unbowed symbol of resistance to marginalization, but the most complacent and passive products of it.

We wear the mask that scowls and lies.

• • •

You could see which way the wind was blowing way back in the early '90s when Dr. Dre was being ripped off by Ruthless Records' white CEO Jerry Heller, and nonetheless got his street cred up by punching and kicking Dee Barnes, a black woman journalist, down a flight of stairs. In this light, hip-hop's obsessive misogyny makes a whole lot more sense. It is literally the logic of domestic violence. A man is abused by a larger society, but there are consequences to striking back at the source of his problems. So he transfers his anger to an acceptable outlet—the women and children in his own household, and by extension, all the black people who constitute his own community.

Nothing better illustrates that point than the recent Oprah debacle. Prior to last month, if you'd heard that a group of rappers had teamed up to attack a billionaire media mogul, you would think that hip-hop had finally produced a moment of collective pride on par with the Black Power fists of the 1968 Olympics. But, nay, just more blackface.

In the past two months, artists as diverse as Ludacris, 50 Cent, and Ice Cube have attacked Oprah Winfrey for her alleged disdain for hip-hop. It is a sad but entirely predictable irony that in the one instance where hip-hop's reigning alpha males have summoned the testicular fortitude to challenge someone more powerful and wealthy than they are, they chose to go after a black woman.

The whole setup was an echo of some bad history. Two centuries ago, professional boxing got its start in America with white slaveholders who pitted their largest slaves against those from competing plantations. Tom Molineaux, the first black heavyweight champion, came up through the ranks breaking the bones of other slaves and making white men rich. After he'd broken enough of them, he was given his freedom. The underlying ethic was clear: an attack on the system that enslaved you will cost you your life, but an attack on another black person might just be the road to emancipation.

The basis for this latest bout of black-on-black pugilism was Oprah's purported stiff-arming of Ludacris during an appearance on her show with the cast of the film *Crash*. Ludacris later complained that the host had made an issue of lyrics she saw as misogynistic. Cube jumped into the act whining that Oprah has had all manner of racist flotsam on her show but has never invited him to appear—proof, in his mind, that she has an irrational contempt for hip-hop. Then 50 threw in his two cents with a claim that Oprah's criticism of hip-hop was an attempt to win points with her largely white, middle-class audience. All told, she was charged with that most heinous of hip-hop's felonies: hateration.

But before we press charges, isn't 50 the same character who openly expressed his love for G. W. Bush as a fellow "gangsta" and demanded that the black community stop criticizing how he handled Hurricane Katrina? Compare that to the multiple millions that Oprah has disseminated to our communities (including building homes for the Katrina families, financing HIV prevention in South Africa, and that $5 million she dropped on Morehouse

College last year), and the idea of an ex–crack dealer challenging her commitment to black folk becomes even more surreal.

In spite of—or, actually, as a *result* of—his impeccable gangsta credentials, 50 basically curtsied before a president who stayed on vacation for three days while black bodies floated down the New Orleans streets. No wonder it took a middle-class preppie with an African name and no criminal record, Kanye West, to man-up and tell the whole world that "George Bush don't care about black folks." No wonder David Banner—a rapper who is just a few credits short of a master's degree in social work—spearheaded hip-hop's Katrina relief concerts, rather than any of his thug counterparts who are eternally shouting out the hoods they allegedly love.

The 50 Cent whose music is a panoramic vision of black-on-black homicide, and who went after crosstown rival Ja Rule with the vengeance of a dictator killing off a hated ethnic minority, did everything but tap dance when Reebok told him to dismantle his porn production company or lose his lucrative sneaker endorsement deal.

But why single out 50? Hip-hop at large was conspicuously silent when Bush press secretary Tony Snow (a rapper's alias if ever there was one) assaulted hip-hop in terms way more inflammatory than Oprah's mild request: "Take a look at the idiotic culture of hip-hop and whaddya have? You have people glorifying failure. You have a bunch of gold-toothed hot dogs become millionaires by running around and telling everybody else that they oughtta be miserable failures and if they're really lucky maybe they can get gunned down in a diner sometime, like Eminem's old running mate." (We're still awaiting an outraged response from the thug community for that one.) Rush Limbaugh has blamed hip-hop for everything short of the avian flu, but I can't recall a single hip-hop artist who has gone after him lyrically, publicly, or physically. Are we seeing a theme yet?

It's worth noting that Ludacris did not devote as much

energy to Bill O'Reilly—who attacked his music on his show regularly and caused him to lose a multimillion-dollar Pepsi endorsement—as he did to criticizing Oprah, who simply stated that she was tired of hip-hop's misogyny. Luda was content to diss O'Reilly on his next record and go about his business. Anyone who heard the interview that Oprah gave on Power 105.1 in New York knew she was speaking for a whole generation of hip-hop heads when she said that she loved the music but wanted the artists to exercise some responsibility. But this response is not really about Oprah, or ultimately about hip-hop, either. It is about black men once again choosing a black woman as the safest target for their aggression, and even one with a billion dollars is still fair game.

Of all their claims, the charge that Oprah sold out to win points with her white audience is the most tragically laughable. The truth is that her audience's white middle-class kids exert *waaay* more influence over 50 and Cube than their parents do over Oprah. I long ago tired of Cube, a thirty-something successful director, entrepreneur, and married father of three children making records about his aged recollections of a thug's life. The gangsta theme went cliché eons ago, but Cube, 50, and a whole array of their musical peers lack either the freedom or the vision to talk about any broader element of our lives. The reality is that the major labels and their majority white fan base will not *accept* anything else from them.

And there we have it again: more masks, more lies.

It is not coincidental that hip-hop has made *nigga* the most common noun in popular music, but you have almost never heard any certified thug utter the word "cracker," "ofay," "honky," "peckerwood," "wop," "dago," "guinea," "kike," or any other white-oriented epithet. The reason for that is simple: Massa ain't havin' it. The word "fag," once a commonplace derisive in the music, has all but disappeared from hip-hop's vocabulary.

(Yes, these thugs fear the backlash from white gays, too.) And "bitch" is still allowed with the common understanding that the term is referring to black women. The point is this: debasement of black communities is entirely acceptable—required even—by hip-hop's predominantly white consumer base.

We have lived enough history to know better by now—to know that "gangsta" is Sonny Liston threatening to kill Cassius Clay but being completely impotent when it came to demanding that his white handlers stop stealing his money. Gangsta is the black men at the Parchman Farm prison in Mississippi who beat civil rights workers Fannie Lou Hamer and Annell Ponder into bloody unconsciousness because their white wardens told them to. Gangsta is Michael Irvin, the former NFL bad boy, remaining conspicuously mute during that ESPN broadcast where Rush Limbaugh dissed Donovan McNabb as an Affirmative Action athlete. Gangsta is Bigger Thomas with dilated pupils and every other sweaty-palmed black boy who saw method acting and an attitude as his ticket out of the ghetto.

Surely our ancestors' struggles were about more than creating millionaires who couldn't care less about us and then tolerating their violent disrespect out of a hunger for black success stories. Surely we are not so desperate for heroes that we uphold cardboard icons because they throw good glare. There's more required than that. The weight of history demands more than simply this. Surely we understand that these men are acting out an age-old script. Taking the Tom Molineaux route. Spitting in the wind and breaking black bones. Hoping to become free.

Or at least a well-paid slave.

June 2006

15

The Hater's Ball

Way back in the ancient times when being politically black was still in vogue, there was a concept called selling out. It occurred when a person—for money or prestige, or the hand-me-down glory of white gratitude—placed their own individual interests ahead of those of the broader black community. That cat on the corner with the swollen pockets hustling crack to his own people? Sell-out. The Negro professional who amasses his wealth legitimately but never shares a penny of it with the community that produced him? Same deal.

But those days are gone.

You still hear faint echoes of it—usually tossed at female presidential appointees and the occasional Supreme Court justice—but the barb has lost its sting. And in its wake, the winds of social disapproval have started blowing in an entirely different direction. These days the worst social sin in black America is not to "sell out," but to "player-hate." It has become so routine to place one's interests ahead of all others that the stigma of it has all but dissolved. And now we throw shade at those who accuse others of selling out, referring to those lost idealists as simply "haters." Got a problem with the cat on the corner profiting from pharmaceutical genocide? You must be a hater.

On some level, you saw this coming ten years ago when Jay-Z issued a player's injunction on his debut release, *Reasonable Doubt*. Beyond being the title of the first track on that CD, "Can't Knock the Hustle" was a statement of a whole new belief system.

Nowhere is that ethic clearer than in the recent ghetto public service announcement "Stop Snitching." The visibility of the Stop Snitching campaign indicates, if nothing else, that the heads on Martin Luther King Avenue understand viral marketing at least as well as those on Madison Avenue do. Having started as a catch phrase of the keep-it-real set, the slogan quickly found its way into a guerilla DVD featuring Denver Nugget Carmelo Anthony. T-shirts bearing the phrase have now become a mandatory fashion accessory of the hood—and therefore everywhere else.

It might be because I'm a sentimentalist with a penchant for lost causes, but this shiznit is wearing me out. Compile an index of the conditions that are most damaging to black America right now, and you would be hard-pressed to find a place for "snitching" in the top ten thousand. Then again, anyone who observed the 2004 presidential election knows that the causes people care about and those that most impact their lives are not necessarily the same thing.

The snitch is the most loathed subspecies of hater. Such is the contempt that silence has now become part of the marketing schemes in hip-hop. Forget gold, these days silence is platinum—and so are the record sales of the most tight-lipped of the artists.

When Busta Rhymes's bodyguard was murdered on the set of his music video, the rapper earned all kinds of boulevard credentials by refusing to speak to the police following the homicide. When Cam'ron was shot in both arms by an alleged carjacker in Washington, D.C., the streets lauded his decision to stonewall the cops from his hospital bed. Or in the best example yet, Li'l Kim was sentenced to 366 days in prison for refusing to admit knowing a man who was involved in a shoot-out in New York—despite the fact that the same man was listed in the acknowledgements for her album.

This refusal to speak derives from an age when all authority was white and black was, by definition, criminal. In an unjust system, the criminal is the equivalent of hero. Given the weight of injustice perpetrated on black people in this country, it's not hard to see how a romantic ideal of the criminal as hero developed. As far back as the 1890s, the murderous exploits of Stagolee, the best known of an entire class of so-called baaad niggers were mythologized and retold in song and story. In the 1970s, the era of Blaxploitation film created a polyester dynasty of outlaw heroes. The Black Panther Party openly hailed the criminal underclass as the most "revolutionary" sector of society—which explains why a journeyman rapist like Eldridge Cleaver could pass off his ravages as part of some broad scheme of political resistance.

Nor can the long history of political subversion be ignored. The Universal Negro Improvement Association, Marcus Garvey's radical anticolonial organization, was infiltrated and derailed in part by informants. Both Martin and Malcolm were followed, harassed, reported on, and undermined by people in the service of the intelligence apparatus of this country. Slave revolts undermined. COINTELPRO. Thus arises a tendency to christen any Negro with a court date as a political prisoner.

But before we run wild with the footnotes, consider this. The current campaign has more in common with the corporate code of silence that allowed the CEOs of Enron and WorldCom to rob innocent people blind than it does with any element of black folks history in this country. It is mafia witness intimidation in black-face. And yeah, we know about other versions of the "stop snitching" coda—the police department's well-known blue wall of silence and the mafia's code of omerta. What these codes all share in common is that they exist as a means of protecting wrongdoers—not those who are their primary victims. The DVD that inspired the Stop Snitching phenomenon did not feature young men urging the black community to develop more political unity in light of police behavior but instead an array of street-level aspiring gangstas issuing threats to people who may be foolish enough to inform on their activities.

Contrary to what you hear in certain precincts of racial self-deprecation, black people in this country are not suffering from a lack of unity. If anything, there's too much of it. Or at least too much of it directed at the most questionable of causes. If you needed further evidence that the world is tilted off its axis, consider exhibit A. Last year, a lawyer friend told me about her experience trying a rape case in a small town. Both the defendant and the victim—an elderly woman—were black, as was the jury and the prosecutor. The state had overwhelming evidence of the suspect's guilt, but the jury acquitted him of the charge. When the DA polled the jury to see what left them with an iota of doubt as to who committed the crime, the response was that they believed he was guilty but "just couldn't see sending another black man to prison." This is the same logic as the Stop Snitching campaign—that victimizing the community is somehow more noble than seeing that the perpetrator is punished.

Between 1976 and 2004, African Americans, who are 13 percent of the population constituted nearly 47 percent of the homicide cases in the United States. A huge chunk of which were never solved. To be a black person in this society is to walk around carrying a statistical burden that makes you six times more likely to die as a victim of homicide than your white counterpart. It is to know that no one will notice. And those who do will say nothing of it in order to uphold a wasted ghetto ethic. The real history of bias and injustice in this country has nothing to do with giving a predator a free pass to make victims of people—predominantly people who look just like him.

So, no, what black America needs is not more unity, but more *haters*. If it means challenging irresponsibility and taking control of our own lives, then yeah, I'm a hater. If it means stating the uncomfortable truths so that we can see our condition precisely as it is, I plead guilty. But on some level, you know that these are acts of love. And self-preservation. The alternative is an endorsement of a skewed fun-house mirror version of the world where hustlers are allowed to sell crack undisturbed and commit homicide without fear of reprisal. Where "unity" allows rapists to continue victimizing their own communities. And in this horror flick of life, we can cling to the false virtue of keeping our mouths shut.

December 2005

16

What Happens in Rio

In 2003, the hip-hop artists Snoop Dog and Pharrell Williams filmed a video for the song "Beautiful" on location in Brazil. The video inspired an avalanche of tourism to Brazil, most of it involving black American men pursuing sex with Brazilian women. At the least, the phenomenon was an ironic commentary on the power of hip-hop and the meaning of manhood in this new century.

1

They notice you the second you walk into the club. There's a ripple effect—two dozen beautiful women competing to establish eye contact with you. Some coo compliments in their accented English. A caramel-colored sister in a short skirt sends a note saying you are the most handsome man she's seen all night. (It was probably written twenty minutes before you ever set foot in the joint, but that's beside the point.) You grab a table. The waiter flips open the menu to display the night's specials. Resting under his thumb is a four-pack of Viagra, which he offers to you for six dollars a pill. You ignore the pills and order a caipirinha. Ten minutes later your table looks like the set of a music video as six stunning women surround you, smiling at you.

Welcome to Rio.

Mention Brazil and you will likely conjure up images of pristine beaches and beautiful women or maybe the strong African cultural traditions that have survived and flourished here for centuries. But there are other attractions driving tourism to this South American nation: Brazil is a hub of the international sex-tourism industry. Its reputation dates all the way back to a time when white men exploited black women during slavery. But times have changed. According to Judith Morrison, executive director of the Inter-Agency Consultation on Race in Latin America, a Washington, D.C., policy organization that addresses issues facing Latinos of African descent, the number of African American men participating in the trade has exploded in recent years. At least one report has charted a 16 percent increase in black American tourism to Brazil in the past two years. This is 15 percent higher than the general increase in Brazilian tourism, and black Americans, who are only 12 percent of the U.S. population, account for 17 percent of the Americans traveling to Brazil.

By most accounts, sex tourism is driving this increase. "At least 80 percent of the black men coming here from the States are pursuing sex," says Don,* an entrepreneur from Los Angeles who relocated to Rio de Janeiro and now runs a travel agency catering to male tourists. "This is the biggest secret in black America that I can think of," observes Jewel Woods, a doctoral candidate in social work and sociology at the University of Michigan and author of *The New Ugly American: Professional Black Men, Sexual Paradise, and Brazil,* a study of African American men who travel to Brazil. "Black women just don't know about this."

But that secrecy was shattered, at least in Brazil, by two

* All names in this piece have been changed.

recent high-profile incidents involving black American men. A year ago authorities raided a boat ride and arrested twenty-eight brothers and forty prostitutes—or *garotas de programas,* as they are called in Brazil. News of the arrests spread throughout message boards and chat rooms with a warning that the organizers of the tour had failed to pay off the right authorities. A similar claim was made two months ago when a high-end men's social club in Rio was busted and forty men—all of them black Americans—were arrested.

Of course, cheap sex with women in Third World countries has long been considered a perk for men of the industrialized world. While prostitution in Brazil is legal (as long as participants are over eighteen), maintaining a place for sexual purposes is technically illegal, though the law is so seldom enforced that the trade thrives, especially in the tourist areas. It's a question of economics: even working-class Americans have vastly more resources than the women who live here. "Despite the stats of Black American men being incarcerated, beat down and unem- ployed, there is a level of affluence that we have gained that allows us to act in the same way Whites have," says Tracy Sharpley-Whiting, a Vanderbilt University professor who has researched the lure of sex tourism in Brazil. As if to prove her point, on my first night in Rio a bartender recounts the story of a brother who had a price quoted to him by a woman and, amazed at how cheap the sex was, replied, "I'll take you—and your four friends over there."

2

At night, the strip in Rio's famed Copacabana section is a gauntlet of fine women running game. It's an intriguing role reversal. The women holler lines at you on the street, asking if your name is Denzel, telling you how well your linen shirt fits as you enter a club. Inside, the place is lined wall to wall with black men. You choose a table and settle down to watch a rotation of incredibly beautiful women of every conceivable description dancing onstage.

Before you know it, a woman about five feet ten inches tall, with green eyes and full lips, slips up to you. Her skin, the color of creamy coffee, is flawless. She's so fine that you feel like the Lord was showing off when He made her. She whispers in fractured English that she noticed you watching her while she was onstage. By way of introduction, she kisses you on each cheek.

After three minutes of language-barrier small talk she leans over, touches your thigh, and announces, "I, two-hundred-fifty dollars." You know you're supposed to come back with a lower bid. That's how the game is played—the bartender at the last club you visited explained it all. But the simple reduction of a person to a monetary figure makes your head spin.

This deal making doesn't seem to bother most of the brothers who visit here. They range from blue collar to blue chip and every category in between: cops, firemen, lawyers, engineers, even one marriage counselor. From early twenties through late sixties; married, single, dating, or engaged, they're lured by an unimaginable scale of sexual possibility and a chance to live as a rate-of-exchange baller. The bawdy or hushed locker-room tales they share with other guys only up the ante. To hear them tell it, the women are willing, the sex is cheap, and Viagra is nearly as common as the sand on Ipanema's immaculate beach. One sixty-nine-year-old from Baltimore, who's been traveling to Brazil for twenty-one years, brags to you about bedding two women nearly every night, and then having a grand finale with six bisexual women on his last night in town. He cuts short the conversation because he has a date for a ménage à trois set for 10:00 p.m. As he leaves, you're thinking this dude wouldn't score a ménage à anything back home.

But this is Rio.

What happens here is as much about validation as it is about sex, explains Woods. "A lot of men go down there after some emotional trauma like divorce or separation," he says. There's Keith, a muscular forty-three-year-old brother from Ohio who could easily pass for a decade younger. He came to Brazil for the first time two years ago when he learned that neither of the two children he was raising with his long-term partner was biologically his. When he returned home, he and his woman split up, and he has been back to Rio five times since then. He laughs easily, but his words have a bitter undertone. "I never sit at a table completely surrounded by dimes [perfect tens] in America," he says. "These girls make you feel like a million dollars. They stroke the hell out of your ego. I have a twenty-year-old who cooks and cleans for me and treats me like a god. I don't get that in America."

Many locals believe the latest outbreak of Rio fever among brothers is inspired at least in part by hip-hop's glamorization of the city. "The numbers of black American men really started increasing after the Snoop video," a cab driver tells me. He is referring to the video for Snoop and Pharrell's 2003 collaboration, "Beautiful," which was shot in Rio and features throngs of gorgeous Brazilian women. "Tourism really took off after that video was shot," agrees Morrison. "We've noticed that there are more black Americans in Brazil generally, and a disproportionate number of them are men. Once, flying out of New York, I was the only African American woman on a plane full of black men." Her observation is borne out by my week in Rio. Though I meet dozens of black men during my time here, I run into only four African American women, three of them traveling together.

That could be because black men represent a tourism market that is being increasingly targeted. In recent years, enterprising guides have put together travel packages specifically designed for African American men. Don, the brother with the travel company, has a Web site advertising "cultural tours" of Brazil. But if you scroll down to the bottom of the page, you'll get a link to porn featuring Brazilian women.

Don's company is an outgrowth of an annual carnival tour he started after visiting Rio ten years ago. "Before long I was making more money from the tours than I was at my job, and I knew it was time to move here full time," he tells me. His company serves a high-end clientele—"men who travel without a budget," as he puts it. "Three or four years ago, you started getting a younger, hip-hop crowd coming to Rio; men who wanted to relive the Snoop video," he observes. The increasing numbers of black American male tourists, he adds, are also driven by the fact that "women here are not trying to be equal to their men." As proof, he offers that his Brazilian wife serves him breakfast in bed every morning and wouldn't dream of letting him wash a plate after dinner.

In Rio the women, even those women who speak virtually no English, run a line that you hear so often it becomes something of an inside joke. Give them two minutes and they'll whisper in your ear, "I love black American men." Ask why, and they will cite reasons ranging from penis size to sexual skill to their belief that we are simply more hygienic than white men. "The black men shower more," says Karla, a twenty-three-year-old who vaguely resembles the singer Ciara. "Like you, I knew you were clean when you sat down." She points to my fingernails and says they are the first thing she notices about a potential client.

It's important to grasp that her compliments are merely part of good customer relations. "I love black men" is a pitch line for a service industry that understands its consumer. But for brothers who face an onslaught of racial slights back home, and live our lives inside a cellblock of damning statistical indexes, the attention is intoxicating. I begin to understand why, of more than sixty black men I speak with in the course of a week, only two or three are here for the first time.

One brother, a forty-something paramedic from Brooklyn with a girlfriend at home, has come here three times in the past thirteen months. Thomas, a married fiftyish accountant from Cleveland, has made annual trips here for almost twenty years. He insists his wife knows why he visits, but that she's adopted a don't-ask-don't-tell policy about his time in Rio. Brian, a thirty-seven-year-old entrepreneur from Atlanta, estimates he's been in Brazil well over forty times in the past decade. "I work like crazy for three months and then spend a couple of weeks here and get taken care of," he says. He doesn't even bother with serious relationships Stateside anymore.

3

The men speak of being "ruined" by the kind of treatment they receive in Brazil. "It definitely changes how you view women," says Ben, thirty-one, an engineer from California with a girlfriend of more than two years back home. He is seated at a table with three women for whom he has just bought drinks. He tells of a friend who came to Rio for a bachelor party and then had to reevaluate his decision to get married. Another brother, in his late twenties with a fiancée back in the Midwest, tells me about Josie, the woman he has spent his vacation with. After detailing her talent for catering to her clients—both in and out of the bed—he observes, "You know, this is only partly about p****. The rest is really about affirmation. Josie's done more for me in these five days than my fiancée has in three years."

What differentiates this from run-of-the-mill vacation skirt-chasing is the underlying sociology. A lot of brothers in Rio are quick to label African American women as "materialistic gold diggers." Many are bitterly disillusioned with sisters back home. "In the States, it's all about financial worth," Don tells me. "Five minutes after meeting you, African American women want to know what you do so they can figure out how much you make. Here they want to know who you are as a person." The fact that his clients pay a lot of money to have beautiful women get to know them "as a person" is an irony that seems lost on Don.

It's also easy to see what's going on in Rio as a kind of backlash against the perceived successes of African American women. Ron, a sixty-year-old marriage counselor, whom I met as he was negotiating with a twenty-four-year-old *garotas de programa,* tells me, "The women are willing to look after and take care of their men in a way that black women in America stopped doing after they got successful." And Don, the tour operator, suggests that the men on the strip are looking for a quick and easy version of the more enduring relationships he finds for his well-heeled clientele— relationships in which the women cater to their partner's every desire. It's no wonder, he says, that his tours have resulted in three marriages between clients and the Brazilian women (not prostitutes, he emphasizes) that he introduced them to.

"The men always speak of getting in Brazil what black women aren't giving them in America," echoes Woods. Whether this is an emotional reality or a convenient rationalization, sex tourism here is driven by an alluring fantasy that receives word-of-mouth marketing every time a return flight touches down in the States. "If nothing else, the men bring back attitudes and expectations about how women should act," observes Sharpley-Whiting. Case in point: "The first time I came back from Brazil," Brian, the entrepreneur, tells me, "it was like I had seen the light! The minute a woman at home said the wrong thing, I would tell her to step. The women in Brazil know that they have to let you be the man." In other words, they defer to you, cook and clean for you, pamper you, and are sexually insatiable.

Or at least they pretend to be.

"What happens in Rio is like a movie," says Carlos, a Brazilian cab driver who went to high school in the United States. "People know what's happening on the screen is not real, but if it's done well enough, they still become emotionally invested." This emotional investment is carefully nurtured by the women to overshadow the financial one. It's why the men frequenting the bars and clubs on the strip almost never mention the money. "They will talk about all the women they had and how she couldn't get enough, but they never talk about the fact that they paid for it," says Sharpley-Whiting. "They imagine it to be something other than what it is." Woods suggests the men are fooling themselves in other ways as well. "The real irony is that these women speak hardly any English," he says, "so the men have this experience of feeling like Denzel or Puffy for a day with women who literally can't even communicate with them."

The fantasy works in part because prostitution doesn't always look like a transaction here. Some women simply seek out tourists to date without asking for cash explicitly. But they derive the benefits of staying in a hotel, dining at fine restaurants, and partying in high-end clubs. Other women charge not for sex but for what they call GFE—local lingo for a "girlfriend experience." GFE women dine with you, take you on tours of the city, cook and clean for you (many tourists rent a suite or an apartment), and have sex whenever you want it. "The guys come away feeling like they've found some unique personal friendship," says Woods. "One guy, a banker who is extremely high-ranking in his field and a deep-thinking kind of person, admitted he once cried when leaving."

4

Still, there are moments when the charade becomes obvious. One night I'm at a corner table taking notes on the scene. There are stares and glances sent my way, but a woman two tables over is by far the most persistent. A slight nod is all it takes to summon her to my table. Lucia has a languid stride and choreographed movements that scream sexual invitation. As she slides into a chair opposite me, she holds my gaze for a long moment and smiles. She leans in when I talk and then makes brazen advertisements about her skills in the bedroom. "I love to f***," she says bluntly. "I would f*** you all night." She follows this with the mandatory sales pitch: "I like the black American men."

After I tell her I'm a journalist and am interested in talking to her, not hiring her, an entirely different person emerges. She relaxes visibly; her entire posture loosens. She is a pretty woman in her late twenties with skin the color of sand, shoulder-length hair, and long, toned legs that her short skirt and heels show off well. She tells me her husband abandoned her and their four-year-old twins three years ago. "I tried other work," she says, "but when I saw my children going hungry, I decided to do this. The money is much better." In Rio the average monthly income is around one hundred dollars, but a *garotas de programa* can bring in more than twenty times that in a good month.

Lucia says some black American men have told her they "feel like they are in prison in the United States, but they are free when they come here." She's built continuing relationships with several of them who seek her out when they come to Rio. Even after they return to the States, the men send her money. "If I am having a difficult time, I send an e-mail, and I know one of them will help me out," she says.

I encounter variations of Lucia's story a dozen times on the strip. Economic conditions in Brazil ensure that the clubs and beaches have a constant supply of attractive women who are willing to sell sex. "In parts of the northeast, the women are giving their bodies away literally for sustenance," says Morrison. According to a United Nations development report, 30 percent of the country's 186 million people live below the poverty line, with some 46 million—a quarter of the population—surviving on less than a dollar per day. The ugliness of this economic reality struck me one night as I wandered back to my hotel. Outside one of the clubs was a cluster of ten- to twelve-year-old girls. A local explained they were glue addicts who sleep with tourists for money. The children aren't welcome in the bars and restaurants, but they walk the strip. They are easy to find. "There is a horrific problem of sex tourism and children," confirms Morrison. "The families of these children literally don't have any food."

5

If you keep your eyes open long enough, you can't avoid recognizing that there is indeed an underside to this sexual Disneyland: a 2004 UN report on AIDS states there are 660,000 HIV-infected persons living in Brazil. Sex work by definition entails exposure to STDs. "Of course I am worried," says a thirty-something firefighter from Connecticut who has made multiple trips here. "I'm very worried. I don't touch anything unless I'm wrapped up." The women, too, say they're careful; that a man won't get much more than a handshake from them without a condom. Brenda, a honey-colored woman in her midtwenties who carries nude pictures of herself to show potential customers, talks about a time that she had to flee a hotel naked because a client refused to cover it up.

"These women will make you shower and insist on a rubber," Keith confirms. I mention there are STDs that condoms won't protect against. Keith merely shrugs and says nothing. We both know that given the tales of men who've fathered children with women here, there's reasonable doubt that every encounter involves the use of protection.

And there are dangers beyond the immunological ones. The week before I arrived in Rio, a tourist at the same bar where the waiter tried to sell me Viagra was caught in the crossfire between a gunman and the police. He was shot in the head and killed. (When I went to the bar, another patron shooed me away from the first table I was about to take, believing that it was bad luck to sit where a man had been killed.)

But these are the kinds of truths that green eyes and full lips will help you push into the far corners of your mind. If you convince yourself that the woman sitting across from you gives you that look because she can't get enough, then you'll miss the fact that the game is really about people getting by. It's about poor people playing a role that those with deeper pockets have scripted for them, and doing it well enough to survive. And in the clubs on the strip where black American men congregate, the game is also about dueling stereotypes—black bucks in pursuit of hot-blooded Latinas—with the truth obscured beneath a sexual mirage. With Rio cast as a sort of crossroads where Latin American poverty and black male insecurities intersect, it's easy to become confused about who is using whom more efficiently. But twenty-five-year-old Josie, whose fresh-faced girl-next-door appearance masks an analytical intelligence and focused ambition—she's writing a book about her experience in the sex trade and is saving to open a beauty salon—is anything but confused. "There are no losers here," she tells me with perfect authority. "Men like to win, even when they know from the start they can't lose."

It's why they come to Rio.

September 2006

First Person

There's a reason why the venerable old composition teachers at I.S. 238 forbade us from using the first person singular for an entire semester. The personal essay is a particular challenge (which is, perhaps, why this is the shortest section of this book). It requires turning a lens that is usually focused outward toward oneself and being willing to describe what you see there. Much easier to just look out the window and observe the world than to describe the world while figuring out your place in it. But on another level, there's a hazy line between the personal and external. Muhammad Ali once crafted a poem that was a masterpiece of economy. The entire poem reads: "Me, we." The essays that follow are personal observations of the world at a particular time, in a particular place, and my understanding of it. They are comments on myself. And maybe on the rest of us, too.

17

My Daughter, Once Removed

When I wake up in the morning, I think about Aiesha, first thing. I haven't spoken to her in a month, but all of her messages are still saved on my answering machine; I still tell her that she is my favorite person. There is a T-shirt in the exact same spot she left it three months ago when she last visited me. Aiesha is eight, spoiling for nine, and she's my ex-daughter.

In my wide-eyed youth I subscribed to wild notions like "biology does not equal paternity" and "twenty-six chromosomes don't make you Daddy." I believed that love makes one a parent; that fatherhood is created every morning at 6:00 a.m. when you creak out of bed to crack eggs, rattle pans, and let yourself be hustled into granting your kid ten more minutes of sleep. A father is the big guy who's there at the end of the table each night to finish everyone else's leftovers. In my adulthood I believe that genes don't make the parent, but now I ask, what does a voided wedding vow make me?

If you listen to the running dialogue on talk radio, barbershops, and from pulpits, the American father has been dispatched, part of some planned obsolescence, done in by feminism and sperm banks. The old Dad model has been discontinued in favor of a newer, sleeker single-parent alternative. I don't subscribe to that theory, but I do think we're in danger of becoming a society of temporary families. The volumes of books and how-to guides for divorce and the divorce workshops make it easier for people to survive the end of the marriage. But as a consequence, I think we run the risk of making divorce a cure-all for marital woe.

I know Aiesha because her mother, Shana, was my college girlfriend and because I broke up with her and then years later found myself wishing for her again. She was wild and reckless and beautiful—the opposite of my self-conscious, bookish way. We were done in less than six months but stayed in touch with each other. Five years later I moved to New York for graduate school. When we threw a surprise party for my mother's fiftieth birthday, I invited Shana and she showed up with a buoyant two-year-old with impossibly round cheeks whose favorite word was "*No!*" as in "You are adorable." "*No!*"

Soon we were hanging out again, back to our old college routine, and when I occasionally spent the night, I slept on the living room sofa so that Aiesha wouldn't get the wrong idea. The first night we slept together again, Shana told me that she wasn't looking for another short-term relationship. I understood; neither was I. At some point in those first months, I realized that I loved Shana again and that Aiesha had already chosen me as her father. Shana and I were married a year and a half later.

I think men secretly want to raise their daughters to be the kind of women who were out of their league when they were young. And so it was with Aiesha. But really, it was about the words, teaching her the words to old classics like "Sittin' on the Dock of the Bay" and "Ain't No Sunshine When She's Gone," and giggling through the part where Bill Withers sings, "And I know, I know, I know, I know, I *know,* I know . . ." Kids dig repetition. She turned out volumes of poems, plays, songs, and stories that were duly typed up and e-mailed to all of my friends, coworkers, and distant relatives as evidence of her burgeoning literary genius.

There were signs, now that I think of it, indicating that the marriage was headed south early on. I saw in gradual degrees that my wife was less and less interested in our relationship, and knew that I was at the point where many men would've bailed. I chose to work harder. When the newspapers ranked Aiesha's public school in the bottom half of those in the city, I reduced my grad classes and worked part-time to send her to a private one. When Shana was stuck at work a few hours before her women's group meeting, I came home early and surprised her by cleaning the apartment and cooking all the food. I was like an outfielder who knows the ball is headed for the bleachers, but smashes face-first into the wall trying to catch it anyway. In my world, there was no such thing as a warning track.

A marital cliché: the spouse is in the kitchen cooking dinner when the other returns from a hard day at the office and announces that it's over. Just like that. It's a scenario that any writing instructor worth his salt would trash, but that's how it really went down. The exact words were: *I don't love you the way a wife should love a husband and I would like for you to move out.* Then silence. It went down that way, and I was broken for a while. She married me because I was the theoretical good catch, not out of a desire to build a lifelong connection. When Shana asked me to leave, I stared at her blankly for about five minutes. When she told Aiesha that I was leaving, Aiesha asked, "Does this mean that I don't have a father anymore?"

There are easy answers. Friends (mainly female) tell me, Once a father, always a father. But experience tells me different—that I could just as easily be evicted again, that Shana could remarry and leave me a parental second-string player. Raising Aiesha for five years was the greatest experience of my life, but in these past months I have loved her from a distance. The truth is that in the wake of a dissolved marriage, I am terrified of the vulnerability that being a stepparent entails, terrified that my parental role could be ended just as abruptly. Experience tells me that *ex-stepfather* does not exist as a census category. That I no longer qualify for a Father's Day card.

Looking at it now, I know that I was trying to single-handedly undo the mythology directed at black men, that I wanted a family who would laugh past the bleak statistics, the damning indices charting black male irresponsibility. When I married Shana, Aiesha had not seen her biological father in over a year. She hasn't seen him since then. I saw tragedy in her growing up as yet another fatherless black girl, another child whose father abandoned her in favor of emptier pursuits. I wanted to be like my old man, quietly heroic in raising my brother, sister, and me and never once letting on that my siblings were not his biological kin. I wanted to be a keeper.

These days I know that the relationship is unwieldy, that it is sagging under the weight of its own ambiguity. Fatherhood is all about watching the daily changes, the new word learned, or noticing that now she doesn't have to stand on a stool to reach her toothbrush. But I also know that in a year or two my work may require that I move to Texas or California or Anchorage and I may fade from her preadolescent memory.

Christmas is a hard, cold, bright day, and I wake up that morning with my head heavy from the last night's bender. Aiesha had left me a message saying she had a gift for me and "please come today so I can give it to you." I have been gone for six months. I don't know her as well as I did in June, and in another six months she'll be a different child altogether. When I see her outside riding her bike in the parking lot of her building, I think how she's grown long and slender like a reed.

I bought her a watch—yellow and red, but with no cartoon characters, because Aiesha fancies herself a sophisticate. The note says, "Dear Aiesha: My father once told me that keeping track of time is the first step toward being a grown-up. I hope you think of me when you wear this. Love, Jelani." She gives me a card written in her best eight-year-old scrawl: simply "I love you," it says. She's chattering, telling me the plot points for her newest story, the one she "wants to publish when she's twelve." A moment later she wants me to toss her into the air and keeps pleading "one more time" until my deltoids are burning. She still remembers most of the words to "Ain't No Sunshine When She's Gone." Today she's my daughter. Today.

January 2001

18

Seeing Double

You slip into a cool sanctuary on a Southern August day and almost make your way to the back before you see her. Circumstance has put her on the front row in a pink floral dress, not quite looking bereaved, but more like she is trying to solve a calculus equation in her head. You say no under your breath and grunt the way your old man used to when his arthritis was acting up. And you know that this will be worse than you imagined.

She is there, trying to bridge the irreconcilable gulf between what she had sweated and pushed into this world and what lies embalmed before her. On the front row beside her are two girl-friends, because the deceased were too young to have wives. Her younger son, nineteen years old and dressed in all white, speaks a single line of scripture: Proverbs 10, verse 2. Brief eulogy for brief life. He speaks those words and then passes his older brother and his first cousin, who lies in a casket beside him, and then he collapses. The preacher lays down a tired prayer, like he has a template for prematurely dead black men. This is a panoramic view of our common wretchedness, and you want to be anywhere but here—in church on a weekday, giving up wasted lamentations. Circumstance is this: two black men, neighbors of yours, young cats with whom you talked shit and lifted weights, found shot in the head in an abandoned building.

Their lives merited several sentences, but no adjectives, in an Associated Press report. Police have suspicions but no leads; their story ends with a cliché: "suspected to be drug-related." You sit there, void and unpowerful, thinking that this is some shit out of an Etheridge Knight poem. You are full with anger that goes deeper than your bones and want nothing of goddamned hymns, no cursed prayers, no useless solace. No nineteen-year-old eulogists and no mothers in floral dresses doing math problems on the front row. No girlfriends in mourning because the deceased were too young to have wives.

In a moment you move from anger to despair and worry for the future of your clan who do not know that a people who slay their own youth are damned to perish. You start thinking philosophically, like: What is a life if not a collection of days with a theme, and if you're lucky you figure the theme out before the final credits roll. But more often its like the movies where the audience sees what's coming long before the lead on the screen is wise to what is in store. And you wish that the two young men in front of you had been given a saga, not a short, an epic instead of a novella.

This is a piece that was turned in late because on the day of my deadline I went to a double funeral for two black men, aged twenty-two and twenty-seven, and couldn't fuck with a computer when I got home.

If you invest your faith in the statistical palm reading of actuaries, you know that a black man at age thirty-four is way overdue for a midlife crisis. This piece was supposed to be about the reflections of a brother on turning thirty-four years and eight days old, about losing a step on your baseline drive and shaving an inch off your vertical. This was supposed to be about hoping that you've gained wisdom enough to merit the colony of gray hairs—eleven of them now—that have taken root in your beard. About having a body that will do most of what it once could, you just have to ask more politely. About being old enough to have loved, lost, and then loved some more. It was going to be about wondering what your old man, gone ten years now, would make of you these days and asking yourself what he was doing at your age. You have his same field Negro frame and Sonny Liston–sized hands, only you remember the distant past for a living, and he lived to put distance between himself and the past. You sweat tenure committees and publication deadlines, and he wrestled with the world for what it would relinquish to a black boy with three grades worth of book learning.

And you could really trip off this kind of shit, wondering what it meant to be thirty-four in 1953, until you recognize that self-reflection is a sucker's game, and what you know is this: being thirty-four in 2003 means being twelve years older than what lies before you in a premature coffin. It means that your people will not live to count gray hairs in beards, to talk about the feats of which they were capable "back in the day," they will not live to ask these kinds of questions.

On the way out you pass two other young brothers, you nod and say *Peace,* but even here, at this hour, they are practicing how to be hard. You know you could hem them both up, because thirty-four or not, you got a field Negro frame and Sonny Liston–sized hands: you could do that and tell them that you know that deep down they are scared like a motherfucker so you don't gotta front for me. You could tell them that you are in the audience and you know how this flick ends. You could tell them that Proverbs 10, verse 2 reads: "Ill-gotten treasures are of no value, but righteousness delivers from death." But instead, you betray your people and maintain decorum.

Outside you reflect on this bitter truth: the hustle is interminable. The preacher is threadbare. The outside is hot and the church is cool. The cousins are their own eternal company, ride or die.

And the world keeps spinning, like a hustler's twenty-inch rims.

August 2004

19

Two-fifth & Hollis

To get there you had to take the downtown A train from 145th and transfer to the E at 42nd. Ride the front subway car and get off at the second-to-last stop, 168th Street. Walk down the hill to the bus terminal—you can't miss it, because the new main branch of the Queens Public Library is right across the street. If you see the El running down Jamaica Avenue, it means you went down too far. Get the Q2 bus at the terminal—that's "Q" like Quincy. The 2 will take you down—what is that, Hillside?—until you get to the underpass and it branches off to Hollis. Right after that you'll start seeing these aluminum-sided one- and two-family houses with a little square patch of yard out front. Don't look like uptown at all. Stay on until you see the supermarket on the left; it used to be Associated, and Pathmark before that, and I don't have any idea what it is now. The street numbers will be going up, and you'll see these wide side streets; the houses on those streets got driveways and little lamps out front that come on automatically as soon as the sun set. Ring the bell when you pass the catering place on the right-hand side, and the bus will put you out right there. On Two-Fifth Street.

For my people, who hail from places with names like Waycross, Bessemer, and Hazlehurst, Queens was a zip code, a time zone, and a continent away from the Southern burgs they were abandoning. This was back in the day when the Mets were the city's new team and people still referred to the largest borough as "Queens, Long Island." Talk to black people of a certain age about Queens and they will pridefully point out the once-exclusive sections of St. Albans, where James Brown and Count Basie owned homes in the Sixties. Listen long enough and you'll hear about W. E. B. Du Bois buying a home in Queens before he quit the country altogether, and that Malcolm X was living in East Elmhurst when his house was firebombed. Some of the oldheads will remember Bob Beamon when he was still just a lanky Jamaica High School student, before his name became synonymous with the Olympic long jump.

In the 1970s Queens was on its way to becoming the most ethnically diverse region of the United States, and to hear the elders tell it, moving out there from Harlem, the Bronx, or Bed-Stuy in those days meant getting the chance to cash in on 350 years of sweat equity in America. A murdered prophet and a hundred burned cities were redeemable for this: a newly laminated union card, a GS-10 government gig, a patch of front yard, and yellow aluminum siding. The truth is that Martin King, Vietnam, and Molotov cocktails got George Jefferson the FHA loan that landed him a crib next door to Archie Bunker in Astoria.

People played up this angle that they were, at long last,

someplace different in time and geography; even though Queens has been part of New York's five municipalities since 1898, taking the train to Manhattan was referred to as "going into the city." They picked up the local particulars, like how people dropped the zero in street numbers, abbreviating 201st Street to simply Two-First—except for 200th, which was called by its full name instead of Two-Zero.

Hollis, Queens. Neighborhood in central Queens, bounded to the north by Grand Central Parkway, to the east by Francis Lewis Boulevard, to the south by Hollis Avenue, and to the west by 184th Street. Established in 1885 by Frederick W. Denton, nephew of the supervisor of what was then called Jamaica Town.

My aunt Elsie was the first. She and my uncle Ray bought themselves a gray, shingled house on Two-Fifth, just off Hollis Avenue in '67. Then her son Lee, known as "Brother," bought a two-family place down on 193rd. Next came Mary C., my mother, who was called by her first name and middle initial to distinguish her from my maternal grandmother, her cousin, and my paternal grandfather's first cousin—all of whom were named Mary. She and my father bought the yellow house at 109–62 200th Street in '69, just before I was born. My cousin Louise—whom I called "Aunt" Lou because she was less than a year younger than my mother—moved over there by Jamaica Park in the early '70s, before she bought her place in Lefrak City. Then came Lou's sister Net, who settled in the 190s, and my mother's younger sister, Pat, who rented a place on Two-Third or Two-Fourth. Between them came scores of cousins, aunts, and distant kin who occupied basements, guest rooms, and couches until they found their own niches in the city.

To them, Queens was a place to come to; for me, though, it was where I was from. This is what I remember of home: redbrick front steps that were eventually painted white, blue carpet and white beads in the living room, and stained glass windows on the stairwell. I remember that our phone number was 465–8162 and that our first answering machine was the size of a VCR. There was a gold Chrysler parked in the driveway; I remember the electric blue convertible Cadillac with whitewall tires that replaced the gold Chrysler, and the pool table in the basement. In the closet there were matching blue suits with white hats worn by my parents to "After 8" receptions and the blue-and-yellow uniforms of St. Pascal-Baylon Elementary School. The collie was named Tony; the Belgian shepherd was called Blue.

For my parents' generation, Queens was tied to an American fantasy of becoming—even as they remained as steadfastly country as the day they crossed the Alabama state line. The Hollis of the 1970s was a community where kids ate fish and grits for breakfast, people consulted the dream books when deciding what number to play, and children were expected to refer to any woman over fifty as Aunt such-and-such. In the years before the community language became spiced with West Indian patois, it was a place where Southern accents were almost ubiquitous among the grown folk: they said "ain't" not "wudn't," "y'all" instead of "you'se," "fittin' to" as opposed to "gonna." Down the street were Aunt Precious (her real name) and her husband, Mr. Jimmy, who came up from Sumter, South Carolina; over on Two-First was Aunt Mary—who was not one of the kinfolk Marys—and her husband, Mr. Sonny, the sometime mechanic. They were from North Carolina. These were Southern Negroes who had known emptiness and hard times and who had, by hook or by crook, scored a piece of real estate in the imperial city of New York. You couldn't do no better than that.

For us, though, the generation of cousins, nephews, and nieces born in Queens, our middle-classness was something to be lived down. God forbid you found yourself caught out there in Union Square in the presence of the rebel factions from Brooklyn.

God help you if you owned a bomber, nameplate, or sheepskin between '84 and '88; kids from other boroughs had ownership rights to your gear once the E train crossed the East River. It was like black America had finally succeeded in creating a generation of youth privileged enough to resent their parents' prosperity.

Social mobility, though, is a two-way street. For better or worse, my own sense of middle-class shame never came to full blossom. I also remember this: my parents at the hand-carved wooden table in the dining room, month after month, trying to figure out how to make it work. The fights over money and the endless, bone-grinding hustle to maintain. The hand-wringing concession that I be taken out of St. Pascal's and sent to PS 34 over on Two-Fourth, near the projects. The Cadillac that broke down and the used station wagon that replaced it. The American dream that comes with taxes, interest, and balloon payments.

They foreclosed on the yellow, aluminum-sided house in 1980, and it felt like the punch line to a joke we hadn't been in on. And yeah, maybe my old man liked to sip a little too much, but he was a decent guy, really. He just got winded chasing his dollars, cramped up because he bit off more America than his Southern black belly could digest. He was only guilty of literal dream interpretation.

My oldest brother, Alan, died of pneumonia that same year. He'd come home from Vietnam with a scag habit that he managed to kick in 1979; it was years, though, before we realized that he'd been an early victim of AIDS. Those two events fell on us like a metaphor for the coming decade. We moved to an apartment in a buckwild zone of 177th Street, four blocks in from Liberty Avenue, then a smaller apartment in Springfield Gardens on Ridgedale Street.

Twenty-two years later I drove down to see my aunt Shirley, known to us as "Sugar." My mother's youngest sister had chosen to stay in Bessemer while her family spread out through the country. She walked me through the overgrown lots of what had once been the coal miner's quarters where they grew up. Only after she had marked the spot in the glass-strewn dirt where their house had stood and then paced the steps to Aunt Gwen's, pointed the direction to Aunt Lou's, and told me the way to Aunt Elsie's did I begin to understand the obvious. My family had been trying to re-create the community they'd had once down South, but minus the crackerism and Jim Crow that had strangled their own parents' aspirations.

Hollis, Queens, was important because it was as close as you could come to home while being 998 miles from Bessemer.

One bitterly cold night last year, I found myself on Two-Second Street. I was, by then, in hot pursuit of my own dreams, living in Atlanta, trying to finish a PhD and write a novel at the same time. I walked over to 200th and took a look at the once-yellow house at 109–62. I thought about my unknown kinship with whoever lives there now, having climbed the same trees, thrown the same rocks, and run from dragonflies in the same backyard. I thought about how these strangers and I held a deed of memory to the same mortgaged sliver of America.

These days, 168th Street is no longer the second-to-last stop on E; the city built new stations at Sutphin and Parsons, what, ten, twelve years ago now? In 1992 my parents bought a smaller house in South Ozone Park. Aunt Elsie and Brother have moved back down South, buying homes in Atlanta (the new black Mecca). My aunt Pat was shot in the head in 1990 by a drug dealer who was angry with her boyfriend. Aunt Lou is still in Lefrak, and Net is still in Hollis. My old man is gone, though, almost ten years now. And my mother is looking for a house to retire to. In Bessemer, Alabama, a zip code, a time zone, a continent away from Queens, New York.

October 2004

20

The More Things Change

Dateline: New Orleans. Five months later.

From a distance, the Crescent City, with its half-blackened sky-line, appears as something out of a science fiction movie. Even five months later, the events of August 2005 still seemed cinematically unreal. I went to New Orleans to see where the city stood on Martin Luther King Day, five months after the waters of Hurricane Katrina receded. What I saw was a city that was tragically undisturbed, one where there were just as many unresolved questions about the future as there had been on the day that the levies failed and the name New Orleans became shorthand for catastrophe.

From the highway during the daytime you saw the famed aboveground cemeteries that now looked like ruins of a past civilization, their crypts smashed by floating debris and stained from days of submersion in the toxic sludge that covered the city. The graveyard was nearly empty, its ancient contents now in some other improvised and surely less noble resting place.

There were reminders of the storm everywhere, but the Lower Ninth Ward resembled something from file footage of Beirut. The structures there were twisted into mad abstractions. On one street a house sat on top of a car. A few blocks away, a sedan sat atop a house. One structure had the front half torn off, making it a haphazard cutaway, a literal window into the disaster. There was one house where the second floor sat in the front yard and other addresses that simply ceased to exist. The stairs led to precisely nothing, a barren lot and an ominous commentary that whatever life had been lived on these premises would not go on—at least not there.

Much of the city was stained with those same black demarcation lines indicating where the waters had crested—except for the places where there were no lines because the water had risen higher than the tallest structures. In those places you could tell how high the waters had been by the elevation of debris in the trees. On one street in the Lower Ninth Ward, a sodden stuffed bear hung from a tree branch twenty feet above the ground; a medical IV hung from a branch nearby. You could not help but wonder who that IV had been attached to and how it had come to be separated from that person.

And then there was the silence. You never encounter silence in a city. There are always the ambient sounds of living—the hum of traffic, a television, a blaring radio, fugitive snatches of a dozen conversations—but here it was absolutely still. No birds, no laughter on the playground, no dogs barking at passersby. And no passersby. The catastrophe stretched on for miles and so did that envelope of quiet.

But it was clear that this was supposed to happen. The battered landscape in New Orleans reminded me of the Mexico City earthquake of 1985, where the casualties were people who lived in cheap buildings thrown together by corrupt contractors and approved by the inspectors they bribed. Or Chicago, where the 1995 heat wave killed seven hundred people, a disproportionate number of them poor and black. They were not any more susceptible to heat; their neighborhoods simply had fewer government buildings, supermarkets, and community centers where people could go to cool off.

The fault lines in Mexico City were as much about economics as they were tectonics. And New Orleans illustrates yet again that disaster, like water, follows the path of least resistance. In the Lower Ninth Ward, I saw a mix of working-class and poor neighborhoods that stretched for blocks, all sharing the fact that whether by design or default they had all been thrown together in harm's way.

The French Quarter was only a short distance away, but it bore no evidence of what had happened. The business owners there literally held the high ground, and at night the inebriated revelry continued as if there had never been a storm compounded by a plague of human failures. But that kind of amnesia was impossible in other parts of the city. In the Third Ward I met a man who was a member of a fraternal lodge and who was thankful that they at least recovered their bodies in his neighborhood. He told me about areas to the east where victims of the flood were swept into the Gulf of Mexico. I thought about that for a minute and realized that the definition of a disaster is a set of circumstances so horrific that one becomes grateful for a body to bury.

The first Martin Luther King holiday after Katrina was freighted with political significance. Instead of the standard municipal blandishments about interracial understanding and "Dr. King's Dream," New Orleans was grappling with a real racial dilemma that had implications for the future of its citizens. Nearly half of the city's population had still not returned after the evacuation, and there were looming doubts about whether vast segments of the black population would ever make it back. The population shift had implications for everything from New Orleans' economy to its politics. With an election only a few months away, strategists had begun to speculate that whites in New Orleans would be poised for the first time in decades to elect a white mayor. Ray Nagin made a speech insisting that the city would once again be majority-black. He welcomed its residents back and urged those who were scattered across the country to return home. God himself, he proclaimed, wanted New Orleans to remain a black city. They would be safe, he assured them. "This," he proclaimed, "is the safest city in America right now."

I talked in a local restaurant with John O'Neal, the playwright whose work with the Student Nonviolent Coordinating Committee (SNCC) and the Free Southern Theater brought him to New Orleans over thirty years ago. He saw the storm and its aftermath in much more local terms. "New Orleans is corrupt and it has been for decades," he told me. And the catastrophic ineptitude that cost so many lives in the city was a result of this decades-long accretion of inefficiency. O'Neal's home was near the center of the city in an area that had been spared from the worst ravages of the flooding, but getting there required that you drive through large swaths of dark territory where electricity had yet to be restored.

In disasters as in disaster flicks, one wrong turn can change everything. In this case an attempt to find a highway on-ramp delivered me directly into the midst of a "second line" celebration. There are thousands gathered on North Dorjenois Street, marching, dancing, laughing, and holding signs representing their various streets. And for a moment it became clear. The gathering wound down the street, past the detritus of a disaster already five months into history, past the shattered storefronts invaded by mold and the decomposing carcass of a Rottweiler, whose jaws are frozen in a macabre grin.

But still there was the "first line," the music, above and beyond all else. At the head of the second line, a band rolled down the street, laying down a rollicking, elliptical rhythm. A twenty-year-old improvised a dance routine on the porch of a gutted house, moving like a marionette with invisible strings. He grabbed his hat and kneeled forward then ricocheted back two steps, a butterfly pattern of improbable movements. It is this insistence upon celebrating life in spite of tragedy, or perhaps because of it, that gave people faith that the city would recover, that its vast reserves of resilience would succeed where engineers and city planners had failed. Like New Yorkers who took comfort in their image of themselves as a thick-skinned breed gifted with an armor-plated sense of perseverance in the days after 9/11. And for that moment it becomes clear.

And then this: gunshots on Martin Luther King Day. They ring out in front of you, just off to the left. The music stops and you notice blood speckled on the street in front of you. A black man about thirty lies on the ground, and a dark woman in a white T-shirt starts to wail. The cops take forever to arrive, but they come in force with seventeen cars. Soon after, there was yellow tape cordoning off the corner of Orleans and North Dorjenois where the shooting took place. The paramedics begin cutting his clothes off. There is an entry wound on his back just under his rib cage. His shredded jeans and bloodstained Timberlands in the street like urban artifacts, and the paramedics prepare to roll him into an ambulance.

And then gunshots happened again. This time in the crowd behind you. This was a taunt to the officers in "the safest city in America"—a shooting as they are on the scene to investigate a shooting. The bullet passed through a young woman and hit a man in the thigh. A cop pulled a shotgun from his trunk and marched toward the activity. Across the street a teenager screamed, "You see! *This* is why they don't want us back here!" A caravan of blue lights and sirens shot down the street in pursuit of the new shooter.

The street began to scowl.

Stripped of its celebrants, the scars on North Dorjenois Street become even more visible. You notice a statue of the Virgin Mother that has endured the storm and now holds court over a haphazard array of broken bricks, shattered wood, and a random confetti of storm-tossed objects. The second line became an unintentional metaphor, a neat encapsulation of everything that was at stake in New Orleans. A signpost of the reasons for hope in the city and the treacherous pitfalls that lay ahead of it. The next day an angry, fatigued Ray Nagin amended his welcome home speech. He said: "If you want to kill, we don't want you back in New Orleans."

The next morning the city was struck by a violent thunderstorm.

January 2006

Black-Owned

It's a small black world. If technology, communications, and travel have turned the planet into a global village, then black America is just a single block in a tiny neighborhood. The six degrees that separate the rest of the world are diminished to 1.5 when dealing with us. It's at least part of the reason why so many of us still cringe when we see a brown assailant doing the perp walk on the 6:00 p.m. news. An idea that skin color will have you damned by association. But that blade cuts two ways. That same sense of collective connection means that the achievements of any of us is understood as a vicarious accomplishment for 31 million other people. These essays are about those people. They range from short comments on extraordinary lives to longer meditations on individuals whose personal fortunes or trials made some broader comment about the state of the world. Or at least our small neighborhood.

21

Kindred's Soul: Words with Octavia Butler

There was a time in the not-so-distant past when black folks had no future. Or at least that's what one would suspect if he or she were taking the reams of blackless speculative fiction as evidence. On both the page and the screen, the future appeared in monochrome. And worse, the vanished brothers and sisters didn't merit so much as a plot point—no ominous backstory that would sooner or later unveil where the Negroes had all gone off to. They were simply not there; evidence that when Ellison spoke of black people being invisible, he was being equal parts reporter and fortune-teller.

Octavia Butler helped change that. Over the course of her career she carved out a niche as a visionary and master of speculative fiction writing. Her brilliant novel Kindred *grappled with the complexities of ancestry and inheritance in a tale where a black woman is confronted with the dilemma of saving her enslaved forebear even if it means that she herself will never be born centuries later. Her cautionary tale* Parable of the Sower *threw a black female protagonist into a near-future dystopian Los Angeles and raised questions about the implications of race, crime, poverty, and war for our common present. Butler—along with Samuel Delaney, and later Tananarive Due and Steven Barnes— helped move black folks from the periphery of science fiction. I met Ms. Butler in Atlanta in July 1994 at the national black arts festival. Two months later, I had the opportunity to interview her for* ONE Magazine. *Her death in early 2006 left a yearning void in the ranks not only of black writers, but also of genuine original thinkers at a time and place when they are in such short supply.*

COBB: How did you start writing?

BUTLER: Well, I began writing when I was ten, and the thing is, I had begun telling myself stories when I was about four, so it was almost a natural progression to write them down—eventually. I just got the idea when I was ten to start writing them down, because I was forgetting some of them. And I enjoyed it so much I kept doing it.

COBB: I read something I thought was interesting. You said your mother or your grandmother would bring home books.

BUTLER: My mother.

COBB: I interviewed Baraka about two weeks ago, and he said the same thing.

BUTLER: Yeah.

COBB: His grandmother worked for some white people, and she would bring home books.

BUTLER: Yeah. Anything she could find that— especially that was intended for children, but she really didn't stop it there. I mean, if they threw away old magazines, she'd stop and bring them home, you know?

COBB: Who actually influenced you as a writer in terms of developing your craft and style and sensibilities?

BUTLER: Do you want to know who encouraged me? Nobody. My mother was less annoyed by it than most people. I mean, most of my family just assumed that it was a good thing, because it kept me out of trouble, but they didn't think that it could actually lead to anything, because they didn't know that there were any black writers. In fact, my aunt assured me that there weren't any and that I couldn't be one.

COBB: That's interesting—

BUTLER: My mother helped me out economically. For instance, when I stupidly—well, I was a kid, what did I know—but I got involved with an agent who charged a reading fee. She scraped up the reading fee, which was more than our monthly rent at the time. She tried to help me, you know. But she even felt that it was kind of silly and it was good for me to stay out of trouble, and she hoped I would be a secretary or something.

COBB: So what kept you going as a writer? What kept you pursuing that goal?

BUTLER: Writing is all I really ever wanted to do. Once I discovered it, I found that I enjoyed it, and my mother just made a remark accidentally when I was about ten. She saw me writing, and I told her I was writing a story, and she said, "Well, maybe you'll be a writer." And at that point I had not realized that there were such things as writers, and it had not occurred to me how books and stories got written somehow. And in that little sentence, I mean, it was like in the cartoons where the light goes on over the guy's head. I suddenly realized that yes, there are such things as writers. People can be writers. I want to be a writer.

COBB: Were there any other difficulties peculiar to being a black woman that confronted you?

BUTLER: Yeah, the total lack of examples. It wasn't so much being black as being ignorant that there were any other black people out there. Gradually, in my teens I became aware of people, but they were like off in the stars somewhere, they seemed so far from me. It was interesting, at the [1994 National Black Arts] Festival hearing some people talk about meeting some of these people—Langston Hughes . . . you think, "My God, it's like meeting . . . Moses or somebody." And I mean I met nobody. When I was in the twelfth grade, the schools I went to had no creative writing classes. So I was on my own—the best I could do was journalism. Anyway, at the end of twelfth grade we were allowed to schedule conferences with people working in our area—the area we hoped to get into. They couldn't find me a fiction writer. They found me a journalist who worked at the local newspaper who kept saying, "Well, I don't know what to tell ya." Then he'd talk a little bit about journalism, and then he'd say, "I really don't know what to tell ya." I mean, you know, he wasn't being hard or anything, he just literally didn't know what direction to tell me to go. I had no examples, I had no idea what I was doing wrong in my work. This is true of a lot of people who are beginning to be writers. They don't know what's wrong. They don't know why it keeps getting rejected. I think with a lot of young black people we sit back and say, "Uh-huh, it's just racism." And some of us give up thinking it's racism and never knowing it's because we're writing so badly.

COBB: So how did you—

BUTLER: I went to Cal State LA, and they had one writing class and it was late at night, and I couldn't take it, because I ride buses. After college I went to a writing class given by the Writers Guild of America, West. Eventually, in the second semester of the program's existence, the writer Harlan Ellison came into the program as one of the teachers, and also another writer, Sid Steeple. I got into their classes. Sid was teaching novelizations—

you know, how to take a movie and turn it into a novel—and Harlan was just teaching screenwriting, except that I knew, because I had a lot of his books, that he wrote a lot of science fiction—print science fiction. Or at least it was called science fiction at the time—he's not real thrilled with that term. I knew that he could probably help me if I could get him to, and he was perfectly willing to, so it turned out great. You know, whatever you wrote he would go over it and talk to you about it, and you might go home feeling like you didn't much like him, but it was the kind of criticism I needed. I was in classes sometimes where I was the only black person, and you tend to either get ignored or get petted on the head a lot. Neither is in the slightest useful, so I was eager to get away from that, and Harlan was not interested in doing either.

COBB: Have you ever been pressured, especially when you first started out, first got published, were you pressured to depoliticize your work?

BUTLER: My work isn't all that political really. Actually, I was pressured in the opposite direction. I was pressured to politicize it more like, "Why are you writing science fiction? Why are you writing something so unreal? Why don't you write something that would be meaningful?" In the Sixties "meaningful" was the big word, and I was supposed to be writing more about black history or about the struggle. The thing is, if you let somebody else tell you what you ought to be writing, you're probably gonna write crap. You need to write about the things that interest you. You can always learn to write about the things that interest you. Something that really stirs you up emotionally. Your passion is driving you along, and when you are alone with that computer or typewriter or whatever, you need all the pushing you can get.

COBB: So what would you say stirs you up?

BUTLER: Well, a lot of things, actually. One of the great things about science fiction is the freedom it allows me to get into anything I want to get into. When I wrote *Parable of the Sower*, the thing that stirred me up the most were the things going on right now. The daily news. There are so many terrible things that are going on that no one is paying attention to, because they aren't quite that bad yet.

In *Parable of the Sower* I talk about the return of slavery, which is real. I mean, that's not something that I pulled out of history; that's something I pulled out of the newspapers. You know, we already have situations where, here in Southern California, in the central valley, or in the south in some of the more rural areas, where they'll either bring in illegal aliens and work them and not pay them and forbid them to leave and generally mistreat them and . . . or they'll do it with black people who are not well enough educated or connected to get out of there, or they'll do it with homeless people who, you know, don't have anywhere to go and are abused.

Right now in the maquiladora plants in Mexico, just the other side of the border, where people are worked under horrible conditions, and they live in horrible conditions in shacks made out of whatever they can make them out of. And when they're around thirty, thirty-five, they're pretty much used up if they haven't been injured or damaged in some way by the kind of work they're required to do, and the chemicals, machinery, whatever, they can be tossed aside for younger workers.

COBB: That's something I should look into myself. You have a description of yourself which I don't . . .

BUTLER: Oh, that's something I've been sending out for years and years. You want to hear it?

COBB: Yes.

BUTLER: Let's see, I should have a copy of it around here somewhere . . . As a matter of fact, I usually have several old copies lying around waiting to be thrown out, because they're outdated as far as the books are concerned. Okay, there's a little of this on the cover of *Parable of the Sower*. It's— the title of it is "A Brief Conversation with Octavia E. Butler," and the first question is "Who is Octavia E. Butler? Where is she headed? Where has she been?" The answer is "Who am I? I am a forty-seven-year-old writer who can remember being a ten-year-old writer and who expects someday to be an eighty-year-old writer. I am also comfortably asocial, a hermit in the middle of Los Angeles. (Actually, I don't live there anymore, but I'm reading you an old one.) A pessimist if I'm not careful, a feminist, a black, a former Baptist, an oil and water combination of ambition, laziness, insecurity, certainty, and drive."

COBB: How do all those qualities interplay in your work, or does all that come out, do you think?

BUTLER: What I do as a writer is mine my own life, mine history, mine the news, mine whatever there is. I mean, it's like the whole universe is ore and I have to mine the gold in it. And, of course, I can see bits of my own life in what I write. As for those qualities, they hamper me and they push me, and there's a lot more to me than that, of course.

COBB: Do your feminist views influence your female characters?

BUTLER: Sure. You see any female characters in my work who just—well, there are a few who seem not to do very much, but they're certainly not top characters.

COBB: In *Parable* I think that Lauren seems like she's really much more suited to working with the group that coalesces than any of the other people—

BUTLER: Well, that's because she's the one causing it to coalesce. I mean, she does have this dream of bringing these people together and forming Earthseed. As a matter of fact, I'm working on *Parable of the Talents* right now, and it's one thing for a teenager to have dreams that other people think are crazy and they kind of put up with them, and it's another thing for a grown woman with a kid or two to have these ideas and people think, "My God, isn't she ever going to grow up?" and "What's wrong with her?" So my character in *Parable of the Talents* has a much harder time with people who don't see her dream as anything but childish nonsense. And the first person among those is her husband.

COBB: There was another question that I had about *Parable.* The recurring fire theme in there—was it at all related to the Los Angeles Rebellion in 1992?

BUTLER: No. It wasn't. It was related to something else entirely. People ask me that a lot. I actually got kind of defensive about it for a while there. But, no, actually I was working on the novel as the riots broke out, and I worried about whether I should go back and change the novel, because I didn't want to seem as if I was either feeding off or promoting some of the things that went on in the riots. They burned down my favorite black bookstore, for heaven's sake. They just seemed to burn down whatever was handy.

I'll tell you where part of the burning thing comes from. One of my earliest memories is being carried out of a burning house in the middle of, I guess you could say it was the burning desert, only it was night. My grandmother had a chicken ranch out between Victorville and Barsdale here in California, and this was very primitive.

And we were so far out and we had nothing like a telephone. We had no electricity at this point. So there was no way to call the fire department. We used candles and kerosene lanterns, and I, to this day I don't know who did it, but somebody had an accident with either a candle or a kerosene lantern, and you know how it is in families—it was my grandmother's—people blame each other.

And so I was only about four years old, so I don't know how it happened. I know I was awakened out of a sound sleep by somebody snatching me up and running out of the house with me. This was a house that my uncles had built with their own hands, so it was especially . . . it had everything in it that my grandmother owned as far as mementos and records of her children's birth. She had all her children at home, so there weren't any other kinds of records. But my biggest memory was being snatched up that way and awakened in that particular way and standing outside watching the house burn down.

COBB: That's understandable. Someone commented to me about *Parable* that they thought it was a scary book.

BUTLER: Good.

COBB: Why do you say that's good?

BUTLER: Well, I mean, it was intended to be a cautionary tale. "Look what we're coming to if we're not careful." And if people see it as scary, it's possible that they'll have their eyes a little wider open. I mean, for instance, before NAFTA passed, I used to go around, in my talks I would talk about the maquiladora plants, and I would talk about the kind of . . . I would sort of, you know, patch them into our future, because after all, if companies can go off to Mexico or someplace and employ workers for almost no money and forget about environmental considerations and on-the-job safety, then what the heck, why wouldn't they do that? And if they can't leave right now, if it would be inconvenient, all they have to do is threaten to leave, and they can lower wages here and get rid of environmental considerations here. We seem to be setting things up so that the poor will get a lot poorer and the middle-class will get a lot poorer, too, and I don't think a lot of members of the middle class have figured that out yet. I had somebody review that book, *Parable*, and say "Well, interesting book, but she should have been more clear about how we could possibly get from where we are to where they are in *Parable*, because I just don't see it." I thought, "You poor baby."

COBB: So humanity is destined to live out that sort of nightmare of a future?

BUTLER: Well, I certainly hope not. It's like I said, it's a cautionary tale. There are a lot of problems that we don't have to walk head-on into. Unfortunately, none of them—very few of them are easy. For instance, there's the conference that's going to be held in Egypt talking about the population problem. How many more people can the Earth support with any degree of comfort and civility? It can support a lot more people if we all wanna have much nastier lives. But if you start talking about something like that, it's gonna start scaring people. "Oh, what are you gonna do?" For instance, with black people, are we gonna find out that we're the ones that they need fewer of? I think the Muslims are wondering the same thing—"Is this a trick so that the non-Muslim world will be more numerous than us? What's going on?" There are always these worries, these concerns. Maybe there is a problem, maybe there isn't, but we don't trust the people who are telling us that there is a problem.

COBB: I only have a few more questions. In Atlanta you said something about people seeking power probably shouldn't have it.

BUTLER: Oh, I was talking about my own feelings. I wasn't talking literally about what should or shouldn't be, but that I had somehow developed the idea—or the personal myth, you could call it—that seeking power was somehow immoral. And that made it very difficult for me to write this book, because I had to first overcome that myth, and it was a lot stronger than I had supposed. I had to, I talked about it in terms of my friend's personal mythology, and the two personal myths that I use when I talk about that are one that's almost dead—that the rich are unhappy, that they are specifically unhappy because they are rich—and the idea that wisdom is power. I go on to talk about that and say the personal myth is kind of self-protective. I mean, if you're poor, it's very convenient for you to believe that the rich are unhappy. If you are powerless, it's very convenient for you to believe that those who've sought and acquired power are immoral. I mean, maybe they are and maybe they aren't, but it's convenient to believe that.

Wisdom and power and money are all tools. They are tools that can be used in any way you like. You can use them to tear things up. You can use them to build things up. I've written about power before, but it was always power that kind of fell on people. Either they were born to it, or somebody thrust it on them in the form of major responsibility as in my Xenogenesis books. So I had two problems. The first, as I said, was writing about a power seeker who is also a sympathetic character, and the second was believing that a black woman could be convincing as not just a power seeker but a power holder over people who were not necessarily black and not necessarily female.

COBB: How do you respond when people ask you what does your work have to do with being black?

BUTLER: Oddly enough, I don't get that question anymore. I haven't heard that question for a very long time. I mentioned that during the Sixties and the Seventies I got it a lot. It's like saying that somehow we are set apart from the future and are a part of only our own past. I mean it's silly. We need to look at the wider world, the wider universe, heck, as much as any other group of people need to.

August 1994

22

Lifecycle of a Butterfly

In the course of fifty-three years the life of Muhammad Ali has become a saga more like some serial drama than the doings and sayings of most of us mortals. He has once again reetched his name all over our consciousness, a fact that says as much of the era we inhabit as it does of Ali's Christlike capacity for resurrection. Case in point: Ali and his trembling hand extended to light the Olympic torch in Atlanta were the high-water mark of an event furiously attempting to put a revisionist spin on Southern history and present reality.

Fighters have an odd way of mirroring the times in which they perform their brutal labors. Jack Johnson was a harbinger of the New Negro, the post–World War, darky-no-more, colored man who, having tasted the "liberties" of France, wasn't trying to jigaboo to the drumbeat of white supremacy at home. His pummeling of white men and consorting with white women led the grand vicar of black life, Booker T. Washington, to criticize Johnson's lifestyle and sent white America frantically searching itself for a "white hope" to redeem Anglo-Saxons everywhere.

A man like Joe Louis would have been more to the Tuskegee Wizard's liking. Louis embodied the hero as race rep ideal at a time when black America was (yet again) attempting to prove itself worthy of not being trampled upon by running what amounts to a massive racial PR campaign. His defeat of Max Schmeling (along with Jesse Owens's four medals in the '36 Olympics) were exhibit A in the case for Negro citizenship, but it was his fight with Primo Carnera, an Italian, at the height of the ethnic bad blood inspired by Mussolini's invasion of Ethiopia that first raised the Brown Bomber to the status of race man. Black people took Il Duce's invasion personally—Ethiopia and (nominally) Liberia were the only countries in Africa that had not fallen victim to European colonialism and were, for that reason, symbols of race pride. The fight wasn't simply a clash hyped by two groups trying to figure out how to become Americans and Louis's victory wasn't just a check in the "W" column— it was a glimmering minute of racial redemption in the middle of what were some real bad times.

It's been said that great men are the embodiment to the time in which they live. In the case of Ali, it seems almost like he was a figure sent over from Central Casting. Or better yet, that he wrote the script for the times in which he worked. He was anti-Vietnam, and damn if he didn't pay for it, sacrificing three and a half years of his prime to prove a point. He returned to boxing minus his title and with legs that no longer supported his buoyantly choreographed violence. His relationship with Malcolm X was public knowledge at a time when Malcolm was probably the most feared man in America. And Malcolm helped mold—literally and metaphorically—clay into a prophet's likeness. (What remains to be seen, though, is how Ali managed to reconcile his antiwar stance with his membership in the apolitical Nation of Islam.)

Muhammad Ali was and remains meta-athletic—one of those near-mythic figures who seems to use sports simply as a means of proving some larger point. Which is not to suggest that his athletic ability took a backseat to his politics. In the ring, the early Ali was a fluid enigma. He threw punches while moving backward, a technical no-no, and held his hands suicidally low, according to the conventional ring wisdom, but was still quick enough to tag his opponents at will. But beyond his supreme talent in his medium, Ali's ability to function as both a comic and critic simultaneously is second only to Richard Pryor's. The man is stuck firmly in the black tradition of shooting the gift. Ali was as articulate verbally as he was in the language of fists, as artful with a phrase as he was in fluently firing jabs like Morse code messages.

Even before this resurgence of interest in him, his life and times had already begun to meld into a concoction of myth and history. His Olympic medal was rumored to have been tossed into the Ohio River as a protest against Jim Crow, and though this never actually occurred, Ali's public opts for it over the more pedestrian explanation for the vanished medallion. His reign began by exiling the awesomely thuggish Sonny Liston to the edges of obscurity and "phantom" punching him into near irrelevance. What he did to Liston was what he continued to do to every other major heavyweight throughout his career—reduce them to supporting actors in the big-screen epic of Ali.

The fights, especially those coming after his banishment from boxing, were as much about ideology as brutality. Or at least Ali always made them seem that way. Ali–Patterson, the prebanishment prototype, featured the upstart champ battling the soft-spoken joe; the humble, would-be citizen versus the loudmouth apostate American. The nightmare nigger versus the signifyin' flunky. No question that a few years earlier, or a few latitudes to the south, there would have been a noose with the name Cassius Clay on it.

But Floyd Patterson also contributed his share to making that fight a metaphor for impending social and generational rumbles in black communities. Refusing to call him by his Arabic name, and instead consigning him to "Clay" like some perverse inversion of the Kunta Kinte scene in *Roots*, Patterson was attempting to refute Ali's identity—and by extension, the militance of a rising generation. Patterson even went so far as to write two articles in *Sports Illustrated* prattling on about how he "couldn't let a Muslim be champ," proving that it was not possible to be a noncitizen and a nativist at the same time. In reality, as opposed to newsprint, what he couldn't do was beat Ali. The bout featured twelve rounds of Ali jabbing into existence a new state of affairs. The whuppin' laid on Patterson was severe by any measure, and Ali's taunting, fist-punctuated queries of "What's my name?" were plain and simple, an exercise in humiliation.

Even in the case of his later fight with George Foreman, a man who never spoke publicly of his politics (or much of anything else), the Ali opponent got construed as the lackey of the establishment. The clash took place in Zaire under the auspices of dictator Joseph Mobutu and the nascent impresario Don King. The Zairians immediately took to Ali as "their" champion, relegating the actual champion, Foreman, to the role of a Tommish stand-in for white America.

Joe Frazier, though, has a special place in the canon of villain-opponents. Ali's genius for spewing yang like some sort of shit-talking rev'rend made Frazier out to be the epitome of Tommishness. In one of his lower moments Ali echoed stereotypes calling Joe a "gorilla." Talked so bad about Joe that two and half decades later, the man still needs an antacid before he can spit Ali's name out of his mouth. Frazier criticized the choice of Ali as Olympic torchbearer because of Ali's past antiwhite and "anti-American" statements. "I," he nearly gloats, "always thought of whites as my brothers," a fact that may or may not have to do with Joe's own shortcomings. (Besides, Cain and Abel were bloods, too!) Or to put the question on the table, why wasn't Smokin' Joe more "anti-American" since he lived in the same world that Ali did? Frazier wasn't selected to carry the torch, because, quite simply, don't nobody owe him anything.

I've always been amazed by the fact that white America devoted so much of its attention to generating new mythologies to dehumanize blacks. Black people staggered into this century carrying the burden of the Sambo-Mammy myths, but keenly aware that the machinery of white paranoia was cranking out new spins on old lies that made us out to be insatiable Jezebels and bestial rapists. And for all slavery and the years in which we were roasted on spits for their amusement, it wasn't until well into this century that black people actually generated corresponding myths. (But we went straight for the jugular, consigning them to the status of devils, saying that those who claimed that Christian redemption required them to put us in chains were in fact evil incarnate.) And maybe that was something that had to be said at that point, a necessary detour that had to be explored before black people could move past that idea and recognize them for their tragically debased humanity. If insanity is the rational response to an irrational situation, then the "irrationale" of the Nation of Islam made perfect sense.

Plus what Frazier never realized was that "anti-Americanism," like the Vietnam protests, is now seen as a good thing by a substantial number of people in this country. Truth is, Ali was way ahead of Frazier, saying what had to be said and moving on into a deeper understanding of the world around him. And that fact might be at the heart of the Ali mystique. In an era of store-bought pros like Jordan and Iverson, who wouldn't protest anything more wide reaching than a salary cap, Ali is symbolic of a bygone age. Michael Jordan has transcended his sport only to become a corporate property, silent as a mime. Shaq stars in a flick where an adolescent white boy has a seven-foot black man at his beck and call and the word "slavery" never even comes to mind. But Ali is a phenomenon of an entirely different sort, an eloquent blasphemer, the man who wove such gorgeous and truthful heresies that even those he talked bad about had to at least grudgingly admire the man. He reemerges like the proverbial butterfly who is somehow capable of respinning its own cocoon. Like most great figures, Ali's life will inevitably be hacked into sound bites that serve whomever's particular agenda. From the standpoint of those who selected Ali to light the torch of the centennial Olympic games, there is a gain to be had from atoning with so vocal a critic.

That Ali's resurfacing was engineered by the Atlanta Olympic committee is central to understanding the current obsession with him. As is the case with most great and controversial figures in America, Ali's life has already begun dissolving into the user-friendly sound bites whose mass marketing enables the wicked to make profit from their most stringent critics. Like Malcolm and King before him, Ali the person has gained a foothold in the mainstream at the expense of his politics. Think of it as the Malcolming of Ali. His debilitating struggle with Parkinson's might only catalyze the making of "Ali lite." The fight game exacts an awful toll, even from its most astute masters. In the case of Ali, his blank expression and voice reduced to a whisper are sure to elicit sympathy—even from people who remember what he was saying in the 1960s.

Atlanta—the city James Baldwin screamed on as "too busy making money to hate"—launched a massive, pre-Olympic Southern redemption campaign amid the still smoldering ashes of black churches. And although Ali never really threw his medal in the Ohio River, the treatment he received in the South after winning it was more than enough to highlight the irony of having won it. Thus, irony of ironies, Ali, the one who so demonized his opponents as representatives of the white establishment, has returned to us as a benefactor of Southern white largesse.

Gaudy sentimentality abounded as the South's Afrostocracy slapped a coat of makeup on the past and held it up for world consumption. James Earl Jones read passages from William Faulkner (too ironic for words), and interracial gospel choirs belted out praises to the Lord (you could almost forget about the poorer Atlantans who were Jim Crowed on the outskirts of town). Atonement on such grand scales nearly outdid the spectacle of Farrakhan's "sorry-in" on the National Mall, nearly a year before the games. And there, in the middle of it all, was Ali, the old brown warrior with the terribly palsied hands. The transgressed and the redeemed.

July 1996

23

The Killing Fields: Notorious B.I.G.

Brooklyn death angels come draped in oversized Tommy Hil and Timberlands. There are ten thousand midnight troopers selling get-high in the borough of Kings, home to three million of New York's stories. Take a look at the infamous zones: Bed-Stuy, East New York, Red Hook, Flatbush, and Brownsville, and it is obvious who owns the night. The burly Brooklynite professionally known as the Notorious B.I.G. was once one of those ranks. When I was coming up, way before the buppies and gentrification, before Spike Lee opened his "joint" and people with designer dreads moved next door, Fort Green was the refuge of the buckwild, with streets as dangerous as a shared needle. It was the city within a city where B.I.G. did his dirt and collected his cash. And it was those same streets that brimmed with brown people lured out to witness the funeral procession of Christopher Wallace, aka Notorious B.I.G.

The spectacle itself was tinged with surrealism, partly a grim final tour of the fat man's stomping grounds, partly a gauche playa's parade showcasing the same culture that contributed to his demise. Twenty-two limos escorted by seventeen police vans, four helicopters, and innumerable Beamers, Benzes, and Pathfinders, trailed a black hearse down Fulton Avenue—all backed by the unearthly rumble of the dead man's music booming from scores of car speakers.

Whatever else he may have been in life, Biggie's death conferred upon him a nearly sanitized status of neighborhood hero, a symbol of the local boy who makes good. Ergo, the convo in greasy bodegas, barbershops, and check-cashing joints centered on his lyrical skill or the fact that he "took his peeps with him" when fame came knocking on his door. No lie, fifty-year-old reverends stood on street corners giving B.I.G. posthumous props for "talking about reality." Two days later, there was an effort under way to rename the street he lived on Biggie Boulevard.

· · ·

Ready to Die opens with the sounds of a woman in labor, the subcurrent of Curtis Mayfield's *Superfly,* and the cries of a newborn. It closes with the gruesome report of a .38, the sickening thud of a body hitting the floor, perishing by its own hand. We hear the heartbeats slow and stop. The listeners shift uncomfortably as audio witness to a suicide. Even set against the shock-value interludes crammed onto nearly every hip-hop CD, the final moments of *Ready to Die* are among the most disturbing in hip-hop.

Between those two poles, birth and self-inflicted death, were seventeen tracks that etched out B.I.G.'s history and worldview. The addition of B.I.G., along with Nas, Wu-Tang, and the Fugees, to the roster of New York emcees shored up the East Coast's fortunes at a time when LA and Oakland had all but become the dominant voices in the industry. What set *Ready to Die* apart from the dozens of blathering would-be playa releases was the combination of B.I.G.'s verbal virtuosity and his willingness to ascribe a level of vulnerability to himself that was, at that point, unparalleled.

Ralph Ellison described blues ethos as "the impulse to keep the painful details and episodes of a brutal existence alive in one's aching consciousness, to finger the jagged edge of life and to transcend it by squeezing from it a near-tragic, near-comic lyricism." The blues exist for the express purpose of alchemizing beauty from pain. But if blues was about acknowledging pain in order to transcend it, most of hip-hop was about swaggering in the face of it. Denying that pain was an element of its reality. While Eazy-E was nagged by the ominously persistent cough and withering into nothingness, he was steadily spinning out yarns in which he played the immortal, almighty nigga supreme. Minus exceptions like Ice Cube's morose *Dead Homiez,* the pre-Notorious gangsta used hip-hop as urban folklore in which he could write his name in the sky, render himself invincible, and stand out from the anonymous precincts of the ghetto. But only in the rarest of moments could hip-hop give light to the fact that suicide trails only murder as a leading cause of death among black men between eighteen and twenty-five.

B.I.G. broke ranks with that. He spoke of pain anesthetized by malt liquor swilled to excess. *Ready to Die* was crass and backward, but it was also the forum for a sublime rapper to exorcise his demons, to lay bare his lacerated soul. He pushed lines like: "All my life I been considered as the worst / lying to my mother, even stealing out her purse / Crime after crime, from drugs to extortion / I know my mother wish she got a fucking abortion." The rapper broods for three or four more verses, then abruptly squeezes the trigger, canceling his own life.

Life After Death picks up—literally—where *Ready to Die* ends. We hear the emergency room drama and the rapper's final moments in an eerie prelude to what actually went down at the LA hospital two weeks ago. Biggie appears on the CD cover, sporting a bowler and overcoat Hitchcock-style and standing in front of a hearse. The twenty-four-track double-disk release showcases B.I.G.'s ability to rip rhymes from every conceivable angle, but the flashes of insight that redeemed its precursor are all but gone. *Life* would have easily continued B.I.G.'s ascent through the ranks of hip-hop with its bicoastal flavor and mix of base-driven heaviness and melodic, R & B–suffused tracks. Almost as if to prove a point, B.I.G. shows up on "Mo' Money, Mo' Problems" in Bone-Thugs mode and proceeds to flip their style better than the song's originators. The irony of *Life* is B.I.G.'s attempt to build a detente between the coasts musically and the fact that, at least indirectly, he became a casualty of that conflict. *Ready to Die* ended with B.I.G.'s on-air suicide; *Life After Death* closes with a death threat being issued to B.I.G. and the rapper divining that "you're nobody 'til somebody kills you." B.I.G. ain't a nobody no more.

• • •

Biggie was ignorant. Or he chose to speak in an ignorant way. There's a difference between speaking ill of the dead and speaking truthfully about history. And the truth is that the emotional honesty of his work was too often drowned by status-obsessed materialism. I learned a long time ago that if you look at people's excesses, you're also looking at whatever they were once deprived of. That logic of poverty explains why to Biggie, life was all about the cash, the women, and a steady flow of Alizé.

His first single was the retrograde "Party and Bullshit," in which he inverted the Last Poets criticism into a credo for big-city living. He spoke of robbing women: "I don't give a fuck if you pregnant / Gimme the baby ring and the number one mom pendant." And in the end, the industry partiers and bullshitters could not stop the tide of homicide that claimed his life on March 9, 1997.

Minutes after his death, Biggie's "assassination" was incorporated into an ever-widening web of conspiracy theories that hold that Suge Knight is an FBI operative and that Tupac, like his hero, Machiavelli, faked his own death in order to kill his enemies (i.e., Biggie). The whole plot sounds only slightly more outlandish than reverends standing on Brooklyn street corners giving props to ex–drug dealing rappers for keeping it real. Only an iota further away from reality than people struggling to rename boulevards so people can sell crack and pay homage simultaneously.

The conspiracies are pathetic evasions of the truth, ugly as it may be. The truth is that if we take hip-hop as a representative demographic sample, there will be many more violent deaths. The truth is that to the music industry, the deaths of Biggie, Tupac, and Eazy-E mean a chance to cash in on the posthumous release market. Dead sells. The truth is that there is more than enough self-contempt to fuel black-on-black homicide without spooky FBI manipulation. And both Tupac's and Biggie's seemingly prescient knowledge of their deaths has more to do with history and the meaningless loss of black life than with clairvoyance. How else do playas lives end?

The truth is that most rappers are apolitical character actors whose first allegiance is to their bank statements. After a moment of silence, the stream of senseless death will continue to wind its way through black communities unabated. The killings have only the symbolic value of setting an everyday occurrence into high-profile relief. The truth is that black people desperately need a new set of heroes—ones who are ready to die *for a cause*. Or better yet, live for one.

March 1997

24

Ore: Requiem for a Neighborhood Badass

1

There it was, plastered to the battered boulevard, slapped recklessly between an advertisement for Jay-Z's latest release and a poster dominated by Li'l Kim's silicone enhancements. This was the image of Mike Tyson, clean-faced and older than his thirty-two years, and Francois Botha, the blanched-out journeyman last seen abusing the fists of southpaw underachiever Michael Moorer. You could tell, even from a distance, that the whole architecture of the flick was off—Tyson's arms crossed like a Brooklyn b-boy circa 1984; Botha, the white interloper, looking less like a potential threat than a sad B movie actor. But not even the specter Tyson, the native son returned, going against a white South African bearing the surname of apartheid's most bloody bureaucrat, could make the masses get it up for this one. And the statement underlying all of this is as explicit as it is sad: this is what it has come to.

The life and career of Mike Tyson have become the most recent of ring parables. The histories of the heavyweight champions, more than any other type of narrative, tell of the tragic arc of the disposable hero: the desperate origins, the hunger-fueled rise, the shimmering pinnacle and meteoric decline. Unlike actors and musicians, who gradually fade from the public radar, fighters—like politicians—tend toward spectacular collapse and personal apocalypse. The man formerly known as Iron Mike has reached that point where the scale of his career is tilted not in favor of his future prospects, but by the weight of his own foolish, epic, and ultimately tragic history.

Think back for a moment and you will remember the kinetic malice he brought with him as a young professional, the way he blew through opponents, inexorable as an act of God, doing the unheard of by knocking out seasoned fighters with body shots. That Tyson, the gifted upstart with the eclectic punch repertoire, was dubbed the perfect heavyweight, the one who could "put it all together" by no less an authority than Cus D'Amato. And despite the aura that surrounded him as a brawler, the record is clear: the vintage Tyson ranks among the most scientific of boxers. The angles from which he threw punches and the wicked geometry of his violence were the creation of an empirical mind, not a savage heart. Early on, he mastered the art of sowing devastation—with either hand—while remaining nearly impossible to hit. Understand, the man once evaded eleven consecutive blows, thrown at close range, bobbing with the internal rhythm of a metronome, only to emerge from the lower reaches with a right hand that was malignance distilled. This was the demon-ghost, the poltergeist, completely absent until the point of impact.

Ali brought sheen and grace to the alleged sweet science; he cast himself as both harlequin and firebrand. But even at his most hostile, Ali allowed for a certain suspension of disbelief; he gave enough psychic breathing room for people to believe that they were witnessing anything but the most graceful and highly refined act of violence imaginable. Never Tyson. The Brownsville Bomber was strictly cinema verite. He came off like a prism for bad intentions, taking in the pure white fear of his opponents and channeling every color of violence in the spectrum. The funk of violence would cling heavily to the air around him before a fight.

The fighter came up out of Brownsville, the crumbling ward at the center of the Crooklyn mythology. It was there that he did his dirt, there that he was not so much raised as brought to a boil. The way the story gets told, the late Cus D'Amato, trainer of Floyd Patterson and the great light heavyweight Jose Torres, found Tyson on a Brooklyn street, a brawny thirteen-year-old fighting with the four cops who were unsuccessfully attempting to arrest him. The ensuing years read like a Prometheus tale in which D'Amato became a sort of fistic missionary, bringing the gospel of the ring to the unschooled street boy. The ascetic professor of the sweet science took Tyson upstate to Peekskill and literally raised him to be the heavyweight champion of the world. And in return, Tyson became the ultimate extension of D'Amato's will. His style was tailor-made for his body type and quickness. The prodigy student was known to spend hours absorbing tapes of the great heavyweights, diligently cataloging the strengths and flaws of his predecessors.

But all of this was before the virus of celebrity effaced his athletic prowess, eroded the discipline, and recast the scientific fighter as the stand-in for all that is menacing, black, and urban. Tyson was the first heavyweight champion of the hip-hop era and, as such, carried the weight of a stigmatized genre. Emerging as he did in the bleak winter of Reagan's administration, it was small wonder that the same crowd whose vision of black life was satirized in *Bonfire of the Vanities* would make Tyson the Negro heavy, the unfinished street nig coming straight out of the asphalt heart of darkness. The Liston of our days.

Recognize: Tyson was complicit with this, speaking to the press of punches thrown "with evil intentions to vital areas" and airing his desire to drive an opponent's nasal bone into his brain. His character was not so much assassinated as it fell victim to an assisted suicide. The Brooklyn heads, though, saw something else when they looked at Tyson. To his boulevard constituents, Tyson represented every worthless black boy to tread that broken ghetto pavement; he delivered the vicarious thrill of flipping the social script, so to speak, and making oneself large by legal means. It was in that "Borough of Kings" and all the other Brooklyns of the world that Tyson first solidified his status as a bona fide working-class idol.

The string of first-round knockouts testified not only to his preternatural talent for violence, but to the sad state of the heavyweight division in the eighties and the fact that not since the era of Ali had any fighter so effectively wielded fear as a weapon. Tyson had all but destroyed Michael Spinks before either man stepped into the ring. Then Trevor Berbick—the once-upon-a-time champion—went out like a virgin being sacrificed to a wide-bodied, pigeon-toed war god.

Fear is as elemental to boxing as lying is to politics, and in this arena, victory belongs to the man who best swallows his own intimidation. It was clear in the opening round that Tyson owned Berbick, that the fear went all the way down to the deep tissues, that it was in the lungs and we were witnessing the sad spectacle of a champion gagging on his own trepidation. This was a gloved saturnalia. The destruction of Berbick made Tyson the youngest heavyweight champion in history. Tyson proved willing to give encores, annihilating bigger, more experienced men. They blur in the memory now, the men, the rounds, the profane array of crumpled bodies heaving on the canvases.

Yet it was his three losses—minuscule in comparison to forty-five wins and thirty-nine knockouts—that have defined the history of Mike Tyson. The first, in which a grief-stricken Buster Douglas dispatched an out-of-shape champion, could be written off as a fluke. Nor was Tyson in top condition for his ill-fated first bout with Evander Holyfield. But here it came to be seen that Tyson had been ruined by the ease of his own dominance. The ardor and grind of round after round of combat at close quarters was new to the man who had destroyed so many so quickly. This was damnation enough, but still, it is the third in the trilogy that became the moment in which his career was defined.

2

Ore (noun): *metal, iron, any material containing valuable constituents that can be mined and worked. Crude material.*

3

The decline begins with a momentary flicker of the eyes—a hiccup on the fear graph. The scripted scenario of predator and prey is not to be acted out this time. And who is to say what was in Tyson's lungs at that point. It opens with Holyfield surging forward to meet Tyson, who assumes the uncharacteristic stance of counterpuncher. What the assembled scribes deemed sluggishness on Tyson's part was in fact a return to the defensive tactics of years gone by. Holyfield head-butts and throws elbows, all of which go unchecked by referee Mills Lane. And in a moment, there is a gash over Tyson's eye and the second bout begins to eerily echo the first one. This is when Tyson does the unthinkable—biting the champion's ear. Holyfield howls and jumps, and for a flash Tyson broadcasts the fury of old. But only for a moment, for Tyson bites Holyfield at the beginning of the third round, bringing bedlam and his own inevitable disqualification.

In the ensuing moments, a retinue of police enters the ring and Tyson scuffles with the lawmen. The scene is a reprisal of that operatic moment years before when Cus had witnessed Tyson brawling with New York's alleged finest. It will seem ironic at this moment in history to note that Evander Holyfield was by no measure a more gifted fighter than Mike Tyson was; he simply believed himself to be so, and in the final calculation this is all that mattered.

The Vegas meltdown marked the ultimate triumph of Tyson the three-dimensional cartoon character over Tyson the man. In the wake of the second Holyfield fight, Tyson's capital as a fighter experienced its own version of Black Monday. The word from the cheap seats was that Holyfield had simply brought fear to the fear-bringer. Tyson seemed scared, not of that eternal fount of gospelism, Evander Holyfield, but scared, perhaps, of the prospect of facing the world shorn of his own mythology. The self-proclaimed baddest man on the planet had relinquished all claims to his baaad nigger status, or, to speak in the tongues of the boulevard, Tyson had played himself lovely. One Spanish-language newspaper led with the caption "*No es humano*"—He is not human. The sentiments in English were not much kinder.

Yet Tyson is all too human, and the mock horror at his Las Vegas implosion—following years in which his capacity for public brutality had made men rich—reeked of hypocrisy. In another sense, Tyson had simply reached the logical conclusion of the preceding two decades. This is a man who was literally raised to fight. Many of these same critics had been aligned in unison, denouncing Tyson's conviction for rape five years earlier. What happened between Tyson and Desiree Washington—a heavy-weight brawler not known for his feminist sympathies and a starstruck young woman who had previously filed a rape charge deemed false—in that Indiana hotel room is unknown and unknowable, but his public behavior had long before gone Shakespearean: all the world's a ring. And this explains why Tyson the man has so often found himself against the ropes.

4

In battle the iron proved untempered; where other athletes reached to the inner reserves to produce sterling performances, Tyson could muster only ore—unfiltered and tragically impure. It remains to be seen how history will treat Tyson; his station in the pantheon of twentieth-century heavyweights is far from unassailable. The revisionists will inevitably march forward to declare him a paper tiger. And truth be told, in another era Tyson would never had been able to inflict the fear that he used as so much currency.

Ali would have frustrated Tyson, moving away, ever away while stinging him with a relentless catalog of jabs. Tyson would be by far the quickest heavyweight that Ali had ever fought, but it is Ali's ability to spend until the point of physical bankruptcy, the immutable will that lifted him over Joe Frazier in Manila, that would have assured Tyson's defeat.

Tyson would've KO'd big George Foreman—who lost to Ali for almost exactly the same reasons that Tyson lost to Holyfield. Tyson would've been hurt by the unhuman power in that sledgehammer arc that Foreman perfected. But Foreman would've missed far more often than he connected, tired himself out and been an easy mark for Tyson's left hand. Joe Frazier's inexorable forward motion would've intimidated Tyson, who in turn would've damaged Smokin' Joe with the quickness of his hands. Tyson–Frazier would've been a meeting of two immovable objects, two punchers equipped with atomic left hands who are perhaps more evenly pitted than Ali and Frazier were. And it is clear that Tyson would've proven too much for either his spiritual ancestor Sonny Liston or the fleet Floyd Patterson.

But for all his ability, Tyson never verged upon heroism; instead he was an idol. Having never transcended the accepted mortal bounds, never authored an indelible epic feat of imagination and will, he is, at his most basic level, antiheroic. Idols, as they are, shatter and are quickly replaced. Such evaluation may well be idle chatter at this point. The fury and desperation, hubris, naiveté, and absence of wisdom that have plagued Tyson for more than a decade have led to this blind alley: fighting journeyman contenders in bouts that, ultimately, no one cares about. Take another look at the dejected banner plastered to Fifth Avenue in Harlem and this much becomes clear: the fat lady has not yet sung, but she's damn sure in the wings, clearing her throat.

POSTSCRIPT

After five unchoreographed rounds in which Tyson swung like a rusty gate, the ex-champ succeeded in leaving the so-called white hunter on his face, tail, and back. A few weeks later Tyson was convicted of assault by a Maryland court and sentenced to one year in prison—proving, yet again, that the obese gal will always sing, but not necessarily in the key we were expecting.

December 1998

25
The Last Race Man

Even before 1863 when black people, bloodied and dizzy, staggered into the semipromised land of emancipation, there was the question of Africa's salvation. The answers may have come as gift-wrapped paternalism or civilizing missions in blackface, but the fact remains that Africa had been hardwired into the circuits of black thought since that first African hit the shores of Jamestown and made the tragic realization that he was a long, long way from Benin. And in the thirty-eight decades since that brutal conclusion was drawn, the world has witnessed the continent as a colonial buffet for a rapacious Europe, seen it as an intellectual blank slate and labor camp to the globe.

But what was seldom noted was the tradition of African

American defenders of their ancestral continent, the artifacts like the blueprint for African independence that originated on the intellectual drafting board of W. E. B. Du Bois, or the vision of depression-era Negroes scraping up pennies to save Ethiopia from the menace of Mussolini and Paul Robeson's tenure as a cultural champion of the so-called dark continent. It is that tradition that finds its most contemporary representative in the person of Randall Robinson, president of TransAfrica.

Robinson is cursed or blessed, endowed or burdened with the weight of human concern in a city, country, and world that understand humanity as suckers for the false god of consumption or cogs who can be made to cheaply manufacture their articles of worship. *Defending the Spirit* is, in part, a poignant unburdening of his soul and in part a jeremiad directed at those self-satisfied black residents of "the city of privilege." This is a book about politics—foreign, domestic, and personal—that simply must be read.

It is no kind precedent that at the end of his life Du Bois was an embittered expatriate and that a battered Robeson slipped through the cracks of sanity and shadowboxed with the ghosts in his head. To attempt to humanize foreign policy—the most Machiavellian of political enterprises—requires either a profound naiveté or a Christlike capacity for self-sacrifice. Robinson has been nailed to the cross of expedience more than once—and judging by the tone of this book, his palms are still bloody. The most brilliant of his victories have consistently been tainted by the stain of bottom-line politics.

Would that Randall Robinson confined his commentary to matters of foreign politics, the body count would be lower. Like a number of his contemporaries, Robinson has come to believe that the accomplishments of the civil rights movement were, on one level, a zero-sum game.

Early on, we learn of an aged Southerner, red of neck and

simple of mind, who refers to the Harvard Law School–educated Robinson as a boy. This happens in 1995. Robinson was fifty-four years old. The incident, one of innumerable slights borne by the author, sparks a moment of reflection. "What have I done with my pain? I am not eager to know. I can find no answer of which I am proud. White-hot hatred would seem the proper reflex. But there is no survival there. In the autumn of my life, I am left regarding white people, before knowing them individually, with an irreducible mistrust and dull dislike."

He speaks longingly of the era before the white people came; the period of his childhood in Jim Crow Virginia. His South is one of congregation, not simply segregation. As he sees it, the forbidden zones of the white world fostered a unity among blacks that has not been seen since. In Robinson's South, whites are themselves Jim Crowed, exiled to the periphery of black people's concerns. He was raised in a loving though poor family that included his brother Max, the nation's first black network news anchor.

But what is curiously absent from Robinson's depiction of the South of his boyhood is the ability of those whites to reach within the confines of black communities and inflict damage. These communities, nurturing as they undoubtedly were, were also under siege from racist white politicians, school boards, and law enforcement. For Robinson, the problems began the moment he passed beyond the womb of black Richmond and into the white world.

Integration, in his view, is a placebo, a decoy that has left black America with its guard down. Last year, in the midst of the Jackie Robinson commemoratives, Hank Aaron penned a sad requiem for the heroic black athlete, a lament that the players who recognized themselves as part of some larger metaphor are now a fixture of history, dead at the hands of narcissistic free-agent individualism. Like Aaron, Robinson is critical of blacks who suffer from "Vernon

Jordan disease," a neurological disorder that causes black people to wrap themselves in the rhetoric of righteousness, climb to the highest perches of society, and instantly forget about those whose struggles helped them to get there in the first place. It is as if a generation of black leaders descended from the metaphorical mountaintop to find priests worshipping the golden calf of privilege.

For his part, Robinson seems to have been well inoculated against the affliction—he has been working on behalf of the over-looked, abused, and oppressed for well over two decades. TransAfrica was organized in 1977 as a means of furthering African and Caribbean causes and pressuring the United States to adopt humane policies toward the black world. The organization frequently finds itself caught in the crosshairs of realpolitiks while insistently attempting to infuse American foreign policy with a moral vision. This is not an enviable position. It was TransAfrica more than any other organization that made Nelson Mandela's name ubiquitous and apartheid the most high-profile human rights cause of the 1980s.

The seeds of the Free South Africa movement germinated in TransAfrica's offices, a political response to the blooming good-will between Ronald Reagan and South Africa's P. W. Botha. Reagan, the cold warrior, understood the world simply in terms of allies, enemies, and people who were too inconsequential to be either. The blacks of South Africa fell into the latter category.

When Robinson received classified State Department documents detailing the administration's plans for South African amity, he made them public (to the dismay of TransAfrica's board members) and set into motion a plan that culminated in a sit-down strike in the offices of the South African consulate. The arrests of Robinson, law professor Mary Frances Berry, Walter Fauntroy, and Eleanor Holmes Norton immediately raised the profile of the South African cause. By 1985, in the middle years of a political depression, Americans nonetheless found themselves quoting the virtues of corporate divestment from South Africa. Both the Reagan administration and business leaders shouted down divestment in the name of cold war strategy and profit.

The passage of the Comprehensive Anti-Apartheid Act over a Reagan veto a year later was largely the product of Robinson's ceaseless politicking and ability to deliver protestors to the South African embassy every day for more than a year. Mandela's eventual release and ascent to the presidency of South Africa was in no small measure a product of the work of TransAfrica.

But not even moral figures of the stature of Mandela can escape the back rooms where political deals get cut. Robinson tells of the South African president's fund-raising deals with the very same corporate executives who vigorously fought against sanctions—a move that caused a rift between the African National Congress and TransAfrica. As he writes: "It all seems so gratuitously self-defeating. Why would a new government, inexperienced in both foreign relations and domestic management, spurn its friends at home and abroad? [Because] government is power and corporations are power and it was with the biggest of governments and largest of corporations with whom they wished to associate." TransAfrica had simply become the minor leagues.

In the case of Haiti, the political lines become even clearer. After the democratically elected prime minister Jean Bertrand Aristide was deposed in a bloody coup in 1992, the new regime initiated the reign of terror that sent fifty thousand Haitians desperately fleeing to American shores. Though Bill Clinton pledged, in the heat of the 1992 election, to end the policy of summarily sending them back to Haiti (while automatically granting asylum to fleeing Cubans), the Slick One ignored Haiti after being elected. Randall Robinson's twenty-four-day hunger strike pressured the administration into overhauling its Haiti policy. But what remains clear is that the human equation had become no more prominent than before. Poor Haitians don't matter. Randall Robinson, Ivy League lawyer and international activist, matters. And the administration simply did not want his emaciated corpse on their hands.

The many elements of *Defending the Spirit* don't always balance out. We learn much about Robinson's passionate commitment to justice for South Africa and the demons that pursued his brother Max to his early grave but virtually nothing about his first marriage, which lasted for seventeen years. But this remains a brilliant book. It is a testament to the fact that those ancient concerns for Africa may have faded, but have never disappeared from the souls of black folk.

May 1998

26

Blood at the Root

Again. Damn. These days the whole world looks like a flick I've seen before.

I could speak the oft-repeated and always ignored cliché that "this madness has got to stop." Or I could be disgusted and stop listening to hip-hop (as I did for almost five years after the Notorious B.I.G. and Tupac Shakur were murdered, thinking the music was the soundtrack to self-genocide). Or I could tell the truth: Jason Mizell was a humble brother from around the way, and I'm feeling blood fury at my own community right about now.

In the ultimate equation, geography makes no difference—a stolen life is an abomination no matter where the theft occurs. Still, as someone who grew up in that neighborhood, Queens, it doesn't go down easy that a pioneer of hip-hop had his life taken on the very same streets where we honed verbal skills, traded our elementary freestyles, and chased reputations for lyrical flow. Hollis Avenue, which runs past the park on 205th Street, where they used to steal power from the streetlights and throw illegal jams back in 1979; Farmers Boulevard, where cats used to get their rhyme skills (and chins) tested on the square; Liberty Avenue, where some of the illest did their dirt and whose residents always rolled deep to the shows at Club Encore. I don't feel the same sadness as when Biggie and Tupac were killed, though, because I'm filled with bitter anger. In place of a local legend who blew up and then actually stayed in the community, we have a name added to the interminable list of the prematurely dead. Again. We have radio stations nostalgically playing a deceased man's music. Again. We have a frantic search for answers that will not be forthcoming. Again.

I think this is where I came in.

Recognize: before middle-aged academics started charting its "globalization," before rappers became unpaid boosters for the booze du jour, before ice was anything but frozen water, there was this—two turntables and a microphone. Before hip-hop was old enough to see over the dashboard of America, the battles weren't between rappers in different time zones—it was all about interborough strife back then. Them Brooklyn cats had it in for the brothers from uptown; Bronx heads were constantly flexing on Brooklynites, and nobody was feeling Queens. I remember when DJs at spots like Union Square and the Latin Quarter would ask if Queens was in the house as a semijoke. Our Benetton-swathed, bomber-wearing delegations kept our mouths shut fearing larceny from the Bed-Stuy, Harlem, South Bronx axis of evil. To cut to the quick: Queens was known for getting played.

Run and them changed that, though.

Jam Master Jay was one-third of the trio that put Queens—a borough that isn't even completely on the New York City subway map—on the musical one. Never the kind of hyperkinetic sound architect that could damn near make the tables speak in tongues, JMJ was still the perfect DJ for Joseph Simmons and Daryl McDaniels. Truth told, Run and DMC didn't need the eye-blurring hand speed of a Grand Master Flash or the pyrotechnics of a Jazzy Jeff, because they had Jay on the ones and twos—a DJ who intrinsically knew how to tailor his cuts and scratches to complement their tightly traded couplets.

> He's Jam Master Jay / The big beat blaster /
> He gets better 'cause / He knows he has-ta
> —"Jam Master Jay" from the album *Run-DMC*

Having opened the doors for acts like LL Cool J, and later MC Shan, Marley Marl, and the Juice Crew, they were responsible for transforming Queens' status from that of ghetto pariah to hip-hop epicenter. For a good block of the music's history—between Kings of Rock and KRS-One's loathsome drive-by, "The Bridge Is Over"—Queens was officially running shit. Cats like JMJ helped make it (slightly) safer to be from the city's largest borough and represent at hip-hop shows. Run, D, and Jay would straight-up claim Hollis on wax so we would in turn shout out "Hollis" (not necessarily "Queens," mind you) at jams.

The irony that Jay's life ended precisely because he remained in the community is enough to make you gag. The number of boulevard stars who go MIA as soon as their bank accounts get into the triple digits is legion. But I remember seeing Jay, still in the neighborhood, still unassuming despite global fame. And thoughts like that are enough to make one angry. I'm thinking now that mourning is played out. Maybe we need more righteous anger because on some battered corner another graffiti epitaph for a murdered black man is being painted; because the truth is that this won't be the last one; because we reproduce hate in ourselves so cavernous that murder has now become a cliché. And because home has been defiled.

To Jam Master Jay: infinite thanks for those memories, one Queens kid to another—may your soul rest in eternal peace. To his family: you have the sympathy of every one of the millions who have ever heard a Run-DMC record. And to the rest of us: be angry enough to do something; be committed enough to love ourselves better. Maybe then we can stop running this tired reel. Live so that we never have to say, "This madness has to stop." Again.

October 2002

27

Rev. Al's Big Score

The big man is punctual and rolls into a room accompanied by a Blaxploitation soundtrack that only he can hear. This fall there are eight Democrats imagining strains of "Hail to the Chief" when they enter a venue, but only Al Sharpton is listening for "Funky President." To the skeptical world, Sharpton may be tilting at his own lofty set of windmills, but for his target audience he is the first legitimate black populist of the new millennium. Sleep if you want to, but beneath the comic appearance, the self-deprecating one-liners—"I understand deficit spending. I was born in deficit spending"—and the deliberately Ebonic diction is a political rationality that Sharpton has parlayed into his present standing as the most influential nonelected black Democrat in the party. Never mind the snickers of the wine-'n'-cheese set, because Al

Sharpton knows he can't win. He also knows he doesn't have to win—all he needs to do is not lose.

Understanding Sharpton's standing as a reputed leader of the race requires understanding of recent history. Understanding Sharpton the presidential candidate requires delving a bit further into the past. Sharpton is a populist, and like most populists dating back to the turn-of-the-century Negrophobe Tom Watson, his approach to politics relies upon equal measures of demagogy and democracy. The reverend who galvanized thousands to confront the near-fascism that was the Giuliani-era NYPD after the rape of Abner Louima and murder of Amadou Diallo is also the clergyman who decried the incursion of "white interlopers" in Harlem and rode the Tawana Brawley enigma to public prominence.

Having copped the elements of his style from James Brown, a Republican, and Rev. Adam Clayton Powell Jr.—quite possibly the two most flamboyant black men of the twentieth century—Sharpton fit right into the era that witnessed his political ascent. New York in the 1980s was the Wild West with a theater district, a town Ed Koch ruled with an aluminum fist. Beneath the veneer of cosmopolitan liberalism was a knotted skein of racial antagonisms. It was an era pockmarked by epidermal hostilities, crack wars, and lawmen who were quick on the draw: Bernard Goetz, subway vigilante; Eleanor Bumpurs, an elderly black woman who was shot to death by NYC housing police; Michael Stewart, a black graffiti artist who was arrested for vandalism and died in police custody; Yusef Hawkins, a black teen gunned down on the streets of Bensonhurst, Brooklyn, for wandering into the wrong neighborhood. And then there was the mad Scottsboro saga of the "Central Park Jogger" rape case. The only thing missing was the tumbleweed.

Times were so hard back then that even a fat preacher with a perm, jogging suit, and gold medallions could get a superhero's welcome. For better or worse, Sharpton parlayed his rapid racial response tactics into a position as unofficial kingmaker among

New York Democrats—the evidence being his nonendorsement of mayoral candidate Mark Green and Green's subsequent defeat by Michael Bloomberg in 2001.

Sharpton the presidential candidate fits into a long historical tradition of symbolic black presidential campaigns. James Ford, a black Communist, was tapped as the Communist Party's vice-presidential candidate in 1932—largely to underscore the CP's commitment to racial equality in the midst of its campaign to save the lives of the nine Scottsboro Boys. Charlotta Bass, the black radical and publisher of the *California Eagle* newspaper ran for VP on the Progressive Party's 1952 ticket, just four years after the defeat of Henry Wallace and burgeoning winds of McCarthyism had relegated them to the sidelines of American politics. Brooklyn congressional representative Shirley Chisholm ran for president in 1972 in a campaign that rejected "soft money" decades before John McCain had ever heard of the term. Her campaign failed to win even the endorsement of the newly formed Congressional Black Caucus. Doug Wilder, the first black governor since Reconstruction, spent a weekend in 1992 running for the high office, and Maryland conservative Alan Keyes threw his hat into the ring in an all but forgotten run in 2000. But the historical reminder that Sharpton wants most explicitly to play up is Jesse Jackson's 1988 campaign.

Jesse's seven million votes didn't win him the party's nomination, but the ripple effect figured into Wilder's election and Ron Brown's ascent to head the Democratic National Committee (and eventual stewardship of Bill Clinton into the Oval Office). Sharpton's platform ranges from the idealistic—an amendment guaranteeing the right to health care—to the unlikely—statehood for Washington, D.C. The first reason he cites for running is to "raise issues that would otherwise be overlooked—for example, affirmative action, anti–death penalty policy, and African and Caribbean policy." But the real ethos behind Sharpton's campaign is his desire to re-create the so-called Jackson Effect. Al Sharpton wants to galvanize black voters into a bloc that can influence, if not determine outright, the direction of the Democratic Party. And, implicitly, extend his own influence inside the party to the national level.

The main problem that confronts the Sharpton campaign is the fact that the Jesse model is ready for retirement. Jesse's "effect" notwithstanding, the DP has become consistently more conservative (or, in their terms, "centrist") in the fifteen years since his campaign. Plus, Sharpton has no hope of garnering even a handful of the votes Jesse received from gays or hard-pressed middle-American farmers. Jackson's civil rights movement pedigree helped him finesse the transition from protest politics to the electoral kind, but it's doubtful that mold can work for another generation of black leadership.

Republican Jesse Jackson Jr.'s recent endorsement of Howard Dean might signify that the handwriting is on the wall for Sharpton. His decision to lash out at Dean—declaring him "antiblack" for his positions on the death penalty, affirmative action, and gun control—was simply bad politics, an echo of Sharpton's "white interloper" days. While Sharpton hopes to build a bloc within the party, there's reason to believe that black people's best hope for furthering their interests within the Democratic Party is to organize outside of it—as evidenced by the thousands of young black people registering as independents. Jesse Sr. famously divided black leadership into "tree-shakers," who stir up social tension and inspire action, and "jelly-makers," who carry out the nuts-and-bolts work of daily organizing. Given his preferences, Al Sharpton would like to shake the hell out of the Democratic Party tree—which might serve some purpose, provided the rest of us don't end up in a jam.

November 2003

28

King, for a Day

Martin Luther King Day, 10:14 p.m. and thirty-something degrees outside. The news vans and cameras, along with the protesters, placards, and the president, were gone by the time I arrived.

Amiri Baraka once told me that things get dangerous once your opponents stop defaming you and start giving you endorsements.

Six-plus hours after the official ceremonies, the block was gradually reverting back to its normal rhythms. Down the block there was a lone white man yelling into his cell phone about the photographer who never showed up and a homeless brother eyeing me while formulating his sales pitch. The barricades were still there, though, as was the windblown wreath, now cocked ace-deuce on the tomb. Look at that tilted floral arrangement over Martin King's memorial for a minute or two, and you realize what it feels like to be slapped in the face with a metaphor.

On its face, George W. Bush's political genuflection to King's memory fits easily into presidential holiday protocol: Arlington ceremonies for Veterans Day, egg-rolling on the White House lawn for Easter, and the most politically expedient center of the Negro populace for January 15. And, for what it matters, Bush's presidential legacy will be tempered by the fact that the two highest-level cabinet appointments of African Americans occurred in his administration. But it doesn't take a historian to recall that only one year ago Bush was singing before a different crowd. Last year his administration chose the Martin Luther King holiday to file their friend-of-the-court brief opposing affirmative action at the University of Michigan. In politics, as in music and comedy, timing is everything.

And not to damn sons for the sins of their fathers, but you can't help but recall that Gulf War, volume 1, was initiated on January 15, 1991. Or that citizens of Bush's home state of Texas have coincidentally chosen King's birthday to neatly coincide with Confederate Remembrance Day. But why should this surprise anyone? These days, conservatives routinely seize upon King's words, trying to prove that his references to being measured by "the content of one's character" show that he would have opposed affirmative action. By that measure, things have gotten way less safe in the six hours since those flowers landed on the white marble memorial.

The problem with dangerous people is that they become extremely safe when they die. And maybe that's dangerous for those of us who are left behind advocating their ideas. Thirty-five years after his assassination, Martin Luther King is as ubiquitous as product placement. His name has been given to 125th Street,

Harlem's carotid artery; there are literally hundreds of King avenues crisscrossing black America. His image is given over to the marketing plans of software companies.

And he is invisible precisely because he is everywhere.

We know the basics of his chronology: born January 15, 1929, at noon; enrolling at Morehouse College at age fifteen; the PhD in theology earned by age twenty-six; and leadership of the Montgomery bus boycott just six months later. The "Dream Speech," 1963. The Nobel Peace Prize at age thirty-five. The horror of his premature death at sunset on April 4, 1968.

But the ideas, the weight of the moral gauntlet that King threw down in his contralto church poetry, is another thing entirely. The scripted sentimentality of Bush's wreath-laying, just beyond the din of protesters, may be politics as usual, but the real statement lies in the fact that he was allowed to visit at all. The White House's last-minute request to participate in the King Center memorial events came with an audacious Secret Service demand that the official ceremonies be cut short to accommodate the president's security concerns. Audacious, but not unique.

This year's affront fits within a pattern of strong-arm approaches to racial reconciliation. Last year's speech on the evils of the slave trade—given near the slaveholding pens on Goree Island—came with the removal of every citizen of the island from their homes and their forced relocation to a local soccer field. This time the implicit deal was that we should be absentminded enough to forget the lawsuits of last winter and the unsanctioned bombing of Iraq. The irony of the Atlanta visit was too obvious to go unnoted: at one point the Kings were on the other side of the protest barricades.

According to the law of unintended consequences, this might be the inevitable effect of having a Martin Luther King national holiday. Official holidays are good for commerce and bad for history. Memorial Day means sales; Thanksgiving is detached from any real grappling with the fate of the Native Americans who were doing the actual giving that first year. Reckoning with the roots of Labor Day—and the history of labor exploitation in this country—might raise too many awkward questions about actual contemporary labor issues and what is being done to address them. Better, perhaps, that we just barbeque. In honoring historic events, we can take but so much history.

In a society where celebrity is the highest stage of citizenship, it's easy to confuse one's idols with one's heroes. (I'm thinking of an e-vite to attend a multicultural King weekend blast to "celebrate the content of our character, not the color of our skin," which also instructed revelers to "break out your finest threads and your sexy stilettos.") Bush's visit, contradictory and calculated as it might have been, was also a form of desegregation. By the most ironic means possible, Martin Luther King has been integrated into the traditions of American history. The benefits include this: a windblown wreath cocked ace-deuce on his tomb.

January 2004

29

Beautiful Struggle: An Interview with Talib Kweli

COBB: The first thing I wanted to ask you about is your musical influences and the way hip-hop artists relate to earlier generations of artists.

KWELI: I definitely feel like hip-hop artists have more musical knowledge than any generation before us, because the nature of hip-hop is to sample and loop and build on the past. And the more you get invested in hip-hop, the more you know about music. I'm willing to bet that every hip-hop artist had music in their house growing up, or at least around them in their neighborhood, because that's how you start to develop your flow, I guess.

My father considered himself a DJ when he was in college, and after that he became a teacher, but after that there was always records all over the house—and he was into everything: funk, jazz, soul, R & B. So when I got into hip-hop, really around the late '80s, people started to sample James Brown and a lot of the soul breaks and stuff, me loving the music made me say, "Rakim sounds good over that," or, "Kane sounds good over that—but where's that music coming from? Where did Marley Marl sample that from?" Then I would look on the back of the record and I'd see—"Oh, that comes from this." Then, walking around my house, I'd notice the James Brown record in my father's record collection—and I'd say, "Oh, that's where they got such-and-such from." Then that became a thing in the culture of DJs in hip-hop who would go around and find records that have been sampled and make tapes, and it's a way to spread musical knowledge in a way that's never been done before.

COBB: I was going to ask you about that Nina Simone sample on "Get By," because you also did a cover of Nina Simone's "Four Women"—was she of particular significance to you?

KWELI: When I was in high school, hip-hop got me. Because I was interested in finding out where those samples came from—especially when Pete Rock was out and Tribe Called Quest was doing all those jazz samples—rock artists and stuff like that. I was always into jazz, but that made me want to get into jazz more, so I started really listening to my father's records. The first thing I noticed about the Nina Simone stuff was that I loved the quality of her voice. She was trained, but it didn't sound trained, it sounded more natural. I loved that she was injecting activism into her music; she didn't look the part of the traditional singer from that era. She looked more African, more dark, and she was talking about social topics, doing hip-hop-style things with her voice. For her to make a song like "Mississippi Goddamn" or to do a song like "Four Women" was like hip-hop to me. I was immediately drawn into Nina's storytelling ability and everything.

Then when me and Hi-Tek did the *Reflection Eternal* album, it was important to me that we connect to the past. I've always wanted to redo songs from the past that I feel like my generation just missed and don't know about. That's why I did "Four Women" on the *Quality* album, and I did "Can I Talk to You" by Eddie Kendricks. Hi-Tek wasn't really familiar with the Nina Simone stuff at first—he'd sampled a lot of her records because he liked the quality of her music—I was more interested in the lyrics. When I told him the idea about "Four Women," he took a version of the song, sampled it, and we did it. Then "In a Blast"—this breakout single I had for the *Reflection* album—I said something about Nina Simone. So when Kanye [West] gave me the beat for "Get By," it already had the Nina Simone sample. I asked him, "Is that Nina?" and he said, "Yeah." Then her daughter asked me to do some work with her on a song. I met [Nina] at a Lauryn Hill concert—I was on tour with Lauryn Hill in Paris, where she lives. And the day I met her I realized that this woman keeps coming into my life in all these different ways. Then when she passed away, I got the phone call from her family before it even hit the news. Then I realized that she had been a sort of spiritual mentor to me—even though I didn't really know her like that, she'd been very involved in my career.

COBB: I wanted to follow up on what you said about Nina Simone injecting activism into her music. I think one of the things that people see with soul music and music from that era is the spillover from the civil rights movement into the popular culture. Do you think hip-hop reflects its political climate that way?

KWELI: Definitely. I think hip-hop is a very accurate reflection of what's going on in people's minds. I think you were accurate in the use of the word "spillover," because some people don't get it; some people don't realize that the context and where the people are at spills over into the music—they want the music, and the artists to lead, and musicians have never played the role of leaders. They've always painted the picture of what's actually going on. And that's what hip-hop does. Because of the breakdown in communication between the generation of the '60s and now, our parents and us, there's certain fundamentals about music and life that just weren't passed down. Kids today don't even know what happened in the '60s and '70s. That's not their fault—they weren't there—but it's the same with music.

Right now, with hip-hop, we've gone through the gangsta thing, the thug thing, the pimp and playa thing, and all that is a real individualistic thing. Like, "I'm just doing me. It's all about what I gotta do for myself, and I'm stacking paper." It's no longer the idea of solidarity between poor people, oppressed people. It's like if you're poor, you're doing something wrong. And if you talk about why somebody else is rich, you hatin' on them. Instead of talking about being poor, if you ain't out there getting it, I don't really have any respect for you. And that's positive and negative; it's a gift and a curse, because it encourages people to be self-sufficient—and that's why we can't shun that mentality—we have to steer it toward positive change. But at the same time, it's dangerous to think that you're not attached to your community and somehow you're gonna be able to stack paper without giving any of it back.

COBB: Right. Exactly. I teach a class here at Spelman on hip-hop culture, and I was talking to my students about "Get By," and I was talking about the social realist movement of the 1930s, and I said that song reminded me of what Diego Rivera had been doing visually—presenting a heroic vision of the lives of everyday people. What were you thinking about when you wrote that?

KWELI: Did you see a movie called *Cradle Will Rock?*

COBB: No. I never saw it.

KWELI: It was a great movie; I think Tim Robbins executive-produced it. Susan Sarandon is in it. It was about those artists in the 1930s and how Nelson Rockefeller had paid Diego Rivera to do a painting and he wanted to do this real political thing. And Rockefeller was like, "I love your art, but you can't do that inside of Rockefeller Plaza. You can't draw a picture of Stalin inside Rockefeller Plaza." It talks about the different plays and how the government was giving money to the theaters, because they wanted to keep jobs, but the theaters wanted to do this antigovernment shit and the different things . . . pretty much what you were talking about.

With "Get By" the label, Rawkus Records, had already shut down, and I'd already recorded my album and Kanye gave me the track. I'd told him that I needed some more tracks for my album to make it hotter, and as soon as the beat came on, I started writing the first verse, and I ended it with "just to get by," because that's what the pianos made me say. I was like, "I need to write something that goes along with these pianos that everyone could say and that everyone could relate to." So as soon as I heard the pianos, I started saying, "Just to get by," and I started writing lyrics in between that. Then I played it for Kanye, and he's very talented, very musical, and he hears melodies. When I played it for him, he said, "You should do the hook like this," and he starts singing the hook—"This morning I woke up . . ." Then he said we should get a choir on it, so he went and got some friends from a church group and they got on it.

COBB: I really like that particular song. When I was talking to the editor about this piece, on the connections between hip-hop and older black music, the example I used was "New World Water," and I pointed out that Mos Def's song was really in the same vein as what Marvin [Gaye] had been singing about on "Mercy, Mercy Me" on the *What's Goin' On* album.

KWELI: I mean, to be real with you, we could sit on the phone and list a thousand hip-hop songs that share those themes. If someone says that the musics aren't related, then they just aren't listening.

March 2004

30

The Stamp of Disapproval

Word on the street has it that the person who told us that hindsight is twenty-twenty vision was blind in one eye his damn self. And that explains why in 2004 it's increasingly difficult to recognize the difference between this country's history and its alibis.

Here history is a mass market of collectible heroes who are bereft of moral conflict and flaws, the dead equivalent of pop stars: *American Idol, 1776*. Time was when there was restricted access to this kind of embalmed celebrity, but in recent years we've become way more democratic with our half-truths. Case in point: on Public Enemy's 1989 incendiary "Fight the Power," the rage prophet Chuck D rhymed: "I'm black and I'm proud / I'm ready and hyped plus I'm amped / Most of my heroes don't appear on no stamps."

But since that song first hit the airwaves, W. E. B. Du Bois, Carter G. Woodson, Langston Hughes, Malcolm X, and, most recently, Paul Robeson have appeared as part of the U.S. Postal Service's Black History stamp series (Robeson's is the twenty-seventh issue in the series to date). On one level, this belated recognition of African American history is an indicator of how hard black people have fought to force the United States to recognize our centrality to the national storyline—and how successful we've been. After centuries of white-listing, black American historical figures have finally begun to emerge in the public consciousness.

Viewed from another angle, though, issuance of postage stamps is curiously ironic, given the relationship the U.S. government has had with black dissenters and the current assault on civil liberties under the guise of fighting terrorism. Fannie Lou Hamer and Martin Luther King were arrested—and Hamer beaten viciously—for having the audacity to demand that the United States obey its own constitution. Marcus Garvey was arrested for mail fraud and deported after his Universal Negro Improvement Association began demanding an end to colonialism in Africa.

The list of those harassed or placed under federal surveillance is even longer: James Baldwin, Medgar Evers, Bayard Rustin, Adam Clayton Powell, and Roy Wilkins, among many others. Langston Hughes was not arrested, but was hauled before Senator Joe McCarthy's House Un-American Activities Committee and coerced into admitting that his early poems were unpatriotic and should be censored. Mary McLeod Bethune was accused of being a Communist sympathizer for advocating equal rights. W. E. B. Du Bois was placed on trial at age eighty-three for allegedly violating the McCarran Act—a piece of McCarthy-era legislation that made it illegal to work on behalf of a foreign government without registering with the State Department. (Du Bois' advocacy of peace amid growing threats of nuclear conflict between the United States and the Soviet Union had been construed as near treason.) It is no coincidence that so many black leaders in the twentieth century have, at one point or another, found themselves behind bars. The accumulated weight of this history raises a question of whether belated recognition marks progress or an attempt to gloss over the undemocratic history of the United States—to provide a racial alibi for America at large.

That Paul Robeson is being honored with a stamp in the current era of repression and political paranoia is the height of historical irony. The catalog of Robeson's achievements is incredible, but his demise, amid allegations of being a Communist in the 1950s, is almost a metaphor for the experience of black heroes who have been enstamped by the U.S. Postal Service. Robeson was born in 1898 to parents who were both former slaves. His mother died in a fire when he was six years old. His father served as minister at a number of churches in New Jersey (being pushed out of at least one post due to racial factors), and settled in as the pastor of St. Luke AME-Zion Church in Westfield. Paul Robeson entered Rutgers College in 1915 as only the third black student to be accepted by the school. He went on to earn fifteen letters in sports during his time there, joined in the debate team, and graduated as valedictorian of the class of 1919. He went on to Columbia University Law School, graduated in 1922, and practiced law briefly before becoming disillusioned with the racism practiced by New York law firms. He decided to embark upon a career as an actor and vocalist.

After landing theatrical roles in *Shuffle Along, Black Boy,* and *The Emperor Jones,* he appeared in a 1930 production of Shakespeare's *Othello,* eventually being recognized as the definitive enactor of the tragic Moor. Robeson had graduated to film in 1924 and starred in Oscar Micheaux's *Body and Soul,* but abandoned the genre because of the limited roles available to black actors. He traveled extensively, visiting Africa in the 1930s and becoming friends with a number of African students, including the Kenyan Jomo

Kenyatta, who were actively fighting against European colonialism. He would eventually learn to speak more than a half dozen languages. Radicalized by his exposure to African struggles, Robeson began to articulate an increasingly critical perspective about racism and American politics. By the beginning of World War II he was widely acclaimed as a vocalist, actor, athlete, and intellectual. Paul Robeson was possibly the best-known American artist in the world.

By 1949, however, the cold war had begun to heat up, and the lines between dissent and treason were deliberately blurred. Robeson's comments at a 1949 peace conference were deliberately misinterpreted to say that African Americans would never fight in a war against the Soviet Union. The denunciations came with fury and swiftness: Walter White, Jackie Robinson, and Mary McLeod Bethune lined up to distance themselves from him. He was called before the House Un-American Activities Committee in 1950, where he refused to state whether or not he was a member of the Communist Party. Robeson, though he had a number of friends who were Communists and had himself visited the Soviet Union more than once, had never been a member of the Communist Party. His issue with the McCarthy inquisition was a moral one: he objected to any form of political expression being criminalized and saw McCarthy as a greater threat to the U.S. Constitution than Communism was. Asked by a committee member why he didn't simply move permanently to the Soviet Union, Robeson famously replied, "Because my father was a slave and my people died to build this country, and no fascist-minded people will drive me from it. Is that clear?"

There would be consequences for this kind of democratic audacity. Robeson was refused permission to perform in venues across the country, and his passport was revoked, making it impossible for him to tour abroad. His alma mater, Rutgers, omitted his name from its list of football greats and all but dismissed his significance as an alumnus of the institution. A planned concert in Peekskill, New York, devolved into a riot when local residents began throwing bricks through the car windows of Robeson's entourage. Within a decade, the most famous black person in the world had quite simply disappeared.

Robeson could have ended his internal exile by simply stating that he was not a Communist, but to do so ran counter to his deep belief in intellectual freedom. He fell into financial ruin. The accumulated strains—along with his discovery of the horrors of Stalin's tyranny in the USSR—took their toll; he suffered a series of nervous breakdowns. Finally, in 1958 the Supreme Court ruled that it was illegal to deny a passport to a citizen on the basis of political beliefs, and Robeson was allowed to travel abroad later that year. He performed internationally, but never came close to his former prominence. He died in 1976, a legend who had been quietly forgotten.

With a sitting president who tells the world, "You are either with us or against us," endorses secret military tribunals, and condones eavesdropping on confidential discussions between a person and his or her attorney, it's almost impossible to ask whether the Robeson stamp is tribute or hypocrisy. These days, presidents visit Martin Luther King's tomb and then appoint former segregationists to the federal bench. And a defamed icon is given accolades a half century after his life was ruined by an overzealous government that had declared Communism its primary threat and that told him he was either with us or against us. With history as an alibi, you can't expect anyone to plead guilty.

February 2004

31

What Black People Should Know by Now

Black people should know by now—should've known long ago, actually—that Ralph Wiley was the real thing. By the time he passed away last weekend, at the age of fifty-two, he had plied his trade as a scribe for three decades, setting high-water marks for prose and blazing trails for black sports journalists along the way. People knew him best for his collections *Why Black People Tend to Shout* and *What Black People Should Do Now*, but that literally wasn't the half. Ralph published ten books during his lifetime, including *Serenity*, the classic though underappreciated memoir of his first ten years covering the fight game. But to really feel what Ralph was laying down, you had to check him on the regular, not the polished collections, but the day-to-day dispatches on the politics, personalities, and drama of the athletic world.

If you read Wiley's dissection of the coming demise of Mike Tyson at the hands of Lennox Lewis (written from Wiley's own home court of Tennessee), you knew just how complete his verb game was. He was good for coming at you with something as unorthodox as a right-hand lead (my friend and fellow Africana columnist Lester Spence reminded me that Wiley had long ago predicted Detroit's coronation as 2004 NBA champions). If you checked his radiant, crackling observations on ESPN.com's "Page 2," you'd see him brush a subject back from the plate with something high and inside and then follow it up with something off-speed on the outside corner. His was all-prose material.

I first met Wiley in 1993 at Vertigo Books in Washington, D.C. I was a twenty-three-year-old with vague inclinations that I could be this thing called a writer, and Ralph had the audacity to tell me that I had some talent and should keep at the craft. He'd already put out *Why Black People Tend to Shout,* and his collaboration with Spike Lee, *By Any Means Necessary,* had recently hit the shelves. From where I stood, words of encouragement from a writer of his standing weighed more than the life advice that the veteran Reggie Jackson was famous for dispensing to wide-eyed rookies in the California Angels' dugout.

Over the next eleven years, our conversations ranged from "How to Write Clean Sentences" to "How to Survive a Divorce Intact." He told me to be persistent, pointing out that his most popular collection was rejected by thirty-five publishers before it found a deal. He warned me away from quick flights toward literary success—"You won't get there overnight, and believe me, you don't want to"—and described the vulnerability inherent in putting your thoughts on paper. "Your books," he said, "are like your children." We had our falling outs, too—as two opinionated Negroes with pens almost certainly would. But invariably I appreciated his friendship and advice too much to remain on the outs with him.

More than once during those years, when I'd written myself into a corner and was trying to find a way to gracefully exit a paragraph (and more than once during this column, as I try to convey the significance of my departed friend), I've heard Ralph's advice echoing in my head. He told me that one's prose must age gracefully and then gracefully set an example of just that. This is what Wiley wrote on Marion Barry:

> There are indelible lessons that the Delta teaches you. You have to be twice as good to go half as far. But of course. We all know that don't we? But more than most, Black people from the Delta know what many White people are capable of and are not surprised by anything they might do in the way of holding up the progress of Black people. So when Barry was videotaped hitting the pipe, he hurt me, not because he was the Black mayor of Washington, D.C., but because he was mayor of Washington, D.C. and a Black man who had come up out of the Delta and had made his way and been twice as good and was now gutted in public because he'd forgotten who he was, what he represented, how he'd gotten there, where he'd come from.

And on Mike Tyson in Memphis:

> Tyson's good to go until he's finally on the slab somewhere. We have a feeling when he's around that somebody's close to the slab. Him, or the guy he's fighting, or maybe, deep down . . . us.
>
> Sounds strange? It is strange. So are mouth-breathing rubberneckers tying up traffic by rolling slowly by a five-car pileup, peering inside, hoping to see what a mangled human being looks like, as a rush, and a cautionary sight, so they can go home to their meat loaf and string beans and tell the little woman and brats what carnage really is.
>
> Tyson is strange? Yeah, he is. Like we're not.

Unlike some lesser scribes who labor in the precincts of sports commentary, Ralph had a broad, erudite understanding of society at large. Sports was merely his metaphor of choice. (The topical, he once told me, should be used only to illustrate broad, recurring themes and questions.) He was capable of channeling both Frederick Douglass and his beloved Mark Twain in a single sentence. Ralph chronicled black kinesthetic genius for a living without ever traveling the well-worn roads of Negro chauvinism. We exchanged views on race-riddled subjects like the standing of Eminem in the pantheon of black musicianship and the pugilistic significance of the white Russian hopes Vladmir and Vitali Klitschko, and Wiley, in grand, content-of-our-character fashion, insisted upon evaluating their bodies of work before any other considerations.

Still, you always knew where Wiley came down, ultimately.

Whether it was in his extension of grace to the far-fallen Barry—"I have to give him a chance, because I never know when I may need redemption myself, as a fallible human being and a Black man in America"—or in his comic apology to white people for black "incompetence, shiftlessness, stupidity, and criminality" (an apology he ended by submitting an invoice for black contributions to America), his was always the perspective of a brother and a witness—unsparing in his criticism, unflinching in his truth-telling, and with the nerve to be funny and lacerating at the same time.

Ralph was a friend and a mentor. An invaluable coach who had faith in my abilities when I was still working on subject-verb agreement. He was a refined talent and a sharp intellect. A sometimes gruff, usually wry, often comic observer. A man—a black one, precisely—who understood the nuances of this sport we all participate in until we're called off the field. Ralph Wiley always brought his A-game.

And I'm not simply talking about sports.

June 2004

32

The Road Ahead of Barack Obama

By the standards of black oratory, the speech heard around the world was a B+. If black political eloquence is your thing, Jesse Jackson—though he's way tired and mired in baby-mama-drama—is still your man. Truth told, Barack Obama's speech to the Democratic National Convention last month was not in the same weight class as Jesse's incandescent address to the 1988 convention. And even Al Sharpton's freestyle on why the Democratic Party was still relevant to black people (a feast of gourmet leftovers) was probably a notch above Obama's keynote speech in terms of form.

But it was not Obama's form so much as it was his content that catapulted him into the political stratosphere. To many he represented a new order, a smooth, nondemagogic brand of leadership that has been advertised as a coming attraction since the decline of the civil rights movement. Harvard-educated, but with an African name; born and raised in the heartland, but representing inner-city Chicago, Obama was a pollster's worst nightmare (which is why he was in a prime position to laugh off the "red states vs. blue states" crowd).

Even the casual observer could see that the Democratic Party needed Obama at least as much as he needed them—and perhaps more than he did. However you slice it, the GOP is responsible for the first black senator elected after Reconstruction (Edward Brooke in 1966), the first black national security adviser, the first black secretary of state, and the only black currently seated on the Supreme Court. With Jesse long past his political expiration date and Ron Brown long deceased, the Democrats are suffering from a melanin deficiency. And it is this specific void that has made for the wildly premature discussion of Obama—who is still just a state legislator—as the party's first black presidential nominee.

The specific brilliance of the Obama speech was that it allowed each of the fragmented constituencies of the Democratic Party to leave Boston's Fleet Center with the belief that at his core Obama represented their specific interests. Even his most widely quoted statements don't place him neatly in either the centrist or liberal wing of the party: "Go into the collar counties around Chicago, and the people will tell you they don't want their tax money wasted by a welfare agency or the Pentagon. Go into any inner-city neighborhood, and folks will tell you that government alone can't teach kids to learn. They know that parents have to parent, that children can't achieve unless we raise their expectations and turn off the television sets and eradicate the slander that says a black youth with a book is acting white."

As a political statement, this is deft, savvy, and intelligent, but as a political blueprint, it's far trickier to pull off. And this is where Obama's political talents will most quickly be tested. The

racial realities of America often come down to either/or predica-
ments, and standing in the middle of the road is the best way to
assure that one is hit by traffic from both directions.

Black leadership has, by necessity, had a long predisposition
toward populism. (Ask yourself where Al Sharpton would be if he
conjugated all of his verbs correctly, and the answer is this:
unemployed.) And the United States Senate is a uniquely challenging forum for black interests. Only four blacks have served in
the Senate since emancipation (three of them Republicans), and
none has left a track record of significant legislative achievement
or party influence. Prior to 1913, senators were elected by state
legislatures—not directly by the population of the state they
were to represent. (This explains why there were no black senators elected after the demise of Reconstruction—when the "Party
of Lincoln" Republicans generally lost interest in the plight of
former slaves.) Still, it took more than a half century for an
African American to be elected after the Seventeenth Amendment provided for direct election of senators.

The first black senator came to office within five years of
emancipation. Hiram Revels, a former barber and AME minister
who had organized black regiments during the Civil War, was
elected to represent Mississippi in 1870. Though Revels was
elected to serve out the final year of his predecessor's term, white
senators representing Delaware and Kentucky challenged his
seating. Revels was eventually seated, but the combination of
race and his lame-duck status prevented him from exerting any
significant influence.

Four years later, however, Blanche K. Bruce—a former slave
who had studied at Oberlin College—was elected from Mississippi. Both Revels and Bruce were products of Southern state
legislatures that were influenced by Reconstructionists and newly
elected black state senators and representatives. But Bruce did
not prove to be any more effective within the halls of the Senate

than his predecessor, failing in his attempts to have pensions paid to black Civil War veterans and to desegregate the army (the latter would require a presidential executive order in 1948). Following the election of 1876, which signaled the end of Reconstruction, there would not be another black senator elected for eighty years.

The first African American to be elected to the Senate by popular vote, in 1966 Edward Brooke was elected as a Republican in a traditionally liberal Democratic state (Massachusetts) just one year after Lyndon B. Johnson—a Democrat—had signed the Voting Rights Act and two years after he had signed the Civil Rights Act into law. Republican or not, Brooke benefited from both the liberalism of New England voters and the Democratic legislation of the civil rights era. Brooke garnered more influence than his predecessors (managing in 1972 to become the only black senator to be reelected) and supported full political representation for the District of Columbia, but lost his bid to retain his seat in 1978.

Carol Mosely-Braun, who was elected from Illinois in 1992 as the first black woman—and the first black Democratic senator— might be most useful in understanding Barack Obama's candidacy. Both Obama and Mosely-Braun served as state legislators from Chicago—a city that counts for 80 percent of the votes in Illinois Democratic primaries. Mosely-Braun's election owed as much—if not more—to the political struggles of women as it did to those of African Americans, and the national outrage over how Anita Hill was treated by pro–Clarence Thomas senators during his confirmation hearings helped Mosely-Braun galvanize the women's vote. During her tenure, she famously challenged Jesse Helms and Strom Thurmond on a bill renewing a patent on the Confederate flag as well as supporting affirmative action to provide "equal economic opportunity not just for minorities, but women as well." Still, Mosely-Braun's single term was marked by questionable expenditures. And her willingness to lend at least rhetorical support to a death penalty for adolescents appeared to be a clear attempt to reach out to white voters, who would support such a measure, rather than African Americans, who would likely be disproportionately impacted by it.

Pundits, party officials, and black people at large see in Obama a new voice and a new style in black leadership. But for what it matters, we may be premature in declaring the old president-of-black-America model of leadership to be deceased. As long as there are outrageous racial offenses, as long as African Americans find themselves unfairly targeted, harassed, and even killed by police—in other words, as long as there is overt racism—there will be a niche for a Negro with a bullhorn. The question is whether or not Obama—or any figure like him—can maintain black support in the midst of a political arena that often splits along racial lines (it should be recalled, for instance, that the majority of white residents of New York City did not believe that the police who shot Amadou Diallo nineteen times should be brought up on charges).

In short, our ancient problems will still confront even new black leadership.

The recent entry of Alan Keyes into the race all but assures that the next senator from Illinois will be an African American. Whatever Keyes's motives (or chances of winning) are, this is significant. Consider the fact that there were eighty-two years between the elections of Blanche K. Bruce and Edward Brooke and fourteen years between Brooke's exit from the Senate in 1978 and Mosely-Braun's election in 1992. There will be only six years between Mosely-Braun and Obama (or if you play the long odds, Keyes.) This might signal a hopeful trend in American politics. But whether or not Barack Obama represents a new page in political history remains to be seen.

June 2004

33

The Tragedy of Colin Powell

I n the cavalcade of heroes that we trot out each Black History
Month, there is a special VIP section reserved for Negro Firsts.
The belief is that each one is a barometer charting the falling
pressures of racism in America. But the truth is that for every
racial pioneer there are hundreds, if not thousands, of black also-
rans who made the mistake of being ahead of history. Still, the
job is not enviable: the First is generally required to perform a
high-wire act in hurricane winds. And in the last months of his
tenure as secretary of state, one starts wishing that Colin Powell
had done so with the benefit of a net.

Since it is unlikely that he will return to the State Department even if a disaster for democracy occurs and Bush is
returned to the White House, we are possibly looking at the

twilight of Powell's career as a professional diplomat. Historians are trained to avoid snap, in-the-moment assessments, but at this juncture Powell's tenure at the State Department appears to have no clear diplomatic legacy, save the dubious distinction of being the First.

Last year, on the verge of the invasion of Iraq, Harry Belafonte denounced Powell as a house Negro. But it's not as simple as Powell being some species of sellout (Negro Domesticus)—because were that merely the case, Powell the political figure would not be nearly as tragic a figure as he ultimately is. Unlike Thomas and Condoleezza Rice, Powell felt no need to disrespect the in-the-street activism that paved the way for his present position. Thomas decried the "specious" social science underpinning the *Brown v. Board of Education* decision and has frequently criticized the Warren Supreme Court that decided it; struck down segregated transportation in Montgomery, Alabama; and outlawed the antimiscegenation laws that would have prevented Thomas himself from living in Virginia with his white wife. Rice, who grew up in Alabama, has taken great pains to point out that her family was not among that set of activist Christians who felt it necessary to march in the streets to end segregation (a statement that runs counter to her own father's political activism, which included traveling the country to give speeches denouncing the war in Vietnam). Powell, on the other hand, wrote in his autobiography of the fury he experienced as a young soldier in Vietnam when Martin Luther King was assassinated, noting that even the radical voices of H. Rap Brown and Stokely Carmichael were "like a fire bell ring in the night, waking up defenders of the status quo with the message that change had better be on the way."

Powell is the most popular of the black Republicans and has more support within black communities than any other institutionally sanctioned black power broker. He has benefited from the perception that he is not among the Negro-loathing mean spirits of the GOP—a grace that does not extend to his son Michael, who as chairman of the Federal Communications Commission presided over the indictment and arrest of Janet Jackson's right nipple when he wasn't busy slackening the laws that inhibit corporate monopolization of the media. (Asked what he planned to do about the alleged "technology gap" that results in poor—presumably black—children having less access to computers, the young Powell remarked something to the effect that "There's a Mercedes gap, too. I want one and can't afford one, but it's not government's job to do anything about it.")

But the house Negro indictment can't be dismissed out of hand, either. Powell took office as the most obvious gesture of racial reconciliation within an administration that required the disenfranchisement of black voters in order to come to power. Powell's own foibles played into the house Negro perception—commissioning a Scottish coat of arms in recognition of his distant European ancestry, with seemingly little concern for the bitter racial circumstances under which that Scotch blood entered his ancestral line. And even more damning is the sad irony of a black secretary of state leading the U.S. delegation's walkout of the United Nations' World Conference Against Racism.

The politics of symbolism permeates Powell's—and to a lesser extent, Rice's—role within the administration. Powell broke ranks with the administration last year to maintain his lifelong support for affirmative action during the University of Michigan case (the same case where the Bush administration filed a friend-of-the-court brief against affirmative action). But it has to be recalled that Condoleezza Rice—a former professor and Stanford University provost who spent her academic career attacking affirmative action—also broke ranks with the administration and supported the Michigan diversity policies. The fact was that Bush benefited from having the top Negroes in his administration disagree with him publicly, because that way Rice and Powell at least maintained a degree of melanin credibility. Dissing the sincere efforts of white academics to attract black students would've made those charges of house Negroism stick like bad rice. And when you get down to it, what good is having a racial token if not even white liberals think they're black enough?

But the ultimate irony of the Powell tragedy is that it is not mainly about race, but character. He took office amid grumblings from the left that his background as a general and former chairman of the Joint Chiefs of Staff would lead him to pursue militarism instead of diplomacy as the secretary of state. But Powell—like Eisenhower before him—was a general who keenly understood the dangers of over-reliance upon warfare. Madeleine Albright, Powell's predecessor as secretary of state, criticized him, in fact, for being too reluctant to commit U.S. troops to activity.

Powell the diplomat was birthed by Powell the soldier. As secretary of state, his vision for the world—the so-called Powell Doctrine—called for the use of military force only in circumstances where there were clear objectives, where there was domestic support and understanding for the action, and where the military could be used in precise and overwhelming forces. He also disdained using warfare to achieve what were essentially political goals. In short, Powell's vision was an attempt to correct everything that had been wrong about his own experience in Vietnam.

In the early days of the Bush administration, and even more clearly after 9/11, though, it became apparent that foreign policy was being run out of the Pentagon and the vice president's office—not the State Department. Powell had set himself up to be the voice of conscience in an administration that did not appear to have one. But there were also other concerns about Powell from the gate: when you get down to it, Powell was smarter, more experienced, and better prepared to be president than George W. Bush was, and his status as secretary of state might be the biggest consolation prize in history.

Powell made his disapproval of the administration's Iraq plans known early on, and as his—and numerous other former generals'—calls for caution went unheeded, the secretary's lack of influence became more publicly apparent. In the past, these kinds of unbreachable gaps had led to extreme statements: Powell's predecessor Cyrus Vance had famously resigned from the Carter administration, and an entire roster of career diplomats resigned in protest when the Bush administration began its long march toward Baghdad.

The job requirements for a Negro First, however, explicitly demand that one remain loyal no matter what happens. Under no circumstances does one quit, lest it be said that members of the race are not suited to handle the pressures of the gig in the first place.

But it's hard to say that Powell was thinking about race in February 2003 when he went before the United Nations and made the case for a war he did not believe was necessary—a gesture that nudged his diplomatic career from the politically ignored over into the historically tragic. Given the nature of his comments to journalist Bob Woodward a year later, Powell recognized even then that the ties between Iraq and Al-Qaeda were tenuous at best and that the war would likely be disastrous.

The central tragedy of Powell's tenure as secretary of state is the failure of history to act as any sort of guide for the present. The present quagmire in Iraq is almost a made-to-order rejection of everything Powell articulated when coming into office. The ideas underpinning the Powell Doctrine were gleaned from Powell's own bitter experiences of combat in Vietnam. Both Donald Rumsfeld and Dick Cheney (along with Paul Wolfowitz) have spoken of the need to erase the failures in Vietnam from the American memory. To avoid history. So in rejecting the Powell Doctrine, Bush and company were not only dismissing the secretary's diplomatic theories, but the administration was also fundamentally rejecting Powell both as an individual and for the portion of history that he represents. And Powell himself aborted history in choosing to remain part of the administration.

Simply put, Powell did not know when to quit.

His name, despite his high-profile and abortive dissents, is tied to one of the worst diplomatic fiascos of the past century. The Black History Month calendars may regard Powell well as a Negro First, but those of us who are concerned with more substantive issues have to hope that Powell is the last of his kind.

July 2004

34

Malcolm: The Unknown

Forty Februarys have come since the one in 1965—the one whose twenty-first day was stained by Malcolm's terrible death—and the balance of history has now tilted in another direction. Having lived only thirty-nine years before that forsaken day in the Audubon Ballroom, Malcolm X has now been gone for longer than he was with us. He is now a figment of our collective memory and imaginings, an article of history understood through the lens of his remaining source material.

Not only is our past imperfect, but our present is as well. In the case of Malcolm X, though, we have an instance in which our contemporary lives have shaped our view of the historical one. In recent years it has become a casual cliché to assert that Tupac Shakur was "our generation's Malcolm X"—a mantle that is surely too heavy to bequeath to a deceased rapper. But even more important, it means that we still wish to have a Malcolm X, the we-have-a-job opening that is as yet unfilled. We read him into our ever-changing present.

You could still see the Audubon when I was growing up, way past its glory, its long-ago shuttered windows and the tattered handbills for forgotten salsa acts glued to its façade. It loomed over Harlem's 163rd Street like a concrete metaphor. Urban legend held that his blood still stained the floors. The ballroom made a cameo in the video for Public Enemy's "Night of the Living Baseheads" in 1988 and returned to attention years later when Columbia University purchased it. There were dispirited protests and demands that the university convert it into a museum in Malcolm's tribute, but municipal momentum remade it as a steel and glass bioresearch center. And now it, too, remains in our memory and imaginings.

And there have been other changes.

In life Malcolm was a rarity; fused in him was an incisive intellect, an ascetic's discipline, and a hustler's spirit. Hard prison time and Elijah Muhammad's teachings made him into Malcolm X, and he made himself El-Hajj Malik El-Shabazz, but he never entirely shook free of "Detroit Red," the uptown hustler who understood all the angles. And that fact alone explains why Malcolm became the patron saint of the hip-hop generation in the late 1980s.

Malcolm articulated that heady moment in America when the Third World was casting off the shackles of colonialism, and he understood the parallels between that struggle and the one being waged by black people in Harlem, Watts, Selma, and Jackson. It is ironic, but not surprising, that in these many years since his death he, like Che Guevara, has been commercially endorsed by many of the same forces he sought to uproot when he was alive. His life has been the subject of a feature film by

Spike Lee, scores of documentaries, dozens of books, and an infinitude of poems. Historians have parsed the details of his life, discovering that he had traveled to the Middle East five years before his 1964 hajj, or pilgrimage, and raising questions about his claim that the sight of white Muslims in 1964 transformed his outlook from the white-man-as-devil teachings of the Nation of Islam into that of an Islamic humanist. The shortcomings and oversights of his ideas have been charted and detailed, the enigma at least partially decoded.

And still, something of him remains undiminished. Not simply hand-me-down nostalgia for a romantic character or a product of his lingering historical charisma, but a shard of something real. The enduring example of a man hand-copying a dictionary to gain literacy; the man who evolved from a pimp into a committed husband and father. The educator, fully aware that his uncompromised lesson plans would cost him his life, but who continued to teach anyway. The individual who did not stop seeking answers.

It is nearly impossible not to play counterfactual games and wonder what would have happened had he missed that appointment, had some random car accident taken his would-be assassins on their way uptown. He would hardly recognize us now: a generation that was in the womb when his life was taken, now grown and reckoning with our own understandings of the world. Thirty million of us in this country who have more assets and economic power as a group than any of us scattered by the slave trade; nine thousand of us who serve as elected officials within this country; our chances to exist as human beings measurably increased by the struggle he helped wage.

Then again, he would have seen heroin peak and decline, only to be replaced by crack, and witnessed HIV and homicide become enduring blights within our communities. He would know that one million men who look like him are incarcerated and that the percentage of our children born in poverty hovers at 40 percent, and he would be puzzled over the rise of bling-ism as a social philosophy.

And one can only imagine the content of his analysis of Condoleezza Rice. At age seventy-nine Malcolm would have lived through the erosion of postcolonial Africa's idealism, seen it dimmed by internal strife, coups and countercoups, and the invisible colonialism of debt to the first world. He would have endured the truculent regimes of Nixon, Reagan, and Bush, versions 1.0 and 2.0. His goal of having newly independent African states present the grievances of African Americans before the United Nations would have been impossible in the era of "structural adjustment" programs and high-interest International Monetary Fund loan hustles. And he would have been challenged by the oppression and enslavement of black Africans in Sudan at the hands of their Muslim countrymen.

And one necessarily wonders how his presence might have mitigated these concerns and wishes that he had been this generation's Malcolm X, too. But it is ultimately useless to speculate, because the history went down as it did. On February 21, 1965. In the Audubon Ballroom on 163rd Street and Broadway. And the weight of that history now rests on our own shoulders.

February 2005

35

The Genius of Harold Cruse, 1916–2005

I've learned enough to know that life doesn't really care about your own individual sense of timing. Still, the recent news that Harold Cruse, the critic, playwright, essayist, activist, professor, and intellectual swordsman superior, had passed away came as a shock.

I first encountered Cruse on the far wall of the "politics" section of Pyramid Bookstore in Washington, D.C. His massive *Crisis of the Negro Intellectual* sat dominating the shelf, its stark black-and-white cover daring me to pick it up. This was back in the late 1980s when I had just discovered that entire canon of black writing—Yosef Ben-Jochannan's *Black Man of the Nile*, J. A. Rogers's *From Superman to Man*, John Henrik Clarke's *Africans at the Crossroads: Notes for an African World*

Revolution, and Cheikh Anta Diop's *The African Origin of Civilization: Myth or Reality*. All of it was new to me, and I had set out to methodically devour every page of it. Cruse was not of that ilk, even though he and Clarke had been friends back in the 1950s and '60s. He was traveling a different road, concerning himself with an entirely different set of questions, and I passed over *The Crisis* in favor of some other now-forgotten piece of Afrocentria.

I came across the book years later, in my midtwenties, and the flair, originality, and straight-up acidity of his prose left my head spinning. It was as if he had taken the dozens and applied them to intellectual discourse. Communists, liberals, muddle-headed race officials of all political stripes—it didn't really matter what they were calling themselves 'cause Cruse analytically Ginsu'ed them anyway. Neither James Baldwin, nor Richard Wright, nor Lorraine Hansberry, nor Paul Robeson escaped his pen unscathed. Unsentimental, unsparing, and, truth told, uncharitable at times, Cruse wasn't concerned with the cotton-mouthed niceties, he wanted to get sharp-tongued truths.

I could not have known it at the time, but I would spend the better part of the next decade grappling with the questions he raised. He was one of the primary reasons that I wound up writing a doctoral dissertation on African American anti-Communists. While researching that project, I came across a cache of Cruse materials at New York University that had never been published. I wrote him a letter and asked if he would consider me as editor of a Harold Cruse reader. I really didn't expect him to agree, but when he did, I flew to meet with him at the Michigan retirement community where he was living. What I found when I arrived was an old man whose quick admissions of failing health were like intellectual versions of Ali's rope-a-dope. Give him a minute and Cruse could still take you to school on the finer points of theater criticism, the failings of American Marxism, the farcical pursuit of reparations ("They'll give 'em to you right after you get on the boat back to Africa"), and the poor state of contemporary black intellectuals ("A bunch of goddamn dummies!").

Cruse was born in Virginia in 1916 and came to New York in his childhood. An aunt dragged him from Queens to Harlem as a child so he could attend the plays and musicals of the waning Harlem Renaissance. He witnessed the tide of radicalism that swept the country in the 1930s, fought in World War II in the 1940s, and joined the Communist Party for a brief period before leaving at the dawn of the McCarthy era. His first love was the theater and he hoped to make a go of it as a playwright. That didn't happen, and by the time his manifesto reached the shelves in 1967, he was already well into middle age.

What Cruse brought to the table was a commitment to resolving the issues that he saw as undermining black leadership—and thereby black people—for decades. He favored the adage that those who fail to understand history are doomed to repeat it, and he therefore applied his massive power of comprehension to the issues lying before us collectively. And unlike a whole lot of others who wear that mantle of public intellectual, Cruse actually did things. With *Crisis* he laid down an intellectual blueprint for the Black Power movement of the latter 1960s. He continued that work in the 1970s at the University of Michigan as a pioneer in the field of black studies. He made big statements and in so doing ran the risk of having large flaws. Successive generations of thinkers criticized Cruse for bias against West Indians, women, the left generally, and the Jewish left in particular. He admitted that *Crisis* was a flawed work, but even now, three-plus decades after its publication, it is a cornerstone—chipped and cracked, but a foundation nonetheless.

He followed *Crisis* with *Rebellion or Revolution?* and then, in the late eighties, *Plural and Equal*, both of which elaborated on the themes he had worked on in the first book. A few months ago he gave me a call and told me that he was working on a book that would respond to his many critics and that he might need my assistance in researching it. And, man, did he have some people in his crosshairs.

By that point, though, his claims to poor health were no longer camouflage, and I didn't know if he was physically strong enough to see the project through to completion. But I will tell you this: there is something to be said about the fact that his time ran out long before his willingness to start an intellectual brawl ever did.

March 2005

36

The Truth about Rosa Parks

It has come down to us as a single moment of moral courage. Tired from a long day of work, a quiet seamstress would no longer accommodate injustice. An isolated instance of dignified refusal, which seemingly wrought a moral revolution. In the treacherous landscape of American race relations, Rosa Parks achieved iconic status by defying the laws of segregation in Alabama. And with her passing we have lost a vital link to the tumultuous history that brought our present world—with all of its opportunities, shortcomings, and ambivalent progress—into being.

But history—even the history of genuine moral heroes—is rarely that simple. Rosa Parks was anything but a passenger on the tides of history. Nothing of her history is as simple as it would seem. She was a reserved, even shy, person who joined the NAACP at a time when membership was literally life-threatening. She married Ray Parks, a gun-carrying barber and longtime NAACP activist, whose gun-toting actively challenged racial injustice in Alabama. And while her actions were brave, they were not unique. December 1, 1955, was not the first time a black person had refused to obey the segregation laws of public transportation. It was not even the first time Parks had refused.

The history of segregation is the history of African Americans resisting segregation. During one twelve-month period in the 1940s, the city of Birmingham witnessed some eighty-eight cases of blacks who refused to obey the segregation laws on public transportation. Five months prior to Parks, fifteen-year-old Claudette Colvin had refused to give up her seat for a white passenger. She had been ejected and arrested, and the local NAACP considered bringing a suit that would challenge segregation on the city's buses, but Colvin was pregnant and unmarried. E. D. Nixon and other activists thought she would not be a sympathetic example. Another young black woman, Mary Louise Smith, was arrested shortly after Colvin, but Nixon thought her dilapidated home and alcoholic father would be a public relations liability.

Parks was the product of a vital community of activists who decided to end segregation. Her grandfather kept a shotgun by his side for dealing with threats posed by the Klan. Ray Parks had raised money for the Scottsboro Boys, nine African American teens who were falsely accused of raping two white women in 1931. Her white friend Virginia Durr, once a raging racist, had become a bitter opponent of segregation and arranged for Parks to attend nonviolent activism classes at the famed Highlander Folk School. Parks herself had attempted to register to vote twice and was told that she had failed the exam. The third time, she made a copy of her answers with the intention of suing the state if she "failed" with the right answers. She passed. In 1943 Parks—then a secretary for the NAACP—boarded a Montgomery bus but refused to exit and reenter through the back door as the law required. The driver seized her and physically threw her off the bus.

History, though, is always a matter of timing: a combination of factors made Rosa Parks's 1955 refusal a powder-keg moment in civil rights history. Just a year earlier, the Supreme Court had handed down the *Brown v. Board of Education* decision, and the segregationist politicians had responded with the "Southern Manifesto," in which they declared their intent to resist integration at all costs. Parks's impromptu sit-in brought tensions that had been simmering for years to a boil. And contrary to the popular retellings, her actions that day were not staged—though they did come at the time when a coalition of activists and local lawyers were planning an assault on the structures of segregation in Montgomery. In the early hours, the local civil rights community found itself scrambling to respond to her arrest and imprisonment. Nor was the idea of boycotting segregated buses, which grew from Parks's arrest, unique. The twenty-six-year-old Martin Luther King Jr. and the newly formed Montgomery Improvement Association (MIA) called upon the Reverend T. J. Jemison for advice. Jemison had organized a two-week boycott of the buses in Baton Rouge, Louisiana, in 1953. Together they formulated a plan by which people would pay the MIA, which would then dispense funds for travel to the drivers in the carpools—in order to avoid tickets for operating unlicensed taxicabs.

None of these details diminish the extraordinary braveness it required for Parks to stare down an infuriated white bus driver—the same one who had thrown her off his bus twelve years earlier—and demand that her humanity be recognized. Southern bus drivers carried guns and routinely dealt out extreme violence. (During World War II, one black soldier who would not comply with Jim Crow seating was bludgeoned with a rifle butt and had his eyes gouged out.) Rosa Parks was literally risking her life for the community.

But the best way to recognize her contributions is not as the exploits of a solo revolutionary, but as the public face of an enduring tradition of resistance. In honoring her life, we honor the hundreds of other anonymous sojourners whose unheralded actions hastened the end of American apartheid.

October 2005

37

Seeing Coretta

The death of Coretta Scott King in February 2006 came on the heels of Rosa Parks's passing and that of the actor Ossie Davis. Death allegedly comes in threes, and the loss of that trio of civil rights icons in such close proximity was yet another reminder that the guard had changed in black America. Fittingly, the three essays that follow trace the meaning and implications of those changes.

When the young Coretta Scott sang publicly, she stood erect and clasped her hands before her, a model of grace, quiet self-assurance, and refinement. Those who were fortunate enough to witness her performance had a unique window into the next five decades of her life. The historian Darlene Clark Hine has written that black women leaders have a long tradition of "dissemblance"—that is, constructing a public persona that serves the race's need for an "ideal black woman" and simultaneously leaving the true individual protected from the antagonism of a racially hostile society. The recognized faces of Mary Church Terrell or Ida B. Wells-Barnett or Ella Baker as the representatives of the race leave us wondering generations later who Ida or Mary or Ella really were. The paradox is that the more we see of these people the less we actually know about them.

We saw a great deal of Coretta Scott, perhaps more than anyone else in these years, and with her death we are not only left bereft of our most vital link to Martin, but we are also made profoundly aware of how little we knew or understood her. The third act of her life—the one that followed her years as an Alabama farm girl and as a famous preacher's wife, the one that began on April 4, 1968—was a public performance that she played with the same grace, quiet self-assurance, and refinement.

If you were able to get beyond the official Coretta, you would have seen the woman whose roots lay in rural Alabama. Her family, unlike most other black Alabamans, owned their own land. But Coretta Scott was not a product of the rural gentry. Few would have known that the closest thing to a First Lady of Black America had grown up picking cotton. Few would have known that she continued to reside in the same working-class community where she and Martin had lived together.

She was a graduate of Antioch College pursuing a graduate degree in music when Martin King, the brash, smooth-tongued city boy from Atlanta, cold-called her. King had been given her number by a mutual friend and within moments got her to agree to have lunch with him.

Coretta endured the open hostility of Martin's father (who had selected another woman for him to marry) and his wedding-day attempt to dissuade them from going through with their marriage plans. As a young wife, she struggled with Martin's refusal to agree with her desire to use her education outside the home (an issue that, interestingly enough, also became a source of conflict between Betty Shabazz, who held a nursing degree, and her husband, Malcolm X).

Beyond the grinding daily pressure of class expectations and confinement to the role of wife and mother, Coretta was married to a man who essentially knew from age twenty-six that his pursuit of justice would lead him to a violent death. Any doubts about that possibility were erased during the Montgomery bus boycott when their home was bombed.

There were other burdens, too.

It was Coretta whom J. Edgar Hoover's FBI sought to turn into King's Achilles heel. In 1965 the agency sent audiotapes of King's sexual liaisons with other women to Coretta as a means of derailing the leader and thereby the movement. What the actual toll of this was is unknown and perhaps unknowable, though years later Coretta wrote that such matters in a union between soul mates are ultimately inconsequential—a profound statement of commitment and love one suspects was written by official Coretta.

Coretta Scott King was frequently compared to Jacqueline Bouvier Kennedy, and on the surface the comparison was apt. Both women were thrust into history by the assassination of a husband whom history has regarded as a great idealist. Both endured unimaginable travail with vast reserves of grace—a feat that anyone who has ever lost a loved one understands as heroic. And the images of Coretta Scott King and Jacqueline Kennedy at their husbands' funerals have been burned into our collective memory. But that is where the similarity ends.

While Kennedy had the weight of the presidential seal to ensure that her husband would remain a cherished icon of his native land, Coretta Scott King was left with only the sad history and official amnesia that has greeted black martyrs since that first African decided not to board a slave ship. Jacqueline Kennedy was free to become Jacqueline Onassis without fear that her husband would be forgotten. Coretta had no such assurances. Ask yourselves how many of us recall and honor Harry T. and Harriette Moore, the NAACP officials who were killed by a firebomb in 1950. Even by 1968 their noble work was remembered as a distant echo. It is possible, in the most ideal of scenarios, that the world had actually been changed by Martin's work and his vision. But such vague hopes are cold comfort to a bereaved wife and a grieving extended community.

It was Coretta's will that ensured that we carried Martin with us and that his vision continues to be spoken of in the present tense. The Martin Luther King Jr. Center for Nonviolent Social Change was literally created in the family basement. It was Coretta's undaunted efforts to have Martin's birthday made into a national holiday that solidified her status as a hero in her own right. A student of the history of this country would have no reason to suspect that it would honor a slain black man with a national holiday. Coretta believed.

With time, she came to use her status in overtly political ways, endorsing Walter Mondale over Jesse Jackson in 1984 and publicly challenging the black community to combat homophobia and address the issue of HIV-AIDS. Last month, Coretta made a surprise appearance at a Salute to Greatness dinner being held in conjunction with the Martin Luther King Day celebrations in Atlanta. The audience was shocked that she had mustered the strength to appear in public after suffering a major stroke. But to those of us who are familiar with her story, there was no reason for surprise. This is the sort of thing that heroes do.

February 2006

38

Auburn Avenue Blues

Even at this point, beyond the ceremony and adjectives, there remains something to be said. Despite the haze of grief and questions of "what next?" looming in front of us, there are still things that the home-going ceremonies of Coretta Scott King this week have made clear. We could focus on her life and her struggle as would be fitting, but we should also know that in a real sense this week was about us, the living.

At the Georgia capitol building some forty thousand people came to see her. But it was at Ebenezer Baptist Church, the home ground of the King family epic that you saw it. The lines. Stretching nearly thirteen blocks, wrapped around corners and up driveways, it was a gathering of black people of all ages and backgrounds, huddled against a rainy and uncharacteristically cold Atlanta night. There was the coffee shop on the corner, packed like the downtown number 2 train at Times Square with people seeking hot beverages.

There were the lines that turned the city's highways into parking lots. Interstate 20, normally an escape route for black professionals that is virtually abandoned between 10:00 a.m. and 4:00 p.m., was jammed into a jigsaw puzzle of traffic—as if the city had chosen to honor Coretta King with her own rush hour. If we paid attention to only the sheer number of mourners, we would have learned that there is still something vital at our center, that there is still a black community no matter how nebulous the term or disparate the group of people who constitute it. New Birth Missionary Baptist Church, the site of the funeral, was itself a metaphor for the broader Atlanta. Flush with the fruits of the local economy and twenty thousand affluent members, it is a new order of megachurch. The sanctuary holds ten thousand, and the mourners could have filled the church several times over. In their municipal exactness, the city's leaders had diverted traffic away from the church and commandeered a mall for offsite parking. And each of those spaces was needed.

We would have also learned that claiming the Lord is not always enough to sway black people.

The reception that George W. Bush received in the New Birth sanctuary was funeral-polite. His presence at the event was simultaneously a measure of how important Coretta's contributions were in life and how safe it has become to claim the legacy of the civil rights struggles of the 1950s and '60s. Bush's speech was theologically sound but politically suspect. Coretta knew something of illegal government wiretaps; she had the products of them delivered to her front door. She knew something of unsanctioned war; she had publicly opposed Vietnam nearly two years earlier than her husband. And she knew that the current occupant of the White House had secured his victory in the last election by opposing gay rights—a cause that Coretta saw as an element of her lifelong struggle for human equality.

Harry Belafonte knew these things and would have spoken them out loud. The noted absence of the man who had escorted Coretta to Martin's funeral from her own final rites sparked rumors that Belafonte had been too recalcitrant, too stuck in the tradition of shouting truth to power to be invited to the funeral.

In the end, it was left in the hands of Joseph Lowery, an eighty-five-year-old stalwart, who remembered that the movement's heart had always been about truth, not politics. They would later say that the old man was wrong, chastising a president for a needless war in that somber forum, but Lowery knew something that perhaps his critics did not. The reverend recognized that perhaps the best tribute to his departed friend was to continue saying the things she no longer could.

We would also have observed that there were beneficiaries of Coretta's commitment to justice far beyond the brown faces in the sanctuary. Jimmy Carter admitted as much when he said that he could not have become president without Coretta Scott King. No Democrat since Lyndon Johnson has won the majority of the Southern white vote, and were it not for the civil rights movement's efforts to break the stranglehold of disenfranchisement, politicians like Carter and Bill Clinton would never have been able to rely upon black voters as part of the party's base.

We know now that our icons are not permanent, and they are not meant to be. The young idealists who had the audacity to believe that democracy could exist in America are now aged and gray elders. But the point beneath all of this is that Coretta Scott King was a descendant in a tradition that stretched for centuries before her and must continue after her. We could believe that this funeral was about her, but no, this is still about the living. And what it is we are prepared to live for.

February 2006

39

Hanging Curve: Barry Bonds as Tragic Hero

If Shakespeare had written about baseball, he would have been hard-pressed to come up with a tragic figure more compelling than Barry Bonds. A young man of noble lineage (the son of one Hall of Famer, the godson of another) ascends through to the pinnacle of his society. The hero attains rewards and accolades, but he possesses a single character trait that will bring about his fall from grace. Not content with his vast riches, he makes an illicit pact to gain even more wealth, more acclaim, more of all of it. But this proves to be his undoing. In Shakespeare a tragic figure has a moment of recognition in which he sees himself as he truly is just before his demise. But this is where the comparison ends. Baseball is not theater, and Barry Bonds is not Othello.

However the recently announced grand jury investigation into Barry Bonds's alleged steroid use plays itself out, the damage to his reputation has already been done. Bonds earned eight gold gloves and maintained a career .307 batting average in the years prior to those marred by steroid allegations—enough to ensure that he would join his father in the Hall of Fame. But facing an overwhelming preponderance of evidence that he did use performance-enhancing substances, he is now in that Shakespearean position of being a great figure whose greatness is eclipsed by his spectacular fall from grace—one who has yet to have his great moment of recognition.

It's no coincidence that Bonds's questionable accomplishments came at precisely the point when age begins to affect most athletes. Time is ruthless—for us mortals it is at least. But for the athlete whose entire life has been shaped by his or her possession of an uncommon physical gift, it is like watching Zeus wake up one morning to discover that he has run out of lightning bolts. Or Mercury suddenly realizing that he's lost a step.

But in a real sense, Bonds's current woes are only half the story; the other half is in the response the allegations have inspired within some sectors of black America. In the weeks following the initial, blistering article on Bonds published by *Sports Illustrated,* Bonds became the latest example of the Racial Defense Reflex. This reflex is triggered when an individual—usually a black man—is publicly assailed by powerful whites. It is a circling of black folks' wagons and a verbal defense offered on every Martin Luther King Avenue in America. It's a skill we have come by honestly, a survival mechanism honed in the centuries when lynching was American recreation and black humanity was considered a contradiction in terms. Far be it from me to lament the wisdom gained from those days of dark experience, but you have to wonder if maybe the threshold should be higher.

We saw the defense reflex at work in 2004 when Ron Artest was suspended by the NBA for leaping into the stands after a beer had been thrown on him and pummeling a man who, as it turned out, had nothing to do with the incident. The talk-show host Tavis Smiley and the sports columnist Steven A. Smith were prominent in the Free Ron Artest chorus. Subsequent months saw Artest hailed in hip-hop magazines and black America at large as the so-called People's Champ—an ironic title given the fact that it was coined for Muhammad Ali during his persecution for refusing to fight in Vietnam.

Nor is this phenomenon confined to athletics. The majority of black America supported Clarence Thomas's nomination to the Supreme Court even as that same majority disagreed with virtually every position he was associated with as a jurist. That support was almost guaranteed the moment he referred to his nomination hearings as a "high-tech lynching." Gone were the questions of whether Thomas actually did sexually harass a black woman lawyer; gone were any questions about where he stood on the issues affecting black America. This was a black man being assailed in public by a group of powerful whites. And this is all that mattered. The reflex is the reason that black people cheered the O. J. verdict—despite the fact that Simpson had a long track record of spousal abuse and virtually no record of concern for black causes.

In the case of Bonds, the words "set up" tend to crop up in discussions of his current plight, and three black sportswriters—William Rhoden in the *New York Times,* Scoop Jackson of ESPN, and, not surprisingly, Stephen A. Smith of the *Philadelphia Inquirer*—penned spirited defenses of the left fielder. All of the articles made the implication—if not the overt statement—that race was a factor in Bonds's current troubles. Surely, they pointed out, Bonds was not the only baseball player to abuse steroids—Jose Canseco said as much in his tell-all book about juicing in baseball. And if Bonds is subject to an investigation, they wonder, why isn't anyone else? It's a good question. Kind of.

On another level, asking why Bonds is being singled out both by baseball and by the federal government is like asking if a driver who runs a red light as a cop pulls into the intersection is being treated unfairly because three other cars got away with it before the cop showed up. Bonds not only owns the single season home-run record (having snatched that title from Mark McGwire in 2001), but he is also the only player in striking distance of the career home-run record—the most prestigious record in professional sports.

While it's true that Bonds is certainly not the only player tainted by steroids, he is also not the only one who has been caught up in an investigation and subjected to questioning on the issue. New York Yankee Jason Giambi was called before a grand jury investigating the BALCO company that supplied designer steroids to professional athletes. He is widely believed to have admitted to using them. Where Bonds stands alone is as the only player to leave behind so large a trail of damning evidence—and to steadfastly deny using the juice. Giambi gave an ambiguously worded apology for whatever failings he'd presented as a player and moved on. Whether the Giambi option was available to Bonds is open to question, but his stonewalling of the grand jury and the press on the subject all but ensured that the next stop would be a more invasive examination of the issue.

No one in baseball, from the managers to the owners and the commissioner, was interested in a wide investigation into steroid abuse. There are a whole lot of reasons for this disinterest, but race wasn't one of them. Bonds is black. But Sammy Sosa—who is black and Latino and whose performance achieved the same kind of sudden meteoric and suspicious lift as Bonds—did not receive any more scrutiny than the white player Mark McGwire did during his banner 1998 season. McGwire's and Sosa's dual pursuit of Roger Maris's single season home-run record breathed life into the sport during a time of declining revenues and real questions about baseball's future appeal. And amid the press scrutiny of the home-run chase, McGwire's cover was blown when it was revealed that he used androstenedione, commonly known as Andro, a performance enhancer that is banned by professional football and track, but is not technically illegal.

Baseball's hand was forced by the immense detail in Mark Fainaru-Wada and Lance Williams's now infamous exposé, *Game of Shadows,* and the aftereffects of a congressional inquiry into steroid abuse. Both Fainaru-Wada and Williams are sportswriters for the *San Francisco Chronicle*—meaning they were supposed to be covering Bonds's performance. Given the prestige and money involved with that book, there's no way that a reporter for the *St. Louis Post-Dispatch* or the *Chicago Sun-Times* wouldn't have exposed McGwire or Sosa if they'd had the information available. It's the stuff Pulitzers, or at least huge book advances, are made of.

Rhoden went so far as to declare Barry Bonds as "this genera-tion's Jack Johnson" (April 7, 2006) and to describe the "growing, angry mob" shouting that Bonds is a cheater in a comparison that was uncomfortably close to lynching (March 13, 2006). The distinction is that Johnson was unjustly pursued and harassed based upon his activities outside the ring—no one can question whether Jack actually knocked Jim Jeffries out. But the nature of Bonds's circumstance is such that it raises a question about how much of his performance is real.

Here is what Stephen Smith had to say in Bonds's defense: "[I]t's difficult to find anyone who would debate his innocence in recent memory. The story, to me, revolves around what provoked Bonds' steroid use in the first place. And what—if in any way at all—anyone else had to do with it" (*Philadelphia Inquirer,* March 9, 2006). Thus, in the haze of questioning double standards, the issue of that individual's guilt becomes secondary.

It is only too clear that Bonds is not Jack Johnson (any more than Ron Artest is Muhammad Ali). Johnson and Ali were persecuted for principled stands—Johnson for refusing to allow the fascist dictates of Jim Crow to determine who he could marry and Ali for refusing to fight in a war he considered unjust. At its best, Bonds's only principle is the right to be as guilty as everyone else.

In baseball terms the most severe irony here is that Bonds is threatening to break a record held by Hank Aaron, an African American Hall of Famer. Aaron's 755 home runs were an example of the kind of mastery and heroism that Bonds fell short of not only statistically, but also as a figure of history. Aaron, for what it matters, never won a home-run title for a single season, but he consistently hit small clusters of home runs over the course of a long career. During his final season, as he threatened to eclipse Babe Ruth, Aaron played with the weight of every backwater racist in the country on his back.

In surpassing Aaron—if Bonds gets that far—we see not only a record eclipsed, but also a certain kind of heroism. It's worth noting that Aaron, in the decades since his retirement from baseball, has become a successful entrepreneur with a track record of giving back to the Atlanta community where he now lives. Neither Bonds, nor Simpson, Artest, or Thomas, for that matter, has demonstrated that kind of concern. And yet their individual trials were the basis for alarm across the race. This is not the meaning of community. And maybe this is the point. For these figures, there is no black community, but more like a black club—one where you never have to pay dues but you're always welcome to use the facilities.

June 2006

40

The Good Example

You had to bypass your automatic race-loyalty circuits in order to fully appreciate the scenario. Under normal circumstances, the sight of a lone, brilliant, and articulate black woman deftly fending off hostile inquiries from a delegation of power-suited white guys would go down as a miniature Great Moment in Negro History. But Condoleezza Rice, the most powerful black woman on the planet, has all but deleted race from the narrative of her personal success, and she certainly doesn't need a partisan racial cheering squad when she has George W. Bush holding it down for her.

Two years before Rice emerged as a talking-head nominee for president, her appearance before the 9/11 Commission on April 8, 2004, defined the catch-22 her career presents to black

America. A public failure on her part would invariably be read as yet another example of black incompetence. And a virtuoso political performance from Rice would simultaneously be a victory for an administration that has squandered international goodwill, undermined the United Nations, used the horror of 9/11 as a political card, run the economy into long-term recession, and started a war to protect us from nonexistent Iraqi weapons of mass destruction. For what it matters, Rice was convincing that day—even as her testimony was starkly at odds with the historical record, her own previous claims, and those of other members of the administration. And the underlying point is this: in the long, tangled history of black people in the United States, we have at last reached the point where black politicians have earned the right to be just as dubious and questionable as their white counterparts.

This ambivalent achievement might explain why black America at large is cool to the recent Internet-based efforts to draft Condoleezza Rice into the 2008 Republican primary. GOP strategists and media commentators have speculated that Rice is perhaps the only counterpoint the party has against the anticipated Democratic nominee Hilary Clinton. For what it matters, the secretary of state has stated numerous times that she is not interested in running for president, but at this stage of the game even the most serious presidential contenders are being coy about their intentions. That said, Rice would be among those rarest of political creatures: a black candidate who has greater support among white voters than black ones.

Putting odds on presidential candidates two years before the nominating convention is like picking World Series matchups in April, but the fact that Rice—an unmarried black woman with no electoral base—is being mentioned in earnest is a statement in itself. Her career is an object lesion in that old truism that nothing succeeds like success. The Republican

Party—the party that Southern whites fled to in order to combat desegregation—has now outflanked their Democratic counterparts. Excluding Lyndon B. Johnson's nomination of Thurgood Marshall for the Supreme Court, the Republican Party is responsible for all three of the most powerful black political appointees in the past four decades. If nothing else, American politics has an abundance of irony.

In black politics, at least since the days when Frederick Douglass screamed at American slaveholders on the Fourth of July, the litmus test has been only partly about legislative success and nuts-and-bolts reforms. The other part of the equation is one's willingness to speak truth to power. (This is also the reason that an outspoken critic like Cynthia McKinney, who is also one of the least effective legislators on Capitol Hill, has inspired fierce loyalty among the constituents of the Fourth District in Georgia.)

But in the case of Rice, Colin Powell, and Clarence Thomas, an additional irony is found in the fact that their powerful positions are enough cause to be suspect in black America. How can one speak truth to power, the thinking goes, when one actually *is* the power? For reasons owing partly to the force of his personality and partly to his willingness to at least mildly question the decisions of the Bush administration, Colin Powell largely escaped the bitter criticism and suspicion that large segments of black America reserved for Clarence Thomas and Condoleezza Rice. Still, it was not uncommon to hear it said of Powell that "if a black man gets that far, he can't possibly be on our side." It's interesting to note that it was Clarence Thomas's disparagement of his sister as a welfare recipient and his contempt for affirmative action far more than the allegations of sexual harassment that placed him on questionable grounds within black America. The harassment could be viewed as a personal failure, but his welfare and affirmative action stances were read as an unforgivable capitulation to the establishment. (Thomas's successful ascent to the Supreme Court earned him two now-famous spots on *Emerge* magazine's cover—in 1993 with an Aunt Jemima–style head wrap, and in 1996 dressed as a porch jockey complete with lantern.)

The doubts about Rice emerged even before the Bush administration had appointed her as national security adviser in 2000. Her affiliation with a candidate whose election hinged upon the disenfranchisement of black voters in Florida was damning enough. At the same time, Rice is a black woman who emerged from the crucible of Alabama segregation to earn a PhD, master concert piano, and learn to speak four languages. She came up in Birmingham, born just six months after the *Brown v. Board of Education* decision desegregated Southern schools. She would later claim that her support for the Second Amendment stemmed from the fact that without it her family would have been unable to defend themselves and their home against the terrorism of segregationists and nightriders. Rice has said that her family was not of the activist brand, choosing to challenge racial bigotry on the individual level by pursuing excellence. She was, to put it simply, to be a good example. Not coincidentally, she shared that perspective with another Alabaman conservative— Booker T. Washington.

Emerging at the turn of the twentieth century, Washington also disdained overt protest in favor of, among other things, example setting. And Washington, coincidentally, served as an adviser—albeit unofficially—to another Republican president, Theodore Roosevelt. For an entire subset of black America, the path to success lay not in picketing and mass rallies, but in the quiet, disciplined, and relentless employment of good behavior. Nor was this an isolated ideal among the moneyed Negro strivers; my mother, born coal-miner poor in Bessemer, Alabama, was given piano and etiquette lessons by an aunt who saw it as the best way of refuting the idea that black was inherently lesser. And for that community, Rice's career is a type of long-awaited validation, literally the substance of things hoped for.

Thus her success before the commission in 2004 was a metaphor for her career and an explanation for the ambivalence that black America holds toward her. It was, quite simply, a case of deliberately nurtured black brilliance at the service of highly questionable political causes. Just over a century ago, W. E. B. Du Bois articulated the idea of "double-consciousness," the antagonistic feud between the black and the American segments of one's identity. The doubts surrounding Rice center on the suspicion that she has resolved that dilemma by aligning herself with purely American interests. Whether this is entirely true can be debated, but in politics perception is reality. Those lingering questions regarding her allegiances were highlighted in September 2005 when she made the politically tone-deaf decision to go shoe shopping and attend a Broadway play while black people were literally drowning in New Orleans. In the strictest sense, her job as secretary of state is to coordinate the nation's foreign policy, and the Gulf Coast disaster was a purely domestic crisis. But the shouts from various quadrants of black America can be distilled down to a single statement: *You should know better.*

Maybe the final paradox of Rice's possible candidacy is just that—we do know better. It may be the case that black America is simply ahead of the curve on the question of Condoleezza Rice and that future generations of observers will see the widespread black disdain for her politics—and those of the George W. Bush presidential administration—as an island of sanity in an era of off-kilter politics. In real terms, a Rice presidential nomination is the longest of political long shots. Then again, Rice has already succeeded against great odds to gain a position that would have been nearly inconceivable for any black girl growing up in 1950s

Alabama. But whether her success amounts to an achievement or a setback for the rest of us is, of course, an entirely different question.

July 2006

41

The Devil and Dave Chappelle

In May 2005 Dave Chappelle walked away from the third season of his highly acclaimed comedy show and a $50 million contract with Comedy Central. A year later the network decided to broadcast sketches that Chappelle felt were not up to his standards. But his decision had as much to do with his political standards as his comedic ones.

The cheap wisdom holds that nothing succeeds like success, but the truth is that nothing fails like it, either. That's the reason there are as many great epics about a hero falling from the pinnacle of glory as there are about one struggling to get there in the first place. It's the reason we have sayings like "a victim of his own success." And it's the reason a great many of us have lined up to view Dave Chappelle's "Lost Episodes."

In Hollywood, where nervous breakdowns are considered a normal stage in career development, Chappelle's flameout last year at least scored points for originality. Where the cliché crises involve overdoses, bad weekend grosses, and cross-dressing hookers, Chappelle's was more like a lost scene from Spike Lee's *Bamboozled*. Blackface, $50 million, and a stint as a fugitive in

South Africa are, at the least, a plot twist. The less benign observers are apt to say the man simply choked under pressure or got turned out by the cash that Comedy Central dropped on him. (The middle-tier talent Mike Epps weighed in, saying that Chappelle's stable suburban upbringing had been his undoing and that a black man like himself with a ghetto pedigree would have no problem handling that kind of situation.) That line of thought came off like a bad joke given that the tagline for Chappelle's show is *"I'm rich, bitch."*

At one point during his appearance on *Oprah,* Chappelle explained that it wasn't the *money* so much as it was everything that came with the money. He spoke of a white man laughing in a way that made him uncomfortable with the direction that his career had taken. That hazy explanation sounds like a lame evasion of his own fears until you reflect upon the events that prefaced his frantic flight to Cape Town.

In the first skit from the "Lost Episodes"—the pieces that Chappelle completed before leaving the show in the third season—a character confesses that no matter how funny the show is, people will say it wasn't as good as last year. Chappelle's character is silent for a moment and then says confessionally, "Yeah, I already know that." And what the viewer already knows is that the brother ain't entirely acting when he makes that statement. But the irony—in a situation that is soaked with it—is that the material from the "Lost Episodes" is easily on par with the work he did in the show's first two seasons.

The problem was not so much the work as it was who was viewing it. It is clear at this point that Chappelle is the inheritor of the mantle held by the late Richard Pryor (and if ever there were occasion to lament his passing, it is now, when there is so much for him to say about this situation). Chappelle mentioned later that he left because he felt he'd been irresponsible with his art. But his work had not changed; the news of his massive contract and his status as the reigning *it* kid of American pop culture had vastly changed the audience he was performing it for. And *that* is what Chappelle meant by "everything that came with the money."

In his brilliant "Bicentennial Nigger" sketch, Pryor starts out by informing his audience that black humor started in slave ships. (In that same tradition, Chappelle's logo features the comic wearing a set of broken shackles and holding two fistfuls of cash.) If Pryor was exaggerating, it wasn't by much. Black humor out of necessity began as a series of inside jokes. The early records of slavery in the United States are filled with accounts of paranoid slave masters who hear slaves laughing and believe they must be the subject of the joke—a fear that works in the same way a person in a room with two others who are speaking a foreign language becomes convinced that they *must* be talking about him. But as the saying goes, just because you're paranoid doesn't mean you're crazy. All the weapons, laws, and shackles in the world couldn't save white people from playing the often unwitting straight man in a satire told just out of earshot of the big house. In the case of Chappelle, you confront the one question at the heart of his dilemma: what happens to an inside joke once the whole world is in on it?

An inside joke is inside for a reason—usually because only a select few people share the references necessary to decipher it, or the background to appreciate where the actual comedy is. In the wrong hands the joke will inevitably be misinterpreted. A profound sense of insider irony allowed black folks to fling the word "nigger" around with no—or at least very few—explanations necessary. And "nigger" was the most inside, the most ironic and complexly encrypted element of both Pryor's and Chappelle's humor. But it's virtually impossible for a white person in America to use the word "nigger" ironically. It would be the equivalent of having an interracial slave revolt—the point being that once white folk get an invitation, well, it ain't really a slave revolt no more. It's no coincidence that both Pryor and Chappelle met career crossroads that entailed traveling to Africa and refusing to use the word "nigger" in their routines when they returned.

Pryor told the *New York Times Magazine* in 1975, "I think there's a thin line between being a Tom and [depicting] human beings. When I do the people, I have to do it true. If I can't do it, I'll stop right in the middle rather than pervert it and turn it into Tomism. There's a thin line between to laugh *with* and to laugh *at*." That line was at the forefront of Pryor's mind when he returned from Africa in 1979. He renounced his use of the word "nigger," later saying in his autobiography that it was "a wretched word. Its connotations weren't funny even when people laughed . . . It was misunderstood by people. They didn't get what I was talking about. Neither did I."

But for all this, race lines weren't even the primary breaking point in Chappelle's crisis. In an era defined by simpleton celebrity gloss, where the lowest denominator is also the primary target audience, Chappelle's real fault line was comedic IQ. His core audience, the people who were drawn to the first two seasons of *Chappelle's Show* is multihued, geographically diverse, and spread across a wide swath of Generations X and Y. They found a common ground in being smart enough to catch the irony—even if only part of that audience could participate in it.

The work he created during those seasons was brilliant precisely because it is so unfiltered and true. His famous skit with Clayton Bigsby, the blind black Klansman, was a sublime dissection of the absurdity of racism. His "Race Draft" piece allowed ethnic groups to trade for people of other races that they'd always wanted to adopt (black folks draft Eminem and trade Colin Powell and Condoleezza Rice; Asians walk off with the Wu-Tang Clan). Those eight minutes of comedy did more to explain the state of American culture than the last dozen academic conferences on "hybridity" and "cultural miscegenation." The series "When Keeping It Real Goes Wrong" ridiculed the street ethics that have metastasized throughout black culture. In other instances, Chappelle put together riffs like the insanely comical Rick James skit that proved he could strip away the politics and still leave you on the floor gasping for air.

By season three, though, *Chappelle's Show* had officially crossed over, meaning he was virtually assured of an audience too big to really dig what exactly he was laughing at. Jimi Hendrix encountered that same paradox when he became big enough to attract an audience that couldn't grasp his guitar genius but did manage to get hung up on their image of him as a black Dionysus who burned guitars onstage. And this is where the demons come in.

Despite his later concerns, Pryor could get away with a skit like "Bicentennial Nigger," in which a slave laughs about two centuries of bondage, rape, and lynching, because his 1976 audience understood the bitter indictment he was actually articulating. It would've been disastrous for the crossover Pryor of the 1980s to undertake that kind of sophisticated irony. The last skit Chappelle did before leaving the show was one in which a minidevil perches on people's shoulders encouraging them to behave in stereotypical ways. In his case, the devil—who appears in blackface—convinces Chappelle's character that he'll be fulfilling a stereotype by ordering chicken on a flight. He dodges that trap by ordering fish, but the minstrel rejoices when he learns it is catfish. The moral of the story is clear: Chappelle's character lives in a catch-22 where anything he does fulfills some trait on an infinite checklist of stereotypes. It is a riff on the racial gymnastics required to negotiate the most routine of daily scenarios. Or it is a hilarious bit about a jigaboo dancing on an airplane. Depending upon who you're talking to.

In retrospect, it made perfect sense that this sketch would strike too close to home. A case of art imitating life. Or vice versa. A man who has demons depicting a man who literally has demons. An effort to deflate a stereotype instead affirms one. A comedian brought down by a single snicker from a single white man he realizes is laughing *with* the blackface devil not *at* him.

There's a reason why people say context is everything.

There are dangers inherent to fighters who forget to duck and comics who become part of their own punch lines. Both Pryor and Chappelle were deeply concerned with humanizing black folk even as they mined their foibles for material. That common concern may be the reason that Pryor designated Chappelle as his comedic successor. And that impulse to humanize is also what primarily separates Chappelle from the nearest in line to Pryor's legacy, Chris Rock, and, to a lesser extent, the cartoonist Aaron McGruder. But it's also the reason that one wrong laugh could put Chappelle—at least in his own mind—on the wrong side of that line between genius and Uncle Tom.

Rock's and McGruder's humor are driven in large part by intraracial anger. Rock's famous "Black People vs. Niggers" bit centers on an alleged civil war pitting the hard-working, respectable members of the race against the kinds of black people that the old folks refer to as "trifling." For Pryor and Chappelle, though, those kinds of divisions were not possible, or even desirable. McGruder's *Boondocks* cartoon—which also airs on the Cartoon Network—both ridicules and reinforces stereotypes of black folk, but, unlike Chappelle, McGruder doesn't seem the least bit conflicted about it. Case in point: the satirical "Survey of the State of the American Black Man" he published in the July 2006 issue of *Esquire*. Loaded questions like "Whose fault is it you don't have a job?" and "Which possession earns more interest: your watch or your house?" were great satirical material if you got past the reality that a sizable portion of *Esquire*'s white, middle-aged, affluent male readership is wondering those same exact questions in earnest.

In that same vein, the young Eddie Murphy dismissed criticism of his Buckwheat character on *Saturday Night Live*, saying that anyone who thought the figure actually represented black folks was ignorant. But if two centuries of American history have established anything, it's that there has never been a deficit of racial ignorance in this country. Damon Wayans had no ambivalence about suing to copyright the word "nigger" so that it could be used on a clothing line he was backing. *The Boondocks* cartoon holds the dubious distinction of using "nigger" more times per minute than Ice Cube circa 1992. But neither Murphy nor Wayans, Rock or McGruder are at risk for a Chappelle-level crisis of conscience, because, to be real for a minute, in black America the question of artistic responsibility went out with Africa medallions and Malcolm X caps. Epps was probably telling the truth when he said he would have had no problems had he been in Chappelle's shoes; then again, there's no guarantee he would've deciphered what was behind that single white man's laugh or even cared if he had. Seriously.

For all of those reasons, it made sense that Chappelle would go back to doing stand-up in small venues like the ones he started out in after his departure from Comedy Central. There's only so much irony that any of us can stand, and all we really want is to be understood. The truth is that we get a little disappointed when our geniuses are fully in control of their gifts. We want them to be slightly conflicted and just far enough ahead of the curve that future generations have the option of lamenting how few of their contemporaries dug where they were really coming from. Chappelle's disappearing act has invested him with an aura of turmoil that all but assures we will think of him as a genius. But whether or not he goes down as a tragically misunderstood one depends entirely upon if you can see a laughing slave and recognize that the joke is on you.

August 2006

4

Past Imperfect

As a child I was witness to a ritual that was infinitely repeated with minor variations. It involved an elder grabbing me by the wrist and tapping a forefinger against my temple, saying, "You got to make sure you get it up here. That's something that they can never take from you"—the implication being that you can and will be deprived of anything else. I am a student of history, because above all else history made sense of the world for me. That sense of vulnerability and an expectation of injustice was the product of a long, specific American history that continues to shape the world we live in. The essays that follow are in some ways riffs on that history—pieces that looked at contemporary events through a historical lens. The past, as the ancient wisdom goes, may be prologue. But just as often it's current events.

42

The Millionth March

You could tell, even ten years ago, where this was headed: the dwindling numbers, the platitudes in demand of a nebulous social justice. The fact that they forgot to sing "Lift Every Voice." We could, at this point, go on mouthing hosannas to the now aged luminaries and reliving that August day through the grainy black-and-white footage. Or we can grapple with what has happened since then.

Karl Marx is attributed saying that history occurs twice, the first time as tragedy and the second time as farce. Forty years after the March on Washington, black leadership is a sitcom without distribution. Civil rights leadership has gone from an advance guard in pursuit of democracy to a gerontocracy that is increasingly preoccupied with the disparagement of its descendants. Last year's overblown conflict surrounding a handful of inconsequential jokes in the movie *Barbershop* illustrated how far things have devolved: faced with unchecked military aggression, a White House that has a renewed and overt commitment of imperialism, a million incarcerated African Americans, and a national conscience that is bereft of moral considerations, Jesse and company were left to film criticism as a form of social protest. The NAACP's political cachet has declined to such an extent that democratic presidential contenders feel confident in blowing off the organization's annual convention and suffering minimal fallout. A half century after *Brown v. Board of Education*, the NAACP's most noted function is its yearly "image" award. The Reverend Jackson wrote a book with the title "It's All About the Money," and Martin Luther King makes commercials for software companies.

The March on Washington, coming as it did, between the deaths of Medgar Evers and the four little girls who perished in Birmingham's Sixteenth Street Baptist Church, was one of those signal events that divides history into before and after. Sojourners—demanding that the government deliver in 1963 what it had promised in 1863—poured through the Baltimore tunnel at a rate of one hundred buses per hour; the death of W. E. B. Du Bois on the eve of the march—like an intellectual Moses who saw the promised land but was destined never to set foot upon it—ordained the day with metaphysical significance. You could have excluded twenty-five letters of the alphabet and the index of attendees would still have included Baldwin, Brando, Baker (as in Josephine), Belafonte, and Baez. Martin Luther King dropped his notes and issued the greatest freestyle oration in black history.

The sheer historical *weight* of that day bestowed a degree of moral authority upon black leadership that had not been seen before—or since. In the haze of nostalgia that surrounds that day, the unpretty details fade. Like the fact that there had to be a march in order to force that great liberal icon John F. Kennedy to push forward with civil rights, or that Student Nonviolent Coordinating Committee president John Lewis's speech was heavily edited to make his tone more politically correct—he fared better than James Baldwin, who was deemed too radical and thus his speech was completely eliminated from the proceedings. Malcolm X riffed on the day, calling it a "Farce on Washington" and charging (inaccurately) that civil rights leaders were taking direct orders on how to protest from the Kennedy administration.

It's not improbable to say that the seeds of our present condition were visible even then; still, there was no way of telling from that vantage point that King's "Dream" would be reduced to the most banal of democratic clichés, or that Andrew Young would ascend to the position of ambassador to the United Nations only to be undone by his position on the Israeli-Palestinian conflict. It was impossible to forecast that Jesse Jackson's titanic ambition and rhyming couplets would gain him seven million votes in the 1988 presidential election— or that he would rewrite himself as a Shakespearean character, undone by his errant erections and left living down the fact that he wasn't important enough to assassinate. The March on Washington would find itself dwarfed by Louis Farrakhan's "sorry-in" on the National Mall, an event with a questionable political agenda that left no visible footprints in history.

In historical terms, the march, along with John Kennedy's fateful trip through Dealey Plaza in Dallas, created the political mandate to pass the Civil Rights Act of 1964, which, among other things, outlawed discrimination in public accommodations. Those of us positioned in the so-deemed hip-hop generation have come of age in a world absent whites-only signs, Jim Crow education, and the outward vestiges of American apartheid. We enjoy more material prosperity than any generation of black people who have preceded us on this soil. And yet there is the nagging suspicion that we've bought America "as is"; that the central irony of this anniversary may be that the March on Washington paved the way for Colin Powell and Condoleezza Rice, the race's representatives at the table of American global domination. That rappers are unofficial ambassadors of American capitalism. That maybe some of us have overcome, and that the rest of the world is none the better for it. In an age of terrorism and unmitigated hypercapitalism, where presidents walk with cowboy swagger across subject nations and world opinion is as relevant as last year's playoffs, black people have finally become shareholders in America, Inc. And whether that is cause for celebration or lament is your question to call.

June 2003

43

Willie Lynch Is Dead (1712?–2003)

I long ago stopped listening to sentences that began with "The problem with black people" or ended with "and that's why black people can't get ahead now," which partly explains my initial disinterest in the now-famous "William Lynch Speech." In the few years since the speech on how to train slaves first appeared, it has been cited by countless college students and a black member of the House of Representatives, and has become the essential verbal footnote in barbershop analysis of what's wrong with black people. The rapper Talib Kweli laments on the song "Know That," "blacks are dyin' / how to make a slave / by Willie Lynch is still applyin'," and one professor at a Midwestern university made the speech required reading for her class. Of late, the frequency of citations to the speech seems to be increasing—at least three people have asked me about it in the last month.

According to the speech's preface, Master Lynch was concerned enough with the fortunes of his slaveholding brethren in the American colonies to give a speech on the bank of the James River explaining how to keep unruly servants disunited. The old, he argued, should be pitted against the young, the dark against the light, the male against the female, and so on. Such disunifying tactics "will control the slaves for at least 300 years," he guaranteed. And that, it seems, is why black people can't get ahead now.

There are many problems with this document—not the least of which is the fact that it is absolutely fake. As a historian, I am generally skeptical of smoking guns. Historical work, like forensic science, is more about the painstaking aggregation of facts that lead researchers to the most likely explanation, but rarely the only one. Slavery was an incredibly complex set of social, economic, and legal relations that literally boiled down to black and white. But given the variation in size of farms, number of enslaved workers, region, crops grown, law, gender ratios, religion, and local economy, it is unlikely that a single letter could explain slave policy for at least 151 years of the institution and its ramifications down to the present day.

Considering the limited number of extant sources from the eighteenth century, if this speech had been "discovered," it would've been the subject of incessant historical panels, scholarly articles, and debates. It would literally be a career-making find. However, the letter was never "discovered," rather it "appeared" in the 1990s—bypassing the official historical circuits and making its way via the Internet directly into the canon of American racial conspiracies.

On a more practical level, the speech is filled with references that are questionable if not completely inaccurate. Lynch makes reference to an invitation reaching him on his "modest plantation in the West Indies." While this is theoretically possible—the plantation system was well established in the Caribbean by 1712—most plantation owners were absentees who chose to remain in the colonizing country while the day-to-day affairs of their holdings were run by hired managers and overseers. But assuming that Mr. Lynch was an exception to this practice, much of the text of his "speech" is anachronistic. Lynch makes consistent reference to "slaves"—which again is possible, though it is far more likely that people during this era would refer to persons in bondage simply as "Negroes." In the first paragraph, he promises, "Ancient Rome would envy us if my program is implemented," but the word "program" did not enter the English language with this connotation until 1837—at the time of this speech it was used to reference a written notice for theater events.

Two paragraphs later he says he will "give an outline of action," for slaveholders; the word "out-line" had appeared only fifty years earlier and was an artistic term meaning a sketch—it didn't convey its present meaning until 1759. Even more damning is the author's use of the terms "indoctrination" and "self-refueling" in the next sentence. The first word didn't carry its current connotation until 1832; the second didn't even enter the language until 1811—a century after the purported date of Lynch's speech. More obviously, Lynch uses the word "Black," with an upper-case "B" to describe African Americans more than two centuries before the word came to be applied as a common ethnic identifier.

In popular citations, Lynch has also been—inexplicably—credited with the term "lynching," which would be odd since the speech promises to provide slaveholders with nonviolent techniques that will save them the expense of killing valuable, if unruly, property. This inaccuracy points to a more basic problem in understanding American history. The violence directed at black people in America was exceptional in that it was racialized and used to reinforce political and social subordination, but it was not unique. Early America was incredibly violent in general—stemming in part from the endemic violence in British society and partly from the violence that tends to be associated with frontier societies. For most of its history, lynching was a nonracial phenomenon—actually it was racial in that it was most often directed at white people. "Lynch law" was derived from the mob violence directed at Tories, or British loyalists, just after the American Revolution. While there is disagreement about the precise origins of the term—some associate it with Charles Lynch, a Revolution-era justice of the peace who imprisoned Tories; others see it as the legacy of an armed militia founded near the Lynche River, or the militia captain named Lynch, who created judicial tribunals in Virginia in 1776—there is no reference to the term earlier than 1768, more than half a century after the date given for the speech.

Given the sparse judicial resources (judges were forced to travel from town to town hearing cases, which is where we get the term "judicial circuit") and the frequency of property crimes in the early republic, lynching was often seen as a form of community justice. Not until the 1880s, after the end of Reconstruction, did "lynching" become associated with African Americans; gradually the number of blacks lynched each year surpassed the number of whites until it became *almost* exclusively directed at black people late in the century.

On another level, the Willie Lynch Speech would seem to give a quick-and-easy explanation of the roots of our much-lamented "black disunity." You could make similar arguments about the lingering effects of a real historical document like the 1845 tract "Religious Instruction of Negroes"—written by a proslavery Presbyterian minister—or the British practice of mixing different African ethnicities on slave ships in order to make communication—and therefore rebellion—more difficult. But this, too, is questionable; it presumes that whites, or any other diverse group, do not face divisive gender issues, generation gaps, and class distinctions. Willie Lynch offers no explanation for the white pro-lifer who guns down a white abortion–provider, or for white-on-white domestic violence. He does not explain political conflicts among different Latino groups or crime in Asian communities. Unity is not the same as unanimity, and in the end, black people are no more disunited than any other group of people.— In fact, we are a lot more united than we give ourselves credit for.

September 2003

44

The Case of the Disappearing Negro

Nostalgia, as the conventional wisdom goes, is one part longing for the past and ten parts resentment of the present. For every sentimentalized reference to the way things allegedly were, there is an implicit anger regarding the way they are now—which is why we so often see disgruntled politicians romanticize the 1950s before demanding an end to affirmative action or denouncing gay marriage. But that kind of mythical, idyllic history only works after you airbrush out the ugly truths about the distant past—and in America, most often this involves evasion of race and racism. And it is a particular brand of American mythology that drives the film *Cold Mountain*.

Set against the backdrop of the Civil War, the film traces the bitter travails of Ada and Inman, lovers separated by the conflict, and the latter's treacherous journey home after deserting the

Confederate ranks. A number of historians have already pointed out the film's historical inaccuracies—most importantly its failure to depict the large number of black soldiers who fought at the Battle of Petersburg in 1864—but it is more difficult to challenge the moral dishonesty that stems from this kind of overblown nostalgia.

The two meet as a new church is being built in the town of Cold Mountain, North Carolina—entirely by white laborers. When the church is opened for services, we see the white citizens of Cold Mountain—but none of the black slaves who likely would have attended but required to remain segregated away from white worshippers. This is perhaps the case because no one in the town appears to actually *own* any slaves—at least none who are actually required to do any work. Ada, the Charleston-bred belle who brings treats to her slaves (who we never see on camera), gives "her Negroes" their freedom during the war—despite the fact that she has no other means of raising enough food to feed herself. This act of white magnanimity is matched by Inman's willingness to risk being discovered by the Confederate Army in order to protect a slave woman whom a white reverend is attempting to drown. When he encounters a band of fugitive slaves in a cornfield, Inman—a Southerner and Confederate—announces that he has no quarrel with them and offers them money for some of their food. He has fought, he professes, for a cause he does not believe in.

Their "cause" is a nebulous one and is steeped in euphemisms about "defending one's way of life." Thus an uninformed viewer might reasonably conclude that the Civil War began because of Northern aggression—not the South's recalcitrant attempts to preserve a way of life based upon the enslavement of four million people of African descent. In reality, both Abraham Lincoln and Congress went to great lengths to assure Southern states that there would be no federal attempt to outlaw slavery—even going so far

as to propose the Crittendon Compromise, a constitutional guarantee that slavery could not be abolished by federal authority. In
reality, nonslaveholding whites like Inman fought for a cause that
they believed in like a religion—which, you might argue, it was.

Yet it is inaccurate to lay the blame for this historical
amnesia solely at the feet of the novelist Charles Frazier or the
screenwriter and filmmaker Anthony Minghella—the problem is
deeper, broader, and older than that. The saccharine racial
politics of *Cold Mountain* are paralleled by Mel Gibson's Revolutionary War flick, *The Patriot,* where we learn that the legions of
black laborers working the fields of a South Carolina plantation
are actually *free*—and Gibson's character, a wealthy South Carolina planter, *pays* them to grow his crops. (The next logical step
would be for him to duck into the nearest phone booth and don
his cape before eliminating hordes or redcoats with his x-ray
vision.) Nor, if history is any judge, should you hold your breath
waiting for a realistic depiction of race and racism in *The
Alamo*—scheduled for release in early 2004. The mythic bravery
of the 185 American holdouts against 5,000 Mexican troops is
too compelling a theme to ruin it by talking about the American
refusal to abide by Mexico's antislavery laws in Texas as a basis
for the war.

Ultimately, this is not about film. In an era where statewide
elections still turn on a candidate's support for the Confederate
flag "as a symbol of Southern pride" and where one still encounters the inane argument that the Civil War was fought over states'
rights, not slavery, it's naïve to think that the movies will be any
more honest about the past. What is at issue here is an American
intolerance of its own history.

Any history of the United States is also a history of race,
whether that is stated explicitly or not. The Civil War was fought
to protect a state's right *to maintain slavery*—a fact established
by the Confederate states' own declarations of secession, which

specifically cite the institution as the reason for the conflict. Ironically, the argument that the war was not about slavery has its roots among Northerners who felt compelled to downplay the Negro issue in favor of something their peers might actually think was worth fighting for—preservation of the Union.

Racism is literally a cornerstone of this country's history—even as it is all but absent from our popular understanding. It is nowhere and it is everywhere. The state of Maine entered the Union only as a counterbalance to the creation of an additional slave state, Missouri, in 1820. Florida became a U.S. possession in 1819—after an impetuous general by the name of Andrew Jackson seized the territory. The seizure was driven by the dual concerns of(1) Native American populations who used the area as grounds from which to attack white settlers, and (2) the fact that the Spaniards did not recognize American slavery laws. Prior to the seizure, fugitive slaves were as likely to flee *south* to the free territory of Florida as they were to head north to the land above the Mason-Dixon Line.

The United States doubled its landmass in 1803 with the Louisiana Purchase—a transaction that would eventually be the basis for thirteen new states. The deal came about because the Haitian Revolution had simultaneously eliminated France's wealthiest Caribbean colony and made its North American holdings a liability. West Virginia became a state when the western portion of the state of Virginia refused to secede from the Union during the Civil War—poor whites felt no compulsion to fight for slaves they could not afford to own. Statehood for Kansas and Nebraska brought a bloody preface to the Civil War when Senator Stephen Douglas's "Popular Sovereignty" scheme—allowing territory-wide referendums to decide whether they would enter the union as free or slave states—devolved into armed combat by proslavery and antislavery forces.

Even California's admission to the Union was facilitated by

the Compromise of 1850, which established it as a free state—in exchange for a strongly enforced Fugitive Slave Act, which legally mandated that any black person who escaped from slavery be returned to the South. History, unlike mythology, is full of difficult realities that raise difficult questions about the present. But don't expect this kind of information to show up on the big screen—or C-Span for that matter—anytime soon. In 2004 a variation of the old adage about history holds true—those who *refuse* to look backward often end up thinking that way.

October 2003

45

The House Negro Blues

By the time he stepped behind that podium in Selma, Alabama, Malcolm was not long for this world. He had come to Alabama to address the young activists of the Student Nonviolent Coordinating Committee in February 1965, just seventeen days before that fateful afternoon at the Audubon Ballroom. Malcolm X spoke at length on the connections between the revolution going on in Alabama and the one under way in the former colonial territories of Africa. Then he dropped a metaphor that has been blowing in the wind ever since. He warned the students that other, allegedly *responsible* Negroes would be sent along to contradict his message, a tactic that he saw as rooted in the history of slavery: "There were two kinds of slaves. There was that old house Negro and the field Negro. And the house Negro always looked out for his master

. . . He ate better, he dressed better and he lived in a better house . . . If his master got sick, he'd say, 'What's the matter, boss, *we*, sick?' When the master's house caught afire, he'd try to put it out. He never wanted his master's property threatened. And he was more defensive of it than the master was." The field Negro, though, "had nothing to lose." They wore the worst clothes, he said. They ate bad food and caught all kinds of hell. "If the master got sick, they'd pray that the master died. If the master's house caught afire, they'd pray for a strong wind to come along—that was the difference between the two."

Malcolm was speaking metaphorically, well aware of the broadening class distinctions within the black community, perhaps even thinking that those same students would eventually have before them a vista of American possibility that no previous generation of black folk had ever witnessed.

The problem with metaphors, though, is that people tend to take them literally. Conduct a search for the phrase "house Negro," and it becomes apparent that right about now, its our pejorative of choice for the black person with questionable race loyalties, the person who is too blinded by position and fake status to realize where his or her *real* interests lie. It was, as Malcolm no doubt knew, never quite that simple. Flip through the pages of John Blassingame's *Slave Community,* Deborah White's *Aren't I a Woman?* Eugene Genovese's *Roll Jordan Roll,* or Herbert Aptheker's old classic *American Negro Slave Revolts,* and a far more complex and subtle portrait of the so-deemed *house Negro* emerges.

It's been 107 years since Paul Lawrence Dunbar hipped us to the fact that the mask that grins also lies, so we would do well not to take the house slave at face value. The slave asking, "Is *we* sick?" might be the same slave who put ground glass or poisonous roots in the stew in the first place. White slave owners existed in a world of perpetual jeopardy, always waiting for the next Nat Turner or Gabriel Prosser to come around the bend. But it was the subtle subversions, the slave plots to poison the plantation whites, the "accidental" fires, and the mysterious deaths of infants whom they nursed that presented the real daily threat to their lives.

No doubt, there were house slaves who fit the obsequious stereotype Malcolm talked about; there were also very many whose evil ways kept slave masters permanently shaken. In one account, a house slave named Clara used her position in the big house to find bullets for her son, who planned to kill his master (he did). In another, a fearful plantation owner recorded in his journal that a house slave named Lethe "had sharp and spiteful eyes" and constantly spoke of her hatred of whites and desire for revenge against the man who sold her husband away from her. "She pointed to the scars upon her face [and] wished to see the day when she could wipe them off in some white man's blood."

Toussaint L'Ouverture, the military strategist and leader of the Haitian Revolution—an insurrection that overthrew the French slave regime and created an independent nation of ex-slaves—was a privileged and literate coachman. L'Ouverture wasn't technically a house slave, but he occupied an envied position in the plantation hierarchy. And that relatively advantaged position gave him opportunities to devour volumes of European history and formulate the strategies that he would later employ in defeating Napoleon's armies.

In many instances, domestic slaves existed inside the citadel of white authority, directly in the line of first fire. If "house" status conferred advantages in terms of food and clothing, it also brought with it its own brand of treachery. For enslaved black women this often meant that a position within the house increased the likelihood of sexual assault, while simultaneously placing them in the most convenient location for spurned white women to seek revenge. After emancipation, one former slave told the story of a mistress who decapitated a peer's newborn child after seeing that it resembled her husband. For the field slave, an accomplice in the house might mean the difference between slavery's slim rations and an extra meal boosted from the big house. During the Civil War, eavesdropping house Negroes carried information to the slave quarters on the status of the war, often facilitating escapes and desertions. The domestic servant was, in Blassingame's words, "the field slave's most important window on the outside world and aides in trying to fathom the planter's psyche."

This might be an arid exercise in historical correction were it not for the fact that slavery's mythology still informs our perspective on the world. In way too many instances, that simple house versus field Negro dichotomy is used to explain class or professional status in the black community. It's no coincidence that the stereotypical attributes of yesterday's house Negro translate almost precisely into the reigning stereotypes of today's black middle class. In the current scramble to lay claim to an ersatz *realness*—meaning *field Negro-ness*—a law degree or non-Ebonic enunciation might be enough to earn honorary house status—and all the suspicion that comes with it. We hear echoes of that same theme with the bogus assertions that academic achievement is somehow *acting white*. House Negroes putting on intellectual airs. Add into the equation legions of middle-class kids copping avenue pretensions, and what you get is a type of class minstrelsy. Call it greenface.

This might not be so ironic were it not for the fact that the rapper—while draped in the latest accoutrements of high capitalism—has become our modern stand-in for the field Negro. We see T-shirts with the tagline "Son of a Field Negro," but ain't nobody trying to lay claim to a house Negro lineage. And truth told, I have to cop to perpetuating the old stereotype, referring to myself alternately as a "millennial field Negro" or "Field Negro

Emeritus." We know, or ought to know by now, that lines of social commitment don't neatly correspond to class (or really race, but that's a whole 'nother column). When it all gets down to the get-down, there were always those among our number who lived inside a house on fire and prayed for a strong wind anyway. For real.

November 2003

46

Ghosts of Tuskegee

B y the time he passed away last month, Ernest Hendon had seen nearly a century of life and earned a reputation as something of a rural sage. He lived through two world wars and eighteen presidential administrations. Shortly before his birth, Theodore Roosevelt had outraged the nation by daring to have lunch in the White House with a Negro—Booker T. Washington—and by the end of his life the president's closest adviser and his secretary of state were both African American. One witnesses a great deal in ninety-six years. Sometimes too much. In addition to being a family man, gardener, and inveterate outdoorsman, Ernest Hendon was also the last surviving member of the United States Public Health Service's study of syphilis—better known as the Tuskegee Experiment.

Between 1932 and 1972, the USPHS monitored the progression

of syphilis in 399 patients in Alabama, most of whom were illiterate sharecroppers, all of whom were black men. The disease brings horrific consequences when left untreated, progressing from a simple, sometimes unnoticeable sore into a second stage, where it assaults bones, tissues, and organs, causing both internal and external lesions, and the final stage, where it causes tumors, attacks the liver, heart, and central nervous system and often leads to paralysis and insanity. The Public Health Service knowingly allowed the disease to progress, deliberately misdiagnosed the patients with so-called bad blood, and offered no treatment—even after penicillin became widely available in the 1940s. The experiment marked a crossroads of modern science and racial superstition; among the oldest of the canon of Negro stereotypes is the idea that Africans are sexually loose and particularly prone to carry sexually transmitted diseases. Mr. Hendon managed to evade bitterness regarding what had been done, but the Tuskegee Experiment remains one of the most horrid episodes in our collective history. And the problem with history is that it refuses to stay in the past.

Tuskegee has been implicated in a raft of medical issues and concerns affecting black communities in 2004. Dr. Stephen Sodeke, the interim director of the Tuskegee University National Center for Bioethics, has pointed out that the infamous experiment has become a central reference point for African American views of the medical establishment: "One of the huge challenges we have is recruitment of African Americans into clinical trials, and the Tuskegee Syphilis Study is always cited as one of the reasons why African Americans are reluctant to participate." Without black participation in clinical trials, "we are forced to make assumptions using the same data that we get from middle-class Caucasian males." This leaves medical researchers with less understanding of how particular drugs or treatments may affect African Americans specifically. And the problems are not limited to clinical trials.

"Within the African American community, the number of organ donors is far, far less than the demand. Proportionately, we need more kidneys than the Caucasian population, but the number of us willing to donate is abysmally low."

But it would be wrong to presume that the syphilis experiment occurred in isolation. Dr. Bill Jenkins, professor of public health at Morehouse College and former manager of the Centers for Disease Control's Health Benefits Program—which handled the medical needs of survivors of the experiment and their affected family members—points out, "It's misleading and not totally respectful of black people to suggest that our mistrust of the medical system is based on one incident—it is based on a history of incidents."

The history of America is a history of race. Medicine was no more immune from the plague of white supremacy than religion, politics, art, or any other area of human endeavor. The early relationship between black people in this country and the medical sciences had the specific goal of restoring health to slaves in order to keep them in the fields producing profit for white slaveholders. Often medicine was directed at reversing the physical injuries to slaves that had been suffered at the hands of those very same slaveholders. In nineteenth-century America, "dissection" of the human body after death was widely considered an abomination and often forbidden by state laws. Entire generations of white medical students perfected their surgical crafts by practicing on the black bodies—either stolen from the graves or purchased— because Negroes were offered no such legal protections. Former slaves often told of "night doctors" who stole bodies from burial grounds for delivery to medical schools. It is no coincidence that Nat Turner's body was turned over to a group of physicians for dissection after he was executed.

Issues of sex and reproduction brought particular violations. One historian reported that in Louisiana Caesarian sections were performed *exclusively* on slave women because of the high mortality rates for abdominal surgery during the era. Black women literally became the practice field for procedures that would later save the lives of white women.

American racial mythology was bolstered by "medical" evidence of black inferiority, complete with bizarre diseases said to be endemic to African-descended peoples. Dr. Sam Cartwright, a nineteenth-century physician, is credited with discovering both *drapetomania,* a mental illness that caused Negroes to run away from plantations (and which could be "cured" through repeated whippings), and *dysaesthia aethiopica,* which caused blacks to suffer sleepiness, dry skin, lesions, bouts of mischievous behavior, and insensitivity to pain. In addition to unique diseases, common ones like tuberculosis were given black designations like "Negro Consumption"—said to differ from the white variety in that it was caused by "superstition."

In the twentieth century, African American men like Ernest Hendon were drafted to serve in World War II, but the army medical establishment segregated their blood from that of whites— jeopardizing the lives of soldiers in need of transfusions in order to maintain racial separation. A decade later, the cancerous cells of a black woman from Baltimore named Henrietta Lacks were harvested without her permission or that of her family members and, because the cells could be cultivated outside the body, came to facilitate modern cancer research.

It is not hard to see the long arm of history in 2004. The reluctance to confront the AIDS pandemic in the black community was partially rooted in fears that to recognize its existence was to confirm the kinds of stereotypes that created the Tuskegee Experiment. African Americans continue to suffer excess mortality—dying disproportionately from treatable illnesses and receiving less aggressive treatments when they do seek medical help. The hazy maze of conspiracy theories surrounding HIV fit neatly into an actual lived experience of medical racism in this country. There are times when paranoia and history become nearly impossible to distinguish. In America the physician's creed to "first do no harm" must be accompanied by a pledge to undo the damage that's already been done.

February 2004

47

OutKasts and Indians

History, according to a wise source of mine, is five minutes ago. And that bond between minutes past and centuries long gone came to mind last month when viewing the now-infamous OutKast performance at the Grammy Awards. Before the smoke signals had settled, charges of racism and minstrelsy were already beginning to swirl. Indigenous groups charged the duo with objectifying Native Americans, disrespecting sacred regalia, and demeaning their historic cultures. In short, redface. Image may not be everything, but it is a whole lot of things, and the Native American groups have a right to be concerned with how their cultures are depicted. On its face, minstrelsy is ethnic exaggeration for popular consumption, a kind of caricature that works best when those being ridiculed are marginalized and disempowered.

In laughing at the profane Sambos conjured up in the nineteenth century, whites were essentially affirming their shared status as Americans. That these charges were being leveled at a group of black artists—given the history of blackface caricature and racial stereotypes that still loom in our collective memory—is bitterly ironic. But not all that surprising.

In the crucible of American history, Africans and Native Americans share a kindred experience. And given that fact, there is a long history of black–Native American interaction, cooperation, and intermarriage. (The long-standing racial cliché about black people claiming to be "part Indian" is not solely an attempt to avoid one's African ancestry; by some estimates at least one-third of African Americans have Native American roots.) And we should bear in mind that grits, that staple of black Southern cuisine, began as a Native American cereal, not African. But this is not an entirely pretty history—as few are. If anything, last month's display at the Grammys fits into an equally long tradition of conflict and contempt between these two groups, whose treatment of each other has often mirrored the very prejudices they both suffered from.

The exploitation and oppression of Native Americans and Africans was a fundamental building block of not only the United States, but also to varying degrees all the nations of North and South America. The European colonization of the alleged New World brought with it the subjugation, enslavement, and decimation of the land's indigenous inhabitants. In Columbus's correspondence to the Spanish crown, he simultaneously commented on the generosity and hospitality shown to him by Native Americans and marveled at how few soldiers he would require to subdue and enslave them. In the Caribbean, groups like the Arawak and Caribs were literally wiped out by European military campaigns, diseases, and the labor conditions imposed upon them. In the early sixteenth century, Bartolome de Las Casas, a

Catholic bishop from Spain, began to intercede on the behalf of the indigenous populations, making the paradoxical argument that their treatment was so inhumane and un-Christian that Africans should be enslaved instead. In large measure the enslavement of Africans by Europeans was facilitated and fueled by the diminishing Native American populations and the constant need for new labor to exploit. In the first four centuries after Columbus's arrival, nearly three-quarters of the people arriving in North and South America were Africans—often replacing the indigenous labor that was rapidly being eradicated.

During the colonial era, fugitive slaves often fled south into Florida and set up maroon communities among Native American populations there. In exchange, they brought with them the West African rice cultivation techniques that contributed to sustaining the Seminole population (and had been the primary reason that South Carolina became a rice-growing colony). The Seminole tradition of giving asylum to black fugitives was, in fact, a motivating factor in General Andrew Jackson's invasion of Florida in 1819. In the 1830s, President Jackson's policy of Indian removal—which led to the famed Trail of Tears—was partially driven by the demands of white slaveholders who wanted to be able to retrieve their black "property" from Florida. The Seminole leader Osceola—whose wife was the daughter of a fugitive slave—famously refused to allow any blacks or black-Indians to be reenslaved. It was not uncommon during colonial-era raids for Native American populations to attack whites, but not the enslaved Africans inhabiting the same settlements. And most notably, black warriors fought fiercely alongside their Native American allies during the Seminole wars of resistance between 1835 and 1842.

But neither group was wholly immune to the prevailing currents of thought regarding the other. As early as 1676, black indentured servants joined their white counterparts in the raids against Native Americans organized by Nathaniel Bacon. Attacking both allied and hostile nations indiscriminately, "Bacon's Rebellion" vastly amplified the general climate of suspicion toward Native Americans in the Virginia colony. (When colonial officials intervened, Bacon turned his forces against them and succeeded in temporarily unseating the British-appointed governor, making the point that it was safer to have poor whites despise Native Americans than the white colonial elite.)

Recognizing the potential problems that African–Native American alliances might create, the British encouraged slaveholding among the Cherokee, Creek, Choctaw, and Chickasaw nations, and even some Seminoles came to participate in the institution. On the verge of the Civil War, the Cherokees allied themselves with the Confederate cause. Given their status as "domestic sovereign nations" within the United States, the Cherokees may have had some sympathy for the banner of "states' rights" that unified the seceding Southern territories. Still, the protection of the institution of slavery cannot be dismissed as a factor in the decision to cast their lot along with the Confederates. (And after the close of the Civil War, emancipation of those slaves held by Native Americans proved a complex matter as tribal leadership cited their sovereign status in claiming exemption from the Emancipation Proclamation.)

In the years following the Civil War, the regiments in which black soldiers fought were reorganized as the 9th and 10th Cavalries—better known as the "Buffalo Soldiers." The cavalries served with distinction—guarding the railroads, handling the treacherous business of escorting the mail, and fighting in border skirmishes with the Mexican forces—but they also participated in the Indian wars, serving as military reinforcement of the United States' long-standing policies of treaty violation and subjugation of Native American populations. Yet another irony is seen in the fact that these black soldiers often served under racist white commanding officers. Later, the histories of African and Native Americans would find themselves intertwined within the historically black college system when Virginia's Hampton Institute served as a normal school aiding in the so-termed civilization of Native American youth.

In the postbellum world, Southern states sought to reinscribe white supremacy through black codes and Jim Crow laws that found their sanction in the 1896 *Plessy v. Ferguson* decision. Among Cherokees—who had been forcibly relocated to Oklahoma—this policy found an unfortunate echo. Blacks who had come west with the Cherokees were segregated from the indigenous populations; black freedmen were allotted less land than their Native American counterparts, grouped into internal homelands, and as early as 1907 were being sent to separate schools.

Most recently, the descendants of African Americans who were enslaved by the Seminoles filed suit against the tribal leadership, which sought to exclude them from sharing in the lucrative legal settlement that had been won against the United States. At the heart of this issue was the question of whether or not the enslaved had ever truly been members of the Seminole nation—a question that has been asked, in different contexts involving black people, for the last four centuries on these shores. Those kinds of conflicts—in conjunction with OutKast's performance—remind us that the past has a way of creeping into the right-now. None of us is immune to racism, all of us have excluded others as a means of including ourselves, and five minutes is far longer than we've ever thought.

March 2004

48

Brown v. **Blacks**

You hear the argument in different contexts, always cited to explain some degree of our present miserable condition: economic decline, loss of communal values, urban decay, dwindling numbers of black marriages—even the inane content of contemporary hip-hop. It has become a catchall explanation, the substance of things we never hoped for and the evidence of bad things we've seen. The mantra is this: *Integration Is to Blame.* "We have," one elder informed me, "lost our minds ever since we got integrated." And at the heart of this indictment is the case of *Brown v. the Board of Education* of Topeka, Kansas.

May 17, 2004, marks the fiftieth anniversary of the most significant legal decision of the twentieth century. *Brown* set into motion titanic forces that have reverberated down to our present days. For what it matters, the current debate over the use of the Confederate emblem in the state flag of Georgia has its roots in the post-*Brown* backlash of Southern nationalism (states adopted Confederate imagery for their national flags during the 1950s as a means of symbolically resisting the federal order to dismantle segregation). The case marked the culmination of four decades of efforts by the NAACP and the NAACP Legal Defense Fund to overturn the doctrine of "separate but equal" that had come out of the 1896 *Plessy v. Ferguson* decision. It became a defining moment for a Supreme Court led by Earl Warren—a newly appointed chief justice who as attorney general for California had presided over the internment of Japanese citizens during World War II.

But the case had its black critics from day one. Zora Neale Hurston wrote: "I regard the ruling of the U.S. Supreme Court to be insulting. I see no tragedy in being too dark to be invited to a white social affair." Hurston believed that the case actually affirmed white supremacy by assuming blacks would learn more when seated next to whites. Sarah Bulah, a Delaware mother whose lawsuit against that state's segregated school system eventually became part of the *Brown* class-action suit, found herself ostracized by friends, neighbors, and even fellow church members (her pastor argued that the colored-only school near the church was "handy"). Some had personal motives for opposing the decision: Southern states frequently offered to pay black applicants' full tuition to their segregated law and graduate schools if they would leave the state and enroll in integrated institutions in the North. Still others argued that the case was evidence of the desire of middle-class Negroes to be next to whites at all costs.

Even then, these arguments required a certain kind of near-sightedness in order to work. A generation of black lawyers had fought against the unequal apportionment of funds to black schools year after year, only to find that their expensive legal victories yielded merely temporary changes—school districts reestablished the old patterns after making cosmetic improvements to the black schools. On one level the push for "integration" hoped to turn the logic of racism against itself, to place black children and white children in the same facilities and thereby make it impossible to underfund any school without harming white children as well as blacks. It was more strategic than critics assumed.

But the criticism of the *Brown* decision has not abated fifty years later. In history, there is something we might call the "Funeral Effect." This phenomenon explains how both deceased individuals and dead traditions are spoken of in warm, nostalgic tones, no matter how much havoc they created when they were alive. The Funeral Effect explains Russians who look at the bleakness of their present and yearn for the halcyon days of Stalinism. It explains the conversation I had with a frustrated young black South African in Cape Town last summer. After detailing his inability to find work and his frustration with the government, he said to me, "Things were better under apartheid."

And the Funeral Effect explains why Joseph Lowery of the SCLC has famously quipped that blacks had fought to get into the mainstream "only to find that it was polluted," and why legal scholar Derrick Bell has publicly questioned the wisdom of the desegregation efforts he helped to organize during the early 1960s. Fueling this perspective is a vision of black life that thrived despite the strictures of Jim Crow: neighborhoods filled with black-owned businesses, Negro League baseball teams, and schools filled with black teachers devoted to nurturing the potential of their charges. This phenomenon almost always requires dimming the spotlight on the injustices of the past.

But nostalgia generally makes for bad history.

Almost all of the stadiums in which Negro League teams

played were white-owned. There were indeed significant black business districts—notably in Pittsburgh, Tulsa, Atlanta, and Washington, D.C. But as early as the 1910s there were complaints of black communities having too few black-owned businesses. James Baldwin wrote of his childhood that he—and most other black Harlemites—resented the poor treatment they received from white (in this case, Jewish) merchants and landlords in the community.

The worst-case scenarios that many feared would be the legacy of "integration" have generally not come to pass. Historically, black colleges have been largely successful in their attempts to attract talented students, despite the option of attending majority institutions. Black churches have remained vital cultural and political institutions. Integration has been cited for the decline of the black press. In the years after *Brown,* periodicals like the *Pittsburgh Courier,* the *Chicago Defender,* the *Amsterdam News*, and the *Baltimore Afro-American* either folded or saw their significance dwindle. Talented black journalists found employment with white newspapers (many were hired on the spot to cover the urban uprisings of the 1960s, when editors feared sending in white reporters to black neighborhoods). Even so, it's hard to solely blame integration for the demise of the black press—the decline of these journals began in the early 1960s, a period when the overall number of newspapers in the United States decreased because of competition with television news coverage.

In a real sense, the concern over "integration" is a straw man. A recent Harvard University report concluded that black children were more likely to go to an all-black school in 2004 than they were in 1968. In criticizing integration, people are ultimately voicing a longing for the signposts of community. (White Republicans are not the only people longing for a simpler, long-gone era.) At a time when it is difficult to understand the complex commonalities tying black people together, many are longing for an era when geography at least was our common denominator. Still, it is possible to value community—voluntary community—without airbrushing the legal fascism practiced in this country between 1896 and 1954.

May 2004

49

The Other L-Word

They have been together for a millennium—or at least look as if they have. They are seated beside each other, arms touching, him shoeless and her head wrapped in cloth, and God only knows what they've seen. They are barely past the bitter years of slavery, and to tell the truth, it's still hard to tell the difference. The photograph is grainy and slightly out of focus, but you can still make out the weathered lines of years and experience on their faces. And you can still sense the connection forged of those years.

The picture speaks of a quiet fortitude, togetherness in the crucible of slavery, an intimacy that is rarely seen in our discussions of black history.

Sometimes it seems like there's a civil war going on between black men and black women. It's ironic that Valentine's Day takes place during Black History Month, but those two events manage to overlap without ever coinciding—as if there is no love or romance within our collective history in this country. We know of husbands sold away from wives and wives taken from husbands to face the sexual exploitation of white overseers. We know of black men and women who were bred like livestock. But what we rarely speak of is love in the context of adversity.

The question goes loudly unasked: who needed love more than the enslaved? Beyond the uprisings and the daily resistance, outside of the escapes, arsons, and thefts, the most subversive act committed by enslaved black people may have been daring to love one another. The ten-plus generations of black men and women who lived through the ordeal of slavery went to extraordinary lengths to give meaning to their own lives, to construct relationships that might, if only momentarily, dull the pain of forced servitude, to care for others in a society that sought to make black love a contradiction in terms. And that reality is all but lost in our present love deficit.

Filtered through the lens of popular media, it seems like there's a civil war going on between black men and black women. African Americans are the least likely segment of the population to marry and have a divorce rate that exceeds 50 percent. We are also far less likely to remarry after a divorce than members of other groups. Black radio's airwaves are congested with loveless ballads; rappers boldly declare themselves love-proof—and thereby pain-proof—and disgruntled sirens sing songs of fiscal obligation. In an era where baby-daddies and baby-mamas replace husbands and wives, it's easy to see the destructive legacy of slavery, segregation, and incarceration playing itself out. But that's only half of the history—and we've never needed to hear the other side of the story more urgently.

The truth is that marriage and family were extremely

important to enslaved black people—despite the obvious difficulties that confronted their relationships. Slave marriages were given no legal recognition, but slaves constructed binding traditions of their own. In addition to "jumping the broom," couples also presented each other with blankets whose acceptance indicated that they were now considered married within the community. Others, who could not find a willing clergyman or who had been denied permission to marry, simply married themselves. Still, recognition of their union was important enough that ex-slaves besieged the Freedman's Bureau with requests for marriage ceremonies after emancipation. Three Mississippi counties accounted for 4,627 marriages in a single year. The end of slavery also brought with it literally thousands of black people wandering throughout the South in search of husbands and wives who had been sold away from them.

Prior to emancipation, people went to great lengths to maintain their relationships. One of the most common reasons why slaves escaped was to see loved ones on distant plantations. One man set out before sunrise each Sunday morning and walked the entire day to spend a few hours with his wife before having to walk back in time to begin the next day's work. George Sally, enslaved on a sugar plantation in Louisiana, ignored the slaveholder's demands and left to visit his wife—an offense for which he was arrested. (He later stated that he did not mind being arrested for seeing his wife.) Others risked their lives to protect their spouses. While sexual exploitation of married black women by overseers was a constant concern, it was not unheard of for husbands to kill whites who had attacked their wives. One unnamed slave attacked an overseer who had attempted to whip his wife and was himself forced to flee into the woods for eleven months.

William Grose, a slave in Loudon County, Virginia, married a free black woman—against the wishes of the plantation owner, who feared that she might help him escape. William was sold to a widower in New Orleans, who demanded that he take another woman as his wife. He wrote in his autobiography, "I was scared half to death, for I had one wife whom I liked and didn't want another." The couple managed to remain in contact and his wife traveled to New Orleans and found work as a domestic in the family that had bought William. When their relationship was discovered, she was forced to leave New Orleans. Incredibly, William devised a plan to escape and fled to Canada, where he and his wife were reunited.

Some black couples managed, despite all odds, to construct long, close-knit unions. In the 1930s, Barbara, a woman who was born into slavery in North Carolina, told an interviewer the story of how she had met her husband, Frank:

> I seen Frank a few times at the Holland's Methodist Church . . . After a while Frank becomes a butcher and he was doing pretty good . . . so he comes to see me and we courts for a year. We was sitting in the kitchen at the house when he asks me to have him. He told me that he knows that he wasn't worthy, but that he loved me and that he'd do anything he could to please me and that he'd always be good to me. When I was fourteen I got married, and when I was fifteen my oldest daughter was born. I had three after her and Frank was as proud of them as could be. We was happy. We lived together fifty-four years and we was always happy, having only a little bit of argument.

Lucy Dunn, who had also been a slave in North Carolina, told a similar tale:

> It was in the little Baptist church where I first seen Jim Dunn

and I fell in love with him then, I reckons. He said that he loved me then too, but it was three Sundays 'fore he asked to see me home. We walked that mile home in front of my mother and I was so happy that I ain't thought it was even a half mile. We ate cornbread and turnips for dinner and it was night before he went home. Mother wouldn't let me walk with him to the gate, so I just sat there on the porch and said goodnight.

He come over every Sunday for a year and finally he proposed. That Sunday night I did walk with Jim to the gate and stood under the honeysuckles that was smelling so sweet. I heard the big old bullfrogs a-croakin' by the river and the whipper-wills a hollerin' in the woods. There was a big yellow moon and I reckon Jim did love me. Anyhow, he said so and asked me to marry him and he squeezed my hand.

She told her suitor that she would have to think about his proposal. She and her mother spent the week discussing the seriousness of marriage. Lucy told her mother that she understood, but "I intends to make a go of it anyhow."

"On Sunday my mother told Jim, and you ought to have seen that black boy grin." They were married a week later. "We lived together fifty-five years and we always loved each other . . . we had our fusses and our troubles, but we trusted in the Lord and we got through." The old woman wiped away tears as she spoke of her husband. "I loved him during life and I love him now, though he's been dead for twelve years. I thinks of him all the time, but it seems like we're young again when I smell honeysuckles or see a yellow moon."

One hundred and thirty-nine years past slavery, we may have something left to learn from those enslaved generations. Near the end of her interview, Barbara spoke a truth that may be more valid now than when she first said it: "My mother died near twenty years ago and father died four years later. He had not cared to live since Mother left him. I've heard some of the young people laugh about slave love, but they should envy the love which kept mother and father so close together in life and even held them in death."

August 2004

50

The 41st Acre

For each of the past fifteen years, Representative John Conyers of Detroit has performed a political ritual: introducing HR 40, a bill authorizing a study on the issue of reparations for African Americans. And in each of the past fifteen years, the House of Representatives has performed a political routine: failing to pass it.

This country may lack for a lot of things, but consistency isn't one of them.

To the American history tourist, the 246 years of black chattel slavery appear as an unfortunate episode best left in the century-old ashes of the Civil War. And according to the three-card hustlers of American "spinocracy", we should be about "color-blindness"—moving past the tangle of racism and into a nirvana of common citizenship. Or, to cut to the real translation: *Just Get Over It.* Think about the prevalence of those two perspectives on race, and you can't help but recognize that the current struggle for reparations is not an uphill battle; it's a vertical one.

In recent years the cause of reparations for slavery, once relegated to the sidelines of black politics, has become an increasingly mainstream concern. A quick index of writings on the subject yields more than a dozen books and scholarly articles that have appeared since 1998. Consider it ironic that the push for reparations has occurred at a juncture when affirmative action is in jeopardy and the Bush administration has scored points by arguing against spending money on health care, but then again, moral claims have a way of being inconvenient no matter when they're raised.

In black America the first faint promises of reparations remain with us like a ghost limb. The ever-referenced, never-received "forty acres and a mule" is the common reference point in discussions of the topic. Ironically, enough, the promise of land to black slaves has its roots not in the desire to redress the vast wrongs of slavery, but rather in the strategic necessities of the Civil War. As General William Tecumseh Sherman made his famed march to the sea, burning all that was in his path, enslaved blacks began abandoning farms and plantations and following the Union forces across the South. (To be accurate, blacks had begun fleeing, pillaging, and in some instances, burning the homes of white slaveholders long before Sherman's 1864–1865 march.) Still, the thousands of civilians literally following in the footsteps of his troops presented a logistical problem for the general, who—importantly—was himself a devout believer in the inferiority of the black race.

As reports of Sherman's ill treatment of the ex-slaves drifted North, Abraham Lincoln dispatched Secretary of War Edwin Stanton to Georgia to resolve the crisis. Black leaders—many of whom were former slaves themselves—told Stanton that the only solution was to provide the fugitives from slavery with land of their own. In response, Sherman issued Special Field Order 15, which seized lands belonging to slaveholders on the South Carolina Sea Islands and along the Atlantic Coast between Charleston and Jacksonville and allocated "forty acres of land" for each ex-slave family.

In the ensuing months, some forty thousand blacks were settled on these lands. With the establishment of the Freedman's Bureau in March 1865, Congress authorized the new agency to take control of abandoned land in the war-ravaged South and dispense "not more than forty acres" to ex-slaves. (The bureau's plan allowed for the three-year rental of land with the option to purchase in the fourth.) Lincoln's assassination, however, brought an abrupt end to the land grants. The president's death brought Andrew Johnson, a Tennessean with sympathies for the defeated South, into office.

Johnson immediately reversed the field order, restored land to its former white owners, and in some instances relied upon the army to forcibly remove those blacks who had been provided with land only months earlier. (Johnson's steadfast opposition to Reconstruction would figure in the scandals that culminated in him becoming the first U.S. president ever to be impeached.)

For what it matters, the claim to black compensation for centuries of unpaid labor was never merely a matter of individual slaveholders who exploited individual black people. The federal government collected hundreds of millions of dollars in taxes on tobacco and cotton grown and harvested by black hands. The financial centers of New York, Philadelphia, and Boston grew rich through their dealings with Southern planters. Northern textile mills relied upon raw materials from the South to grow into modern industries. Shipping lines established trade routes throughout Europe to sell goods whose production would have been impossible without black labor. Indeed, slavery is literally the cornerstone of American wealth.

It would be easy to argue that it is impossible to grapple with the debts generated by a fledgling economy a century and a half ago, but racism might be the great constant of American history. Factor in the generational impact of state-sponsored undereducation of blacks for a century after slavery. Then add the billions of dollars in lost home equity owed to the fact that the Federal Housing Authority issued mortgage subsidies in areas where blacks were legally restricted from living. It becomes clear that we are not dealing with ambiguous claims of long-deceased ancestry.

Importantly, the descendants of the racial terrorism that destroyed Rosewood, Florida, in January 1923 were awarded a $2.1 million settlement in 1994, and Harvard law professor Charles Ogletree has spearheaded a similar suit for the descendants and survivors of the Tulsa massacre of 1921. But for all the historical and legal weight of this claim, America will never reckon with this debt in the grand sense—meaning, beyond the vague endorsements of "better race relations" and the occasional MLK television special.

In an era where profligate billions are spent to erase nonexistent foreign threats and the country tolerates a vice president's company profiteering while death tolls rise daily, you can still count on a public outcry over blacks being given too much. Guilt is just too twentieth century. If we are to gain that next metaphorical acre, it will be through our own cooperative efforts to support black colleges and nurture community development. The historian and critic Harold Cruse once told me with deadpan certainty that black people will definitely get reparations one day—right before they put us on the boats heading back to Africa.

October 2004

51

The Good Ol' Days of Slavery

These days it's getting harder to tell whether history is repeating itself or human beings are just becoming more cliché. This was underscored last week when it came to light that Cary Christian Academy, a private school in North Carolina, was using the deceptively titled pamphlet "Southern Slavery, As It Was" in their curriculum. Among the more notable claims presented by authors Doug Wilson and Stephen Wilkins were neglected virtues like: "Many Southern blacks supported the South because of long established bonds of affection and trust that had been forged over generations with their white masters and friends." Or this gem: "There has never been a multi-racial society which has existed with such mutual intimacy and harmony in the history of the world." Listen closely and you can almost hear the banjoes strumming in the background.

Officials at the school defended the forty-three-page tract, arguing that they want to present students with "both sides" of the Civil War story and that students also read speeches by Abraham Lincoln. Ironically enough, the "both sides" approach does not include the perspectives of the actual black people who *lived* through slavery. A random selection from John Blassingame's *Slave Testimony* yields this first-person dissenting opinion:

> [The mistress] took her in the morning, before sunrise, into a room and had all the doors shut. She tied her hands and then took her frock over her head, and gathered it up in her left hand, and with her right commenced to beating her naked body with bunches of willow twigs. She would beat her until her arm was tired and then thrash her on the floor, and stamp on her with her foot and kick her and choke her to stop her screams. She continued the torture until ten o'clock. The poor child never recovered. A white swelling came from the bruises on her legs of which she died in two or three years.

Any few pages in your college-worn copy of *The Narrative of the Life of Frederick Douglass* would put the lie to Wilson and Wilkins's claim that "Slave life was to them a life of plenty, of simple pleasures, of food, clothes, and good medical care." And one wonders where Harriet Tubman, bludgeoned so badly as a child that she suffered from bouts of narcolepsy for the rest of her life, fits into this backdrop of happy plantation scenery. And far from supporting the South out of their "bonds of affection," nearly all black Confederates, as James McPherson points out in *The Negro's Civil War,* were conscript laborers who constantly sought means to escape across Union lines. To put it simply, this was a case of bond*age* not bonds.

It is pathetic that five years into the twenty-first century, the societal learning curve is so obtuse that we must still make statements like: *American slavery was a violent, oppressive institution responsible for the brutal subjugation and dehumanization of millions of people over the course of three centuries.* Wilson and Wilkins's claim that slave life was characterized by "good medical care" is particularly bizarre given the fact that enslaved black people were frequently used as subjects of nineteenth-century medical experimentation. The historian Katherine Bankole, in fact, pointed out in her book *Slavery and Medicine* that because of the high mortality rates for even the most minor surgeries during the era, doctors in antebellum Louisiana "perfected" their Caesarian-section technique on black women before applying it to white ones.

This is not about accurate history, but about providing the South with a human rights alibi, 139 years past slavery. It is about a vast capacity for willful self-delusion, the need to provide self-absolution for the sins of the so-deemed peculiar institution. Thus you see the kind of historical hair-splitting of "Southern Slavery, As It Was": slavery was wrong . . . but not as bad you might think.

And sadly enough, it's not only in the far precincts of the Christian right that you hear these kinds of weak rationales. The Southern alibi tradition rests upon the now-outmoded arguments of historian Ulrich B. Phillips's *American Negro Slavery*. First published in 1918, the book glazed over the old arguments that slavery had been a benign and beneficial institution to the enslaved with a new scholarly sheen. Phillips's perspective had a striking longevity, finding expression even in the dissenting works that appeared in the 1950s and 1960s, all the way down to Robert Fogel and Stanley Engerman's *Time on the Cross*, which appeared in 1974, arguing that poor treatment of blacks would have made slavery unprofitable as an economic institution. Back in my graduate school days, my friend and fellow historian Khalil Muhammad and I were amazed to find that we—and a single white student—were the sole voices in a fifteen-person

colloquium who were willing to argue that slavery was an unqualified moral wrong.

All of these defenses—whether presented at academic conferences or passed out to adolescents in private academies of the far
right—are invested in viewing slavery as a labor system operated
by rational, managerial white folk, the plantation equivalents of
Jack Welch or Lee Iacocca. But in order for these theories to work,
they also have to overlook the concomitant cruelties of sexual
exploitation of enslaved black women, which was common enough
to be a defining characteristic of the institution. Again, even commonplace texts like Harriet Jacobs's *Incidents in the Life of a Slave
Girl* or Deborah White's *Aren't I a Woman* would illustrate the fact
that rape was an intricate part of enslavement in this country. Nor
can these depictions of "slavery lite" explain away the dissolution
of families for profit and the inhuman breeding of blacks to produce additional chattel for the slave owners.

It would be easy to dismiss these disputes as the arid exer-
cises of some "History Forensics Society" if the implications for
our everyday lives were not so serious. Truth told, Wilkins and
Wilson are only inches away from the "happy darky" illustrations
of black life, and if this is "Southern Slavery, As It Was," then
they would be hard-pressed to explain the literally hundreds of
slave revolts, attempted revolts, poisonings, and fires that
defined the South between the Revolutionary and Civil Wars. In
airbrushing the brutality of slavery, we make it possible to ignore
the tremendous power that race had—and continues to have—in
shaping this society. To cut to the quick, until we are willing to
grapple with slavery as it really was, we will remain incapable of
dealing with America as it is.

December 2004

52

Slavery.edu

History never fails to make you wonder where irony ends and hypocrisy begins. Or vice versa. I came to that conclusion a few weeks ago as I sat on a panel listening to emaciated arguments about the unfairness of affirmative action. It is no secret that affirmative action and "diversity" programs in higher education have found themselves under assault in recent years. The University of California jettisoned its affirmative action program and watched its black enrollments decline precipitously, and the University of Michigan required a Supreme Court decision to maintain its programs. But even with that decision in the books, a prominent fellowship for minorities that I received as a graduate student recently announced that it would no longer target solely people of color for their philanthropy.

In the just-get-over-it age, even proponents of affirmative

action in hiring and education hang their arguments on the benefits of diversity in the workplace and the classroom. The more daring proponents point to indexes of ongoing discrimination in society. Rarely does the history of slavery enter into the discussion these days. But the fact is that it is impossible to separate the history of race and racism from that of higher education in this country. For more reasons than one.

A hypothetical scenario: in 1831 a fledgling business is started. It faces the monumental challenges that confront all start-ups, but through perseverance and skilled planning it grows into a major fixture on the landscape. As demand increases, the owners utilize slaves to literally build the institution. Pristine new buildings begin to dot the landscape, showcasing the skill of the black laborers constructing them. An array of enslaved black men and women perform the manual labor that allows the institution to function daily and fulfill its mission statement. There are, of course, whippings, but they are handled by the higher personnel to avoid unnecessary brutality. And 174 year later, some of those same buildings still stand.

Now a confession: this is not the history of a long-forgotten antebellum plantation, but that of the University of Alabama.

The University of Alabama owned slaves and used slave labor for construction, repairs, and as assistants to the faculty—who were also responsible for whipping unruly black chattel. Its faculty counted among them some of the most vociferous defenders of the peculiar institution, and F. A. P. Barnard, who later became the president of the University of Mississippi, had an enslaved lab assistant during his time on the UA faculty. He later presided over the closing of the University of Mississippi, known as "Ole Miss," during the Civil War as significant portions of the all-male student body left to join the Confederate cause. (Until 1856, matriculating students had been allowed to bring their slaves to college with them.)

Nor can this be dismissed as simply a Southern peculiarity;

even the prestigious and famously liberal institutions of the Northeast are implicated in this history. Georgetown University owned slaves up until the 1840s, when the institution sold all of its human property. As Yale University celebrated its three-hundredth birthday in 2001, three doctoral students released a report titled "Yale, Slavery and Abolition," which pointed out that nine of the school's twelve colleges were named after slave-holders and that Timothy Dwight, a former Yale president and opponent of slavery, had, in fact, purchased a female slave named Naomi. And Brown University was named after the Rhode Island family that provided them with nearly $160,000 in their early years—money earned in part from their activities within the slave trade.

F. A. P. Barnard—the same Barnard who had shut down Ole Miss during the Civil War and permitted the establishment of a university Confederate regiment on campus—later became president of Columbia University. He was, ironically, a fierce advocate for the education of women, and Barnard College at Columbia University was named after him.

Given the fact that cotton alone accounted for nearly 40 percent of the United States' exports between 1800 and the onset of the Civil War, the "benefits" of slavery go beyond those institutions clearly implicated in trading Africans or using slave labor on campus. Slavery—both directly and indirectly—created the climate in which countless institutions of higher education could prosper.

To their credit, the faculty at the University of Alabama issued an apology for the university's ties to slavery, and Brown University—the first Ivy League institution with an African American president—has established a commission to study slavery and reparations in light of the institution's history. Whether these are sufficient or window dressing remains to be seen. What is not up to question is that slavery provided tangible benefits that are still being reaped today. Which brings us back to the issue of affirmative action. The loudly unasked question is this: if slavery's economic benefits have echoed down to the present generation, is it that hard to believe that its damages might have also?

May 2005

53

Forgetting Where We Came From

A familiar scenario: millions of migrants come north, crossing borders in pursuit of economic opportunities. Many of them are poorly educated, unskilled. But they are willing to work. They are enticed by industries that promise jobs. And since they are willing to work for less money than the employees they are hired to replace, resentment builds. Soon that resentment hardens into open hostility amid charges that the migrants are "stealing our jobs" or "driving down wages." Then comes the violence.

This is not the story of the illegal Mexican immigrants who are at the center of the current immigration debate; it is the story of the nearly six million African Americans who left the South during the Great Migration. In the haze of historical amnesia, we overlook the fact that the issues we are debating over immigration are nearly identical to the issues that confronted African Americans in our recent past. Perhaps we need a collective reminder that we were this country's original illegal immigrants as the ships dragging us from the African continent arrived on American shores for decades after the "legal" slave trade ended in 1808. The point is this: our history in this country is the strongest argument for supporting immigrant rights—not only as a moral issue, but because it is also in the best interests of the black community economically.

Because "immigration" is one of those conveniently loaded racial code words, it's easy to forget that this is a question of labor and resources, not race. The same resentments show up even when race is not a factor. More than a few black Northerners were disturbed by the arrival of their Southern kin. (And you can see a reverse form of that resentment now as Southern cities like Atlanta fill up with Northern migrants.) And in the 1930s, as drought ravaged their farmlands, thousands of white Midwesterners migrated to California, where they were met by the hostility of white native Californians with whom they competed for jobs. (Ironically enough, many of those "Okies," as the migrants were called, found work picking fruit—the precise work that Mexican laborers are now doing in the state.)

The Great Migration and the subsequent competition between blacks and whites in the labor market sparked an epidemic of mob violence in the early twentieth century. We would do well to recall the days when black workers accepted whatever pittance was offered to us, not because we wanted to, but because we had no other choice. For the first half of the twentieth century, black people were locked out of the legal process, denied access to unions, and left with few avenues to challenge unequal pay.

The labor leader and activist A. Phillip Randolph spent the

better part of his career trying to convince whites that it was in their interest to let blacks into their unions.

Randolph was right.

Some of the biggest beneficiaries of the civil rights struggles were working-class white men. As blacks gained political power and access to those unions, we could demand better wages—and white workers no longer had to compete with "cheap" black labor.

The sad reality is that cheap labor *does* drive down wages. But this is because of the legal status of the workers, not because they don't want to make more money. (Remove the minimum wage laws, and you would have the same dynamic with native-born Americans underbidding each other for employment.) Given the realities of poverty in this country, black America is disproportionately impacted by competition with illegal labor. "Sending them back" is no solution to this dilemma: by some estimates there are as many as eleven million undocumented workers in this country. At the conclusion of the Civil War there were only four million ex-slaves, and despite their best efforts, they never succeeded in "sending us back," either.

There is an unspoken irony in this discussion. Few in the most stringently anti-immigrant sectors of black America care to recall the years when African American illegal immigrants fled into Mexico seeking freedom from hunger and persecution. The war that led to the secession of Texas from Mexico was driven in large part by the Mexican government's refusal to allow white settlers to bring black slaves into the territory. As a result, in the years between 1836, when Texas declared its independence, and the American Civil War, enslaved blacks actually fled *south*, knowing they would be given their freedom upon arrival in Mexico. (Mexico, which had received between two- and three-hundred thousand Africans as part of the slave trade, had abolished slavery in 1829.) This migration continued well after slavery when numerous African Americans—including James Hughes, father of the poet Langston Hughes—migrated south of the border and set up communities where they felt they would be relatively free of racial prejudice. As the historian Gerald Horne writes in his excellent history *Black and Brown: African Americans and the Mexican Revolution:* "After the death of Reconstruction, some African Americans organized to migrate en masse to Mexico . . . Hundreds left Alabama and were 'warmly supported by the Mexican government.'" Many of these colonies, which were driven by Mexico's interest in developing cotton agriculture, failed, but the perspective that African Americans would fare better in Mexico than in the United States persisted for decades.

North of the border, African Americans and Mexican Americans often found themselves subjected to the same brands of social repression and discrimination. As early as 1836, Texas denied the right to vote to anyone remaining loyal to the Mexican government—a law that was indiscriminately applied to anyone of Mexican descent in the new republic. This trend persisted even after Texas was admitted to the Union, and after 1850 similar voter eligibility laws prevented Mexican Americans from voting in California. After the passage of the Fifteenth Amendment, these kinds of antidemocratic laws and the constant threat of lynching were employed to strip African American men of their newly acquired voting rights.

But this history of common struggle is all but drowned out in the clamor of the current immigration debate. Still, it remains clear that the only way to prevent fruitless competition is to give illegal labor a path to full citizenship—and with it legal avenues to demand decent wages. No one wants to volunteer to be underpaid, and yet as long as we have a two-tier system of employment in this country, both blacks and Latinos will continue to compete for crumbs at the bottom of the economic barrel.

We, if no one else, should understand what it means to be

cheap labor with no citizenship rights. In the midst of this debate, black America literally cannot afford to forget where we came from.

March 2006